Keeping the Dream Alive

My Quest for Peace and Justice

A memoir by
TERRY AHWAL

PathBinder
Publishing LLC
COLUMBUS, INDIANA

Published by PathBinder Publishing
P.O. Box 2611
Columbus, IN 47202
www.PathBinderPublishing.com

Edited by Doug Showalter
Covers designed by Anna Perlich

On the cover: Terry (right) with her sister, Ghada (left), and her brother, Michael, in the garden of St. Joseph School.

First published in 2023
Manufactured in the United States

ISBN: 978-1-955088-63-3
Library of Congress Control Number: 2023912792

To the many people who lifted me up in my journey:

To my husband, Bob Morris, you believed in me every step of the way. You encouraged me to thrive even when I wanted to give up. Thank you is not enough. You are my shining light. I love you.

To my parents. My relationship with them was complex, but both taught me lessons when I least expected. My father taught me the value of listening. Both taught me the value of forgiveness, even when it seems impossible. They did the best they could with the tools they had. My siblings and I are who we are because of them.

To my extended family. I am lucky to have an extended family that cares about me. When I was young and misunderstood, my grandfather, grandmother, aunts and uncles protected me and gave me the much-needed love I craved, and for that I am always grateful.

To the leaders at my Catholic school. I was lucky to attend a Catholic school where the nuns, priests, and teachers dedicated their lives to teach and mold us for the future. I learned from them the value of love, respect, justice, kindness, acceptance, and tenacity to thrive. They taught me that love trumps hate. I carry my formative years' lessons with me wherever I go.

To those who believed in me, gave me opportunities, and urged me not to give up. My siblings, friends, teachers, coworkers, and others paved the road for me.

To the numerous people who helped me in my professional life. It would not have been what it became without them. There are not enough pages to list all of them, but I would be remiss if I didn't pay tribute to my boss and hero, former Wayne County Executive Edward H. McNamara. He showed my colleagues and me the value of integrity, public service, and long-lasting relationships. I met my husband and all my best friends while working for him. These friends— my sisters, and brothers from other mothers—are my guiding stars.

To the founders of the Arab American Anti-Discrimination Committee, who taught me to stand up for my rights even when I am afraid. They took a chance on me and gave me opportunities to fight for the Palestinian cause. Through the ADC, I met and worked with many activists and inspiring people who became my lifelong friends, including Samar Sakakini and Ghada Mansour Barakat.

This book would not have been written had social sciences Professor Ron Stockton not given me a makeup assignment for the Middle East class I dropped at the University of Michigan-Dearborn. Many powerful people weaponize hate toward the Palestinian people, and that silenced many of us. Professor Stockton taught us that the facts and the truth will prevail regardless of the power that stands in our way.

To the many editors who made this memoir a product that I am proud to share with others. My grammar editor and my friend, Diane Kawegoma, David Dempsey, and Dinah Talbert ... thank you is not enough. Your edits made it possible for me to have a product that is good for publishing.

To the Palestinian people and all the indigenous people who never give up on their homeland. Some paid with their lives; others are lingering in political jail. The majority live under merciless apartheid rules fighting for dignity. I hope my story will shed light on the trauma the Palestinians face daily under the Israeli apartheid regime. Keep the hope alive! May our quest for justice and freedom be achieved during my lifetime.

Foreword

This can't be a normal introduction; the project is far too personal. This is really my story of Terry's memoir, and it is a complex story.

Terry was my student in the early 1980s in a class on the Israel-Palestinian Conflict. I had been trained as an African specialist, so this was a new area for me. To be honest, at that point she probably knew more about the issues than I did. But when the Israelis invaded Lebanon in 1978, there were clashes on campus between Lebanese students putting up flyers and a Jewish faculty member tearing them down. A colleague and I decided that for the sake of the curriculum, and the campus community, we should develop a course on that conflict. He was a specialist on Arabic history and culture, and I had taught units on Zionism and Palestinian nationalism. We agreed to divide up the lectures and bring in guest speakers to cover the gaps. It was a successful class.

Unfortunately for me, he left the university the next year. At that point, I was not confident I could continue on my own, but I decided to try. I began to attend the Middle East Studies Conference, to read extensively, and to spend part of my sabbatical in Israel to orient myself to the region. By 1987 I had my first publication on the conflict (which is the point at which faculty are considered credible).

I remember Terry as a charming young woman who often spoke to me after class about growing up in Ramallah. Then halfway through the semester she disappeared. She had taken a job with the newly formed American-Arab Anti-discrimination Committee. This was a new organization committed to resisting stereotyping of Arabs. It was an admirable and necessary organization, established by retired Senator James Abourezk and activist James Zogby.

In time, Terry became the head of the local chapter, in some ways the most important in the country. Then she began to work for Ed McNamara, the mayor of Livonia and soon the county executive of Wayne County. He was one of the most influential political figures in the Detroit area. She quickly became one of his assistant county executives. She worked with various political groups and once even went with Senator Carl Levin to the Middle East. She was on the White House lawn when Yasser Arafat and Yitzak Rabin shook hands.

We stayed in touch during those years. Then one day, she said she wanted to talk to me. She was hoping to get her degree and wanted to know if she could finish those three hours of incomplete credit. She proposed that she write essays on whatever topics I thought would demonstrate her competence.

Her request created two problems. First, universities are not kind to people who return after two decades and want to make up an incomplete grade. But I agreed to carry water for her with the campus bureaucracy (and had a helpful dean to sign off).

The other question was more complex. What would be an appropriate assignment. Perhaps I was being a stuffy professor, but it did not seem that writing five essays on various topics was sufficiently challenging.

Fortunately, I had a backup plan. I had started a program called the Immigrant Memoir Project. In the 1990s our campus had enjoyed a wave of new students from Eastern Europe. We also had students from Iraq, Lebanon, Syria, and other places such as Yugoslavia, Pakistan, India, and Bangladesh. Many had shocking personal stories of growing up in refugee camps, of fleeing massacres, of choosing between flight or arrest. Knowing how quickly America can absorb people and erase their past, I decided to invite these students to write these stories. The intended audience would be their descendants. They would talk about their family history, their life before they emigrated, the decision to emigrate, their first few years in America, and their ultimate success as students at the university.

At the time Terry and I spoke, there were 40 students in the project. We arranged that the memoirs would be put into a special collection in the Bentley Library, a state history archive on the Ann Arbor campus. The writers would meet on a regular basis at my house to discuss their progress. I always told them that "you should not ignore the bad things but don't whine. Let your descendants in 50 or 60 years realize that you were tough enough to face whatever life threw at you."

I suggested to Terry that for her semester assignment she write a memoir of her experiences. She thought that was a good idea and disappeared. A year later, she sent me her paper. It was over 50 pages long. I read it and asked her for a meeting. I told her I was rejecting the paper. I suspect she was as shocked as I was. After all, why should a professor reject a thoughtful 50-page paper from someone trying to finish up an incomplete grade from 20 years ago? But I had a good reason. As I told her, she had just written the Palestinian Narrative: "We have lived here from time immemorial. Jews and Palestinians lived together in peace. Then the Zionists came from Europe with a political plan. In 1948 we became refugees and strangers in our own land. Then in 1967 the rest of Palestine was conquered, and even more people became refugees. The occupation is cruel. We formed organizations to affirm our identity and to resist conquest." And so it goes.

I told her that any thoughtful Palestinian could write the same narrative. There was nothing of her in it. I reminded her of what she had told me in the past about her life. Telling that story would be unique and valuable. I told her to go back and do it again. Tell me about your family. Tell me about your parents and your grandparents. What was it like being a girl in Ramallah? What was your favorite holiday? Tell me about church. Tell me about school. What was it like to walk to school with armed Israeli soldiers watching as you walked along with your books? Tell me about leaving Palestine. That must have been a difficult decision. Why did they decide to leave?

Terry said she would go back and start over. To be honest, I was not sure I would ever see her again. Having such a fine first effort rejected must have been a blow. But a year later she contacted me once again. She had done what I had suggested. She had a new manuscript, 120-pages this time. She wanted me to see it. To be honest, as I read it, I was delighted. It was everything I wanted. It was not just a political activist or an intellectual discussing the Palestinian cause, but a young girl talking about her life. It was what the Palestinian narrative needed—the human dimension.

Terry was soon elected president of the American Federation of Ramallah, Palestine, a national American organization based in the city of Westland, Michigan. They had records going back over fifty years, listing every single marriage or baby or death. They had a real sense of their history, both in Palestine and in America. I suggested to Terry that she add some photos and documents to her memoir and have the Federation publish it. It could be sold at cost and would be a real inspiration to young Palestinians trying to figure out their American lives. She said she would consider it.

Once again, Terry disappeared. And once again, she popped to the surface several years later, in 2019. She said she had vastly expanded her memoir, adding quite a bit about her family and other topics skipped over in the first draft. The new draft was more than twice as long as the first draft. She said she was looking for a publisher. She asked if I would write the foreword.

I told her that not only would I write it, but I would be honored to write it. What I did not say what that if she had asked someone else to write it, I would have been disappointed.

As you read this you will see a young girl leading a normal life. You will see a young girl trembling in fear as bombs explode near her house. You will see a young girl watching her father beaten by soldiers, in his own home. You will see an assassination through the eyes of a child. You will see a girl ripped from her home and taken to a new country, a young girl working long hours to help keep her family afloat, a young woman learning to fit into a new land, a young American who has not forgotten the land she left behind, and an adult woman who mixes with presidents and prime ministers.

To anyone who has gotten this far, I offer the following suggestions:

• If you are a Palestinian American, read this memoir.
• If you are an Arab-American, read this memoir.
• If you are an immigrant of any kind, read this memoir.
• If you are feeling off balance or marginalized by the injustices rife in our land, and wondering how to take advantage of all that this wonderful country has to offer, read this memoir.
• And if you are just interested in a fascinating story, read this memoir.
• And please remember that in fifty years you may have family members who are at loose ends and wondering how to recover their balance. Perhaps you should write something of your own to let those who come after realize that those in your generation did not exactly have it easy, and maybe they should just get on with it.

—Ron Stockton
January 25, 2019

Introduction

The story and glory of the creation of the State of Israel has been written about in thousands of books. Almost all these books created an Israeli history by erasing or ignoring the history of my country, my villages, and my family. I was born into a Palestinian Christian, lower-middle-class family in the ancient land of Palestine. This was a place with very few natural resources, but because of religion, it was coveted by many powers who use my birthplace to their advantage.

My family traces our ancestry to this land from 1300 AD on my mother's side and from 1500 AD on my father's side. Like all indigenous people of this land, we lived through many colonial occupying powers and learned how to survive by tending to our families, staying away from politics, and working hard. In recent history, we have survived the Ottoman Empire, the British Mandate, and now Israel. The regimes came and went, while my family steadfastly tried to live in our homeland. It was not a choice; my family lived there because it was our home! If you look at their official papers, you will note that they are all identified as Palestinians, with different government stamps used as rulers. My great-grandfather was born in Yaffa under the Ottoman Empire. His son, my grandfather, and my mother were also born in Yaffa, under British rulers. I was born in 1956 under the Jordanian rule and my younger sister Maggie was born in 1969 in the Israeli-occupied territories. Despite living in the same region and area, my family's legal papers show that colonial powers governed our regions. They did not have our best interest in mind.

The people of ancient and current Palestine, like my family, mostly identified themselves as Arabs. Some in my family are Christians, and others, like my neighbor, are Muslim. Peppered between us are some Jewish people who lived just like us. We did not have armies, government, or a defense department. We lived off the land and lived a simple life. We were farmers and fishermen. Some members of my family went on to become professionals, working in the trades and as teachers, nuns, priests, judges, accountants, and merchants.

I am writing this memoir to tell the story of my family and how we lived under one occupying country. I chose to write about Israel because this is what I experienced. Everything I write in this book is something I lived through and experienced first-hand. This is my story. It is not a pro-Palestine or anti-Israel story; it is simply the story of my life as I lived it and remember it. Some readers will try to label it as anti-Semitic. That is their problem, not mine. I live by a mantra: I believe we are all brothers and sisters, and we all belong to the human tribe. No one is better or worse than anyone else.

I have wanted to tell this story since I was a child, but some of the memories are horrific, and no child should live through them. To this day, fifty-one years after I immigrated to the United States, I still have a recurring dream of soldiers coming after my family and me. In the dream, I have nowhere to go and nowhere to hide.

My family traces its heritage in Palestine back to the 1300s, yet Israel and its supporters continue to deny our existence. Or as Newt Gingrich and others said, we are "the invented people."[1]

The fact that I am a Palestinian is simply an accident of birth. I have no enemies and would never want enemies. Having an enemy means I must hate. I grew up in extreme circumstances, but was taught to love all people regardless of who they are. My story will be challenged, not because it is wrong, but because to some observers I am a "dehumanized" Palestinian. Someone will challenge even my memories. Again, that is their problem, not mine.

A friend from the Jewish community once told me, "If we want peace, we should stop rehashing our history and look to the future." I disagree with him. We cannot erase our history or our tragedy, just as history cannot erase the Holocaust, slavery, and the many pogroms faced by the African American community and the people of Jewish heritage.

The powers that occupied my birthplace committed various degrees of brutalities, and I wish I could forget some of the atrocities to which I was exposed. I desire peace more than anything else in my life, but peace is not about forgetting. It is about forgiving and moving forward. I forgave people who committed crimes against us. I wake up every day hoping children all over the world are free of a world that values military might and political divisions — the East against the West; Jews against Arabs; Christians against Muslims; and so, on and so on. I pray for a life filled with compassion, love, and brotherhood.

My story is the story of the Palestinian people, even though my family's suffering was less than the suffering of the Palestinian population that has languished in refugee camps since 1948 or been detained without charges in Israeli jails.

If one looks at the United Nations statistics,[2] Israel has been trying to purge my birthplace of its inhabitants. They managed to do so with the support of many peace-loving people who simply bought into the narratives Israel supplied them with daily. They criminalized, dehumanized, and labeled all Palestinians as terrorists. Israel is not afraid of our military might; we don't have any. Most of our armed resistors are small town comical fighters who make Barney Fife look like a master in the battlefield.

1 "Gingrich calls Palestinians 'an invented people,'" by Amy Gardner and Philip Rucker, *Washington Post*, December 9, 2011
2 "How Israel is 'cleansing' Palestinians from Greater Jewish Jerusalem" by Jonathan Cook, Jonathan-Cook.net, November 23, 2017.

Israel is more afraid of our birthrate.[3] They came to my country claiming, "A land without a people for people without a land."[4] In reality, they expelled 726,000, according to the Final Report of the United Nations Economic Survey Mission for the Middle East, published by the United Nations Conciliation Commission. That total of 726,000 includes my twelve-year-old mother and her family at gun point. They gave my family two hours to vacate their homes.

"Every birth of a Palestinian in Palestine puts a dagger in Israel's heart."[5]

For years, Israel sold a false history to an unsuspecting world. Our country and people of goodwill (America and other European countries) provided Israel with financial and military support because they viewed Israel as victims of a hostile Arab world. The data collected by respected Israeli historians show a different story.[6] The truth is as obvious as the rising of the sun in the east. The indigenous people of Palestine have been victims of circumstances beyond their control. Eight out of the twelve prime ministers who governed Israel since its inception were Eastern European natives who had little to do with religion or the region. Everyone was secular, disdaining religious Jews while using Judaism to advance their Zionist European dreams.

The occupation of Palestine affected me not only while I was living under the Israeli occupation but continues to haunt me today and to impact my life in the United States. On a daily basis, I have to dispel the notion that my people are terrorists. As I forged a new life in the United States, I constantly had to show people I was a peace-loving human being who did not want to kill or terrorize people.

The only time a member of my family owned a gun was when I joined the Livonia, Michigan, Police Reserve for a few years. Even then, I was always reminded that as a Palestinian I must be an expert on shooting people. In fact, I was a lousy shot. It took everything in my power to qualify at the shooting range so I could stay on the force. After a particularly bad target practice training session, my trainer shouted through a megaphone for me to stop. He proceeded to berate me by saying, "I can't believe my fucking luck; I inherited the only Palestinian who cannot shoot a gun!" I must admit, I laughed, and I continue to laugh at that story, but the reality is: I don't know any Palestinian in my family or my circle of friends who has ever used a gun or a weapon.

Since we are viewed as aggressors, people fear us regardless of where we reside.

I have been subjected to numerous threats in the United States. Since I frequently write letters to the editors or opinion pieces in the local newspaper on the issue of Palestine, people in power still try to destroy my career or my reputation. After I authored an article about the atrocities suffered by the Palestinians, an influential and politically connected man urged the Wayne County executive to fire me from my job. To his benefit, the county executive refused.

---

3 "Israel's soaring population: Promised Land running out of room?" by Tova Cohen and Steven Scheer, Reuters, September 25, 2015

4 "Zionism for the standpoints of its victims" by Edward Said, *The Reader* (Duke University Press), 1979

5 United Nations Economic Survey Mission for the Middle East, Final Report, page 74, 1949

6 *The Ethnic Cleansing of Palestine* (Oneworld Publications) by Ilan Papp, 2007

I am one of the few lucky people; many Palestinians all over the world have suffered simply because they are Palestinians.

Since becoming an American citizen, I have taken solace in the fact that I have rights, and am protected by our Constitution and by our government. Yet when I visit my homeland, the Israeli government views me, and many of my American Palestinian brethren, as less than United States citizens. We are subjected to humiliation and detention. On July 8, 2014, I was banned from entering my homeland for five years. Yet my Jewish cousin, who has no connection to Palestine, can become a citizen without any problem.

I am not writing this book to play the victim. I am writing this in the hope that people will see the truth and begin to search for a solution that will bring peace to both the Palestinian and Israeli people. For years, the American and European political leaders allowed fright, propaganda, and military power to rule. Israel possesses the 16th largest military forces in the world, but does not see itself as safe. Its citizens live in panic every moment of their lives. The reality is, the Palestinians could never destroy them. Even most fanatics believe that is impossible.

Israel is destroying itself by thinking it can subjugate millions of people. If history is a guide for the future, Israel will self-destruct. That is not what I want. I can't fathom the idea that Israelis should suffer my fate. I believe we must find ways to live as equals in peace based on justice.

This Arabic song, "I Breathe Freedom, Don't Cut Off My Air," sung by singer Julia Boutros, sums up what I believe:

> I breathe freedom, don't cut off my air
> When you cut my air, we both fall together
> You can never erase me, you need to listen to me and to talk to me, and if you think your force is curing, this is not the remedy
> If only you would listen to me, all that happened should be enough
> Force always falls, stopped in the face of ideas and truth
> This world is big enough for everyone, the truth alone remains
> And if you want us to find the solution, it will only happen if we think together
> The voice of freedom remains louder than all the voices
> However violently the wind of oppression blows and the night covers the spaces
> You could never color the universe all the same color
> Or replace the order of the earth or change the current of the wind

The truth will always prevail. The wheels of justice grind slowly, but in the end, they do turn. I hope this book will serve to open a genuine, reflective dialogue about the Palestinian plight. I hope it is the beginning of our work together to end fear and suffering.

Table of Contents

Part I
A Palestinian Girlhood

1 / Everyday Life

Life for the Hebrews is the center of the universe; my neighborhood was the epicenter of my world. Before 1967, the center of our Palestinian universe was our simple and basic neighborhood in Ramallah, a city in the central West Bank that now serves as the de facto administrative capital of the State of Palestine. It consisted of my family, school, church, and our neighbors. My family included six girls. We had a feisty and argumentative mom, whose temper sparked like a wildfire in a dry forest and was always ready to combust and flare. She spoke with a loud voice, even when she was not angry, and we knew early on not to argue with her. My father, on the other hand, was gentle and quiet. He was like a sheltering rock in the middle of a constant storm. You could always count on him to be serene during the chaos.

Even with these differences, they worked as a team to raise their daughters. We lived in a two-room, crumbling home with a large dark basement. Our home was next to two flats; one on the second level and one three steps from our front door.

In the house nearest to us lived an older woman and her husband. I believe they were our fourth cousins once removed on my mother's side. The older man was an active farmer who lived to be 100. He walked to his farm six days a week, rain or shine, and had three spoons of olive oil before breakfast. His wife kept their spacious one-room apartment clean. They were always entertaining their children and grandchildren, including my nemesis, Jamal.

On the second level lived a widow who went by the name of Um Farid (Farid's mother). My memories of her are vague. In the summer she pickled lemons for lemonade. In the winter she was constantly sounding off about the leaks in her roof. We all shared an outhouse across the street on a vacant lot full of weeds and small rocks. It had a rickety door and little peek holes carved by mischievous teenagers who were getting sexually aroused from seeing some woman shit in the shithole.

Our rented home sat at the end of the block and was at the top of a man-made hill. Below us lived our only Muslim neighbor, the local baker, with his wife and four children, all younger than us. Next to the baker lived another old lady with a face that looked like a prune. She lived by herself. Her husband died a few days before I was born, and her five children married and moved to the United States.

Next to the vacant lot where the outhouse stood, lived my mother's first cousin and her new husband. Like my mom, her cousin was lively and loud with the looks of Sophia Loren. Her hair was shiny black, always coiffed and her nails were always long, filed, and covered with beautiful colored nail polish. Her husband was a functioning alcoholic who was always struggling to find a job as an electrician, even during a time when there were few electricians and demand was high.

Next to my mom's cousins lived two middle-aged sisters; they looked ancient as if they were relics from Christ's era. One wore traditional Palestinian embroidered dress, and the other wore the latest clothes from the latest fashions. Their nearest neighbors were two elderly women who were the epitome of busybodies, always butting into our business. They spent most of their day sitting behind their bay windows monitoring the people going and coming into the neighborhood. They chit-chatted with people and occasionally yelled at and threatened kids who were misbehaving.

Across the street lived some friends, cousins, and playmates. Their homes were bigger and had inside plumbing. Economically, we were all considered lower middle class. Religiously, except for the baker and three other families, we were all Christians of various sects; even one of our Muslim neighbors baptized his only boy as a pledge to God after his wife had several miscarriages.

For the most part, our lives were simple. Men went to work, women stayed home — except for my mother. Young children went to school; some went to public schools; others, like my family, went to Catholic or private schools. After school, when and if we convinced our parents and the curious neighbors who sat at the windows all day that we had finished our homework, we took to the streets and played until supper or until our parents called us home.

Our road was paved, but the sidewalks were not. In the summer they were full of dust, and in the winter, they were full of mud. I managed to have hours of playtime, which I spent playing soccer and climbing and twisting myself on the monkey bars. I played marbles with the boys and Tagga Wegri, a local game which resembled baseball, with bases, but instead of a ball, we hit a rock with a stick.

My favorite hobby was chasing butterflies. I chased them like a police officer hunted thieves. I kept after the butterflies until I caught them. Even my stern mother admired my unique skills. Occasionally, I joined the girls in playing hopscotch, jumping ropes, and a game called hassway, a favorite game played by little girls that consisted of juggling five small rocks in the air and catching them before they fell. It was like hopscotch.

I was the third of six girls. I was a tomboy, or as they called me in Arabic, Hassen Sabi or Alsayed. I barely knew my oldest sister. She was always sick and in and out of the hospital. She was always pale, but gorgeous. My second oldest, Ghada, was a good girl. She listened to my parents more than I did. I don't recall her ever getting in trouble with my mother. My younger sisters and I were continually in trouble because Ghada always told on us. She reported every little imperfection and every failure to finish our assigned tasks on time to my mom. My fourth oldest sister, Stella, was just as mischievous as me. The youngest of our brood, Sylvia and Esperance, were fraternal twins who were so different from each other it was funny. They were an adorable little duo.

Esperance was fat and round and barely moved, while Sylvia was squirmy and scrawny. She had "Bette Davis eyes" and was always getting into fights with other girls in the neighborhood.

We went to school Monday through Thursday, and Saturday. We were off on Friday and Sunday. One could tell what school we went to by the uniforms we wore. Our Catholic school uniform was a bright, ugly turquoise color and could be seen from miles away. The nun who chose our school uniform either had a wicked sense of humor or was color-blind. Public school girls wore striped blue and green dresses that resembled my dad's pajamas. The public-school boys did not wear uniforms. The Catholic school boys wore dark blazers with gray or khaki pants and black shoes.

Everyone over the age of three went to school, without exception. The kids at our school, St. Joseph, started school at age two. St. Joseph was, and is still, run by French-order Catholic School nuns who have been serving the community since the mid-1800s. Some of the nuns who taught my sisters and I are still at the school.

On Sunday, we went to church, without exception, as our afterlife salvation depended on it. We were promised heaven if we attended every Sunday and went to confession. A couple of older nuns threatened us with the fire of Hell if we missed church. Luckily for us, we loved going to church and therefore were guaranteed to go to Heaven. Since we are Catholic, of the Latin rites (or so I thought — I found out later that we are Melkite Catholic), we walked to the Holy Family Church in Ramallah.

The church is situated in the middle of the city adjacent to the main street. As a child, I thought it was gigantic. It stood on a hill on the main road. Its steeple and bells could be seen from every corner of the city. I loved hearing the bells ring. They had a particular melody that gave me comfort. Unlike the Orthodox Church, their bells rhymed to the tone of "Taou Salou, Jibou Shiling" (Come on and pray and bring a shilling with you). Kids who went to the Catholic Church used to sing along these words when the Orthodox bells rang.

There were two ways to go to church. One was by my mom's parents' home. The other was to go by Crazy George's home. We preferred to go via my grandparents' home. We avoided George's home for fear he might chase us. We later found out that George was a simple, mentally ill man who never bothered anyone unless he was provoked.

We left home right on time every Sunday. We left the house when the first bell rang and arrived at the sound of the third bell. Father Lewis, the Italian Parish priest, started the service exactly at 9 a.m. He did not tolerate tardiness from anyone, especially children. We were required to wear special Sunday uniforms unless it was the holidays. We all dressed in nice, clean, tailored, and pleated navy-blue skirts. We looked like French expatriates. Our shoes were shined and clean, and we had French berets on our heads. Unless our parents were with us, a nun directed us to the front of the church where she kept an eye on us. The sisters ruled! No one dared to question them even when they were in church.

In the pews, one could see the regular churchgoers. Mrs. Rizqaulla, a classmate's mother, knelt in the front pew with her head cupped in her hands and a rosary dangled right in front of her. We could only see the lacy scarf that she wore every Sunday to church. She was very pious. She came to church early and left late.

The Sylvana family and the Karam Family always arrived late, but sat in the pews across from the students, next to the choir. They always looked like they popped up from the latest French fashion magazine. An old Armenian lady sat by the confessional booth next to the sacristy where the priest and the altar boys enter the church for Mass. I knew her as the grandmother of Hiratche, a young boy who went to school with us. Two of the nuns sat in the back and kept an eye on who was coming and going.

A painting of the risen Christ adorned the wall above the main altar. On the right side of the altar was a picture of St. Joseph and the toddler Jesus, and on the left side was a painting of young Jesus with the Virgin Mary. The church was sectioned by large arches, and every section had a picture of a saint. Unlike our humble home, the church was majestic.

Like all Catholic services, the ritual was predictable and solemn. I tried to listen to the homily, but most times I never understood what the priest was talking about. He was always admonishing someone or something. When I felt I had enough courage, I went to the bathroom. I tried not to make noise, but with patent leather shoes, I tapped, tapped, tapped to the back door and to the bathroom. When I did this, one of the nuns always followed to see if I really had to go to the bathroom. I also suspected that they needed a break from the homily too! I guess I will never know.

Except for the homily, I liked going to church. I stayed clean before the service, because I wanted to be loved by the young associate priest and because I did not want to be punished or lose my meager allowance, and I did not want to go to purgatory or hell. I tried not to play marbles or soccer before Mass. Most of the time I succeeded, but sometimes, I could not resist the temptation of playing a good game of marbles with kids who didn't go to church with us. When I failed, the nuns shamed me and had me sit next to them during the service. "You need to behave, your mom has enough problems … shame on you … do you want the people to say that you are a filthy little girl?" I pretended to care, but playing with the boys was more important than my appearance.

After church, we stopped at my grandparents' home to say hello and get some treats or breakfast. Occasionally, we met my mother there. Anyone who was receiving communion was forbidden from eating two hours before Mass. So, by the time church was over, we were usually starving. Sometimes I ate when no one else could see me. My grandfather was always ready to feed a starving bunch! "Taa'y taa'y ya sidi, kully … come, my grandchildren, eat."

My maternal grandfather was always welcoming and eager to greet, feed and spoil us. He was full of fun, vigor, and joie de vivre. To him, life was meant to be lived fully. He beamed like a sunrise at a lake in early spring. My grandfather was like the bright stars; he was always beaming with warmth and love. Sedo was old and sick yet was young and vigorous. He was so kind and loving and always cheerful. He rarely went to church but had more faith than anyone I knew, including the nuns. However, I was always worried that he might go to

Hell because he did not attend church regularly. When I mentioned my concern to him several times, he told me not to worry, he and God were best friends. He had a great sense of humor. He cuddled us and loved us and was very affectionate to us. When we arrived at his house after church, he opened his arms for a hug and a kiss from each one of us.

My grandmother was a few years younger than him, had a sunbaked face, was sensitive, practical, and supportive of her family. She was the glue that held everything together. She was happy to see us but was always wary of the mess we made for her. Sunday was her day off, and she wanted to spend the time with her neighbors. She was always yelling at us to keep the house clean. "ta-s-khouse al-beyt. Don't mess up the house."

When she was not working at school and cooking at home, she was sitting with her neighbor friends talking about the good old days in Yaffa (just south of Tel-Aviv on the Mediterranean Sea) and how her life had turned into dread after their eviction in 1948. Whenever she mentioned Yaffa, her face lit up and she looked like a different person entirely. Her neighbors had the same expressions. There was something mystical about Yaffa; it was a place where happiness was endless. The mention of Yaffa brought them joy and pain. I did not understand it until later in my life when I was banned from returning to my homeland. Their plight and eviction from their birthplace affected every aspect of their lives. They tried to forge a better life, but they ached for what had once been. "Yaffa Arroust Albahar ... Yaffa is the bride of the sea."

My grandmother was just as loving but was more aware of the practical reality of her life. She was in her forties but saw so much in her life and was anxious about what might come her way. She eloped with my grandfather at age 15 and lived with her mother-in-law, a woman she feared and loved at the same time.

Her mother-in-law taught her how to manage a household on a shoestring budget and live through all kinds of hardships My grandmother always worked to supplement her growing family's income and put food on the table since my grandfather had been sick with congestive heart disease from an early age. She was the manager of both the house and the budget. She tried to save money to ensure that her family did not go without.

In 1948, she was able to sustain the health and well-being of her family by her ingenuity and resourcefulness. My grandfather and his family were expelled from their home on a moment's notice and forced to live in a tent with a donkey for six months, but they managed to survive. This period of devastation had a great impact on her and our family. She wanted her children to go to school, but they did not have the means to do so. When they were able to find a decent home to live in, she always dedicated herself to keeping the house clean. So, when my sisters and I visited her, she demanded the same of us.

She secretly loved to spoil us but wanted us to learn the value of cleanliness. I remember my grandmother smoking, cleaning, cooking, and visiting with her neighbors when she was not at work. Since her home was in a central location, most of the women gathered there. They sat for hours sipping strong Arabic coffee, tipping the cup after they drank the muddy coffee so that my grandmother could read their fortune. The ritual was the same day in and day out. After leisurely drinking their coffee, one or two of the women would ask my grandmother to read their fortunes. Although she loved reading her neighbors' fortunes, she pretended to resist as a show of modesty and humility. When my grandmother was not in the mood for telling fortunes, the friends resorted to begging: "Come on Em Ibrahim (Mother of Abraham). I had a nightmare, and I want to hear my fortune." She did not want to appear too eager. After a few seconds of praise and pleading from the neighbors, she would succumb and read the fortune. "Shayefeh (Do you see)?" This routine sometimes lasted for a couple of hours.

My grandmother would take the small, emptied cup of coffee after it was turned upside down and images and shapes were made from the coffee grounds. She then began to interpret the patterns. She looked silently at the cup for a moment, found a shape and turned her face to the person who drank the coffee and said, "Look! Look at the fish. You are going to receive money."

The woman whose cup was read would smile and say "Inshallah, mn thoumick ela alsama" (It is God's will from your mouth to God's ears), a basic anecdote in Arabic. Or if the woman had children of marriage age, my grand-mother would look in the cup and exclaim the good news by saying, "Do you see this ring? It is evident, you are going to have a wedding soon." With each prediction, the women would ooh and aah and comment in approval if the pre-dictions were positive or lament their luck and say "Yekhefee Alshar" (May the evil thing disappear) if my grandmother saw something negative in the arrays formed by the coffee grounds.

While visiting, some of the women would bring with them their knitting or embroidery materials. After a couple of hours, everyone would return to their homes, and my grandmother would go back to her cleaning and making dinner while she had a cigarette hanging from her mouth. We often ignored my grand-mother and her friends and waited until the next group of neighbors came to visit. When not working, visiting with friends and taking care of her home, she went to visit her family and mother in Jifna, a village about ten miles away from our hometown, Ramallah.

We tended to follow my grandfather. In the winter, we sat with him in the living room, next to a small electrical heater where he weaved magical stories full of fairy tales with jennies, powerful heroes, or Christian saints who defied the devil and the mean people.

He told us stories about his life in Yaffa and talked endlessly about his twin brother who stayed behind. "akhou Shukry can hadi ... can yehbni ktheir ... rah ala elsijin mahaly ... my brother Shukry was a quite nice man, he went to jail instead of me because I had a family and he did not." We heard stories about his childhood and his adventures in the orange orchard and the sea. He told us tales of fishing and swimming in the Mediterranean, a few blocks from his home. Our favorite story was of the boy he rescued in the Mediterranean Sea. "jarna aja ysarakh...alwalid gire'e alwalide." gire'e ... rouhna ana wa ibn ami zey almajanin wa ghtasna fee albahar wa assafnah ..." our neighbor shouted the boy is drowning, the boy is drowning, my cousin and I ran like crazy people and jumped in the water and rescued the boy." Since we never saw the sea, we did not have any concept of its size. I must have heard the story a million times, but my grandfather always captured my imagination with it.

He wore a traditional Palestinian ombaz (an ankle-length robe) with a black jacket. In his pocket, he seemed to have an endless supply of Sylvana chocolate. In the middle of telling us his stories, he used to reach inside his long pocket and produce pieces of chocolate or gum. "khoudy ya sidi, bss ma tahkee lasitik. Take this my grandchild, but don't tell your grandmother."

Frequently when my aunts were visiting, they peeked into the room to say hello and give us a hug. When they had time, they sat with my grandmother and the neighbors and talked about the family, what they were going to cook, the price of food, the latest fashion, and music. But somehow the conversation always veered to the good old days when they lived in Yaffa.

They reminisced about everything that had to do with residing in Yaffa. Yaffa, to my family, was the epicenter of the universe. If they were eating melon, they would say "Ah, these melons are not as sweet as the fruits we had in Yaffa." Since Yaffa was known for its citrus, the savory taste of oranges brought tears and smiles to their faces as they described the sweetness and the nectars of the fresh cut oranges they had in the good old days before they became refugees.

Since the city of Yaffa was an ancient seaport, it was once called the bride of the sea and was famous for its fresh fish and fishermen, including members of my family who made a living fishing in the Mediterranean. My aunts and uncles who did not live in Yaffa did not like fish and rarely cooked it. But my mom and her family ate fish with reverence.

As my family recalled their years in Yaffa, they talked about Sultan Ibrahim and the bushels of crabs they ate with Arabic salad and fried potatoes. They spoke of the holidays and picnics they used to have with families and friends. Of course, we had fish, oranges, and other citrus fruits, and we forged a good life in Ramallah, but nothing seemed to measure up to the standard of living in Yaffa. There was always an ache for what was and what could have been. Since most of our neighbors and friends were refugees from Yaffa, Lud, and Ramleh, they had a collective memory of the simplicity of life, the joy and the great camaraderie that centered around family and food. Yaffa was never far away from our lives.

During the summer, we often had dinner at my grandparents' home. My two aunts, who worked as nurses in Jerusalem in the Army hospital on the outskirts of Ramallah, joined us when they could. After dinner we took naps. After our rest, we waited for my aunts to give us treats or money. As the adults sat in the front yard, drinking disgusting black Arabic coffee with some of the neighbors, my grandfather would have us walk with him to the end of the street to buy ice cream. Any kid who was in sight of my grandfather was treated to ice cream. Rukab popsicles were the best! Of course, as we slurped the ice cream, we dripped it all over our clean church uniforms, which infuriated my mom. However, as long as my grandfather was around, we were safe from my mother's fury.

During the late afternoons, we either went to a picnic, or to Jifna, where my grandmother's mom and her brother lived. At the picnic, we swam in the "balou," a minuscule natural lake. My uncle and aunts brought with them a transistor radio and listened to music. They were joined by my Uncle Zouzou and his cool friends, Manuel, Hanna, and Fouad. Dressed fashionably, my aunts would flirt and tease the boys.

In Jifna, we terrorized the town, by running after farm animals and climbing trees. The townspeople viewed us as spoiled city folks, but no one dared touch us because they had to answer to Grandma Hana, who adored us.

Time marched on in our daily lives. Our favorite hobby and activity was to sit with my grandfather and gaze at the wonders we saw in the clouds. The night skies did not interest us as much as the phenomena and the images we saw in the clouds. My grandfather spun a thousand stories from each and every cloud.

We often sat on short twill-woven kitchen stools across the street from his home and listened to story after story embroidered in the clouds. Each powdered puff cloud was a story about either a saint or a martyr from the Bible. When the clouds were disconnected and pure white, my grandfather would point with his index finger and say, "See, the Virgin Mary is washing her sheets." With our mouths open, we absorbed and stored them in our memories for life. His stories were best when we had rolling clouds covering the blue sky or there were cumulus clouds with a bit of sun hiding behind them. We did not fret or move when he told us the stories of the Bible through the images of the clouds. We sat, listened and were "at the moment." Our happiness derived from the many small moments we spent in our neighborhood with our family and friends.

Our life was not unique or extraordinary; it was the only life we knew. It was routine. We lived an average life day in and day out. We were not happy; we were not sad. We were not poor, but we were not wealthy. Our lives consisted of little and no drama … until my oldest sister died.

2 / Death in My Family

They say when Death decides to visit, no one can stop it. It does not discriminate. Death does not fear nor care about who it grabs. Death just happens to all. When the angel of death takes a young child, it leaves behind shattered and devastated families, friends, neighborhoods, and communities.

In 1964, Death decided that my older sister Hilda, who was only ten, was a prime candidate for its clutches. It did not visit our house suddenly because my sister was sick for a long time, but that did not prepare us for its devastation. Before then, our lives consisted of joy, fun, and sun and poverty. My friends and I climbed trees, skinned our knees, and learned silly rhymes. We were engulfed with love and security in a neighborhood that did not know isolation. Our rolling seasons of fun stopped when Death sneaked into our home and stole my sister without preparing us.

When Death came and took Hilda, it brought with it years of profound and lasting hurt. The heartbreak dashed away from our joy and hope. Misery became our constant companion.

Throughout my young life, my older sister was often sick. I did not know why, but I knew when my dad and mom were not busy at work, they were at the hospital tending to their daughter. She was thin and pale with light brown wavy hair. When my folks were at the hospital, our neighbors stepped in to keep an eye on us. So did my mom's cousin, Mansoura, who became our surrogate babysitter from hell.

During that period, I got into a lot of trouble. As usual, I did not think I was doing anything wrong, but Mansoura had no tolerance for children who didn't listen to her. Since I did not see any problem playing with the boys and coming home with dirty, ripped clothes, we butted heads. I was only six years old. She began to call me "Alsayed," our garbage collector's name. The name stuck, and the rest of the neighbors began to use it, too. I really did not mind the name, at least I was getting some attention.

Preoccupied with my older sister, my parents did not pay much attention to our troubles. We saw our parents only a few minutes a day. In time, my parents stopped going to work. The neighbors still pitched in by cooking meals for us and washing our clothes. One day, I was in bed, pretending to be asleep, when I heard Mansoura tell our next-door neighbor that Hilda was not going to live beyond the weekend. They were whispering and crying at the same time. I was so afraid that I began to cry without knowing why. My dad and mom did not come home that night. Death arrived at our door and took my sister away.

Someone woke us up and told us that we would not be going to school. My Uncle Zouzou came over to help Mansoura. He was not himself; my Uncle Zouzou was the personification of love and fun. Like my grandfather, he gave us pure joy. He lifted our spirits with his love of life. He was young with curly black hair and two dimples that melted the hearts of every teenage girl in our neighborhood. He was always running around with the most popular boys in the city. Young teenage girls liked us because we were his nieces.

That day, he tried to be funny, like usual, but he failed miserably. He and Mansoura kept whispering to each other about what needed to be done. By mid-morning, our neighbors arrived at our house. Some helped us get dressed and made sure we were fed. Others were cleaning the rooms and the basement. Some murmured about the mess. Others tearfully talked about my family. I heard someone say. "Poor Hilda; she is now an angel." I wondered why she was poor if she was an angel. I thought angels were happy. As one of the neighbors combed my hair, she whispered in my ear, "Why couldn't it be you, Alsayed, instead of your beautiful sister?" I answered her with a smile, "I can't be an angel yet!" She hit me lightly with the brush and told me to be nice.

By noon, our home was clean. My dad's hearing-impaired sister Maria, someone I barely knew, came to our house and started to inspect us. She stopped to talk to Um Farid, our neighbor on the second floor. She was trying to be discreet, but because of her hearing, she was practically shouting about how her brother and sister-in-law were going to survive the loss of their daughter. She was crying, and so was Um Farid.

By 3 p.m., someone determined that all the furniture had to be removed to make room for the coffin, as was the tradition. We did not have funeral homes. It was odd that my grandma, grandpa, and my aunts did not come to visit us. Mansoura told us to stay in the yard where she could see us. Somehow, I complied without complaint. I did not fret; I was bewitched by everything going on around me. Everyone was nice to us that day, including Jamal, the boy I hated.

The neighbors and relatives came and left. Some brought food; others brought chairs. Some brought flowers. I had, of course, heard of dead people in the past, but I had never been to a wake or a funeral.

My great-grandmother arrived from her village in Jifna. I loved this woman; she was always happy and allowed us to do anything we wanted when we visited her every other Sunday afternoon. She had a wrinkled light-skinned face, which characterized a life well lived.

In the summer, we often visited her and her son Farid and his family from around 3 to 8 p.m. A private taxicab picked us up from our home and drove us to her home in Jifna. She lived in the middle of almond and apricot groves and she raised chickens and lambs. She allowed us to climb trees and pick apricots when no one else in the village was allowed to. When one of her daughters-in-law protested the unfair treatment; she silenced her by saying, "It is my land, and I do with it as I please. These girls can climb all they want; it is none of your business."

When she arrived this time, she wailed and started to hit her face and head "My poor Hilda! God, my poor Hilda! Why did she have to die? Why did you not take me instead?" Women began to gather around her and in unison began to chant and wail.

I was scared but enthralled. I could not understand what was happening all around me, but for the first time in my young life, I did not feel the urge to go out and play with my friends. In fact, some were peering from around the corner but were afraid to come by.

At 6 p.m., my deaf aunt ushered us to my uncle's home in the next neighborhood. The remaining oldest children held hands and walked in silence with my aunt. She was kind but scary. She wore a traditional Palestinian dress. Since we did not know her well; she scared us. We were wrong; she was a lovely woman. My uncle's wife greeted us at the door and told us to take our shoes off before we could enter her home. We did as she said. My cousins, who were older than us, watched as we sat, as instructed.

Within minutes my sister Ghada began to cry. My aunt began to comfort and soothe her. She swooned in her ears, "It is okay; don't cry. Your sister is an angel." She cried as she whispered to all of us again and again, "It is alright. Everything will be alright."

Since there were not enough beds to go around in the small house, my aunt put some mattresses in the living room for us. After we had eaten supper, we changed into our pajamas and were fast asleep within an hour. I wet my bed that night. That was the first time that I wet the bed. I was embarrassed to move, but my aunt noticed my wet pajamas. She was not happy with me. I ruined her mattress, but she was not really angry.

We ate breakfast with my cousins, who were trying to be polite, at a Japanese low dining table in the basement. I asked my aunt if I could go home, she said "Yes, later," and that she would take us as soon as they brought Hilda home. She looked at my older cousin and told her that she would have to babysit my twin sisters and Jouliana, my newest sister, while she and my deaf aunt would take us to say goodbye to Hilda. My cousin nodded yes without saying a word; it was all mechanically done.

We walked the two blocks holding hands. There was little wind, and my long hair was covering my face. However, I was afraid to move it to avoid being scolded by my aunt. Although I could barely see, I saw women and men dressed in black coming from all directions. I saw my favorite priest dressed in dark vestments. He was walking with another priest from the Melkite Church. Three altar boys were walking ahead of them. One was holding an incense burner, and two were carrying big icons. They were about ten steps ahead of everyone else. Although there were people everywhere, the streets were silent. No one was talking. As we approached our neighbor's home, we saw our grandfather. My sisters and I were about to rush over to him, but my aunt stopped us in our tracks. She yelled with a stern voice, "Don't!" My grandfather did not even look at us. He kept his doleful eyes on the ground.

The walkway between our home and our neighbor' homes was full of men. Some I knew; others were strangers. They were all sitting on woven mismatched chairs collected by our friends, so people could sit while waiting. Many people sat next to and near my father, who was in a trance — tears running down his face.

The incense smoke filled the air, and it made unusual cloud shapes.

We arrived at our neighbor's shortly after the two priests and the altar boys. The altar boys stood on the side by the wall, while the priests went to shake hands with everyone in the room. They spoke to my grandfather, who was openly crying, and then they went to see my father. This is when I saw my Baba (father) begin to sob uncontrollably. It was the first time I saw my dad cry.

Seeing my dad cry was more than we could handle; my sisters and I ran to my dad and began to cry with him. Everyone tried to console us. My Baba, who was utterly despondent, sought to hug us but failed. My Uncle Zouzou and my grandfather picked us up and gently moved us away. My aunt left us and went inside and began to wail and chant a dull, aching, and rhythmic tune meant to touch the soul. The noise from the house was melancholy and sad. My favorite priest tousled my hair and gave my sisters and me a peck on our heads. He ushered my father and the men toward the white coffin, where all the women were seated surrounding it.

Led by my uncle, my grandfather and a neighbor, my sisters and I were escorted to the middle of the room, where my mother, grandmother and the rest of the relatives were seated around that beautiful white coffin with its wreaths of flowers.

Dressed in her communion dress and veil, Hilda looked like she was sleeping. She had flowers around her body like the flowers the dead saints have around their bodies in church photos. Hilda also had a beautiful pink rosary. She looked like she was smiling. As we approached the coffin, my mother leaned in and began to kiss Hilda. My grandmother was slapping her face and chanting; the women and men were making a commotion, as was the custom. The priests stood aside for a few minutes to allow us to say our last goodbyes. As I knelt down to kiss Hilda, as ordered by my neighbor, one of my distant cousins yelled, "It should have been Alsayed, not beautiful Hilda."

Like everyone else, I kissed Hilda on the forehead; she was cold, even though it was April. I was afraid to say or do anything. I looked at my mother; she did not look back. She was leaning with her head on my sister's chest and whispering, "Take me with you, habibty (my love)."

We were gently moved back by our neighbor. My father was escorted by his brother and nephew toward the coffin and my mother. He was about to collapse. He leaned on the coffin and began to scream "No, no, no - she was not supposed to die!" As he uttered these words, everyone in the room began sobbing, wailing, chanting, and screaming.

People made room as the two priests came toward the coffin. The Melkite priest began to pray and chant the Evlogitaria of the Dead, and the other priest responded to his chant. Minutes passed, and my grandfather, my uncle Zouzou, my dad's brother and his nephew moved toward the coffin; they gently tried to move my dad, mother, and grandmother away from Hilda. Some of the nuns and neighbors were also trying to help in this effort. My mom collapsed. A nun began to tend to her. She was trying to have her smell something from a small bottle. One of them softly slapped her on her cheeks. When she was revived, she began to scream "Hilda, Hilda, Habibity."

My father was escorted to the front of the coffin, behind the two priests. The four pallbearers lifted the coffin on their shoulders and began walking downstairs to the street. My mother, grandmother, and aunts were wailing as they were led by other women, including my great-grandmother. They all walked behind the coffin as if they were in a daze. My wailing aunt and the two old ladies from across the street took our hands and walked us behind my mother.

As we left the house, I saw our schoolmates lined up, two to a line, in the streets. They were all carrying wreaths with different names. I also saw my uncle Zouzou, Henry, Giovanni, and Tony. Also, I saw the baker and his wife walking toward the church with us. It seemed like everyone, including the mayor of the city, came to my sister's funeral.

The service was at the Melkite Church, not our usual church. It turned out that my family was of the Melkite rites and not the Latin rites. We just went to the Latin Church because it was where almost everyone in our school went to pray.

The funeral service was over in an hour. Afterward, we went to the cemetery at the edge of town, where Christians bury their dead, to bury Hilda. Nothing was the same after the funeral. For a week, people came to our home to offer their condolences to my parents. Per tradition, we celebrated the third- and ninth-day memorial for my sister, where the women wailed chants and cried with my mom. My sisters and I slept at my aunt's or my grandparent's home. After the ninth day, we returned to school. Everyone, including Sister Filippa, the mean nun, was kind to us. We did not do our homework. During chapel, the priest prayed for my sister's soul and my family. At recess, I did not play soccer for fear my sister would tell my mother that I was naughty. Although I was six years old, something inside me told me not to cause any trouble. My sadness was overwhelming. Seeing my dad and grandfather crying so deeply affected my soul. It put a tear in my heart.

Something else happened. My mom, instead of being feisty, became depressed, sad, bitter and most of all, impatient with us, especially with me. She picked on me before my sister's death, but after her death, I became the object of her distress. If I came home disheveled because I was playing with the boys, she would scream and yell, and beat the crap out of me. I could not do anything right. After several months of moping around the house and making my life a living hell, she went back to work. My second sister, who now became my oldest sister, became the object of her affection.

My father immersed himself in his work. He left home early and came back after dark. My mom fretted and screamed her way around the house. She yelled, slammed, and hit anyone who was in her way. She stopped calling me by my name and began to refer to me as the devil. It was rare to see her relaxed; she was always angry. Some of the neighbors tried to ease her burdens by offering to help her with the cleaning. She refused, instead, she demanded that we scrub, clean and re-clean the house until it was time to finish our homework or time to go to bed.

We learned to whisper to each other; even the twins learned to be discreet. We began to spend more time in the dark basement. We ate in silence and were afraid to complain about the food. My father knew something was wrong but was worried that if he spoke, she would go nuts and end up in the nut house. Occasionally we saw some tenderness, but most times, we watched her cry silently in the corner of the room.

My Uncle Zouzou stopped by after work often to check on us. Our neighbors and our cousin, Mansoura, did not yell at us as much as before. I continued to get in unnecessary trouble by chasing butterflies, bats, and boys older and younger than I. I was always scaling walls and trees to catch a butterfly or discover a bird's nest. I had a knack for balance—I could walk horizontally or vertically to reach my prey. Although she always hollered at me for being a tomboy, on more than one occasion, I heard the pride in my mom's voice as she and the neighbors discussed my ability to catch butterflies and beat out the boys.

However, after Hilda's death, our life had a touch of anger and sadness, but like with everything else, we marched into a new era of our lives with the memories of my dead sister, who did not live long enough.

3 / The Fun Summer of 1965

The summer represented freedom, picnics, hours sitting with my grand-father, a blazing hot sun, fig trees, chasing butterflies, marble games, eating colorful ice cream, and going to church without a uniform. I loved summer. However, I have dark skin and dark cascading hair, and in the summer my skin would turn a dark bronze. People in my neighborhood equated fair skin with beauty, so in their eyes, I didn't have an ideal look.

Anyway, I began each day with my hair combed neatly (in a ponytail or with two braids) and came home messy, with scruffy and skinned knees and elbows, and with new scars on my face from fighting with boys over a soccer or marble game.

It had been a year since my sister died, but the effects of her death still lingered in our lives. The summer of 1965 was a little different. With my sister's death, my mom stayed home or close to home more often than usual. Although I was only six, I wanted to play in the neighborhood, but was having a hard time roaming the streets while my mom was home moping around the house. I had a more difficult time leaving home without finishing my endless chores. She assigned me tasks and expected me to complete them. To make matters worse, my mother, who considered me the black sheep of the family, insisted I stick around and play with my shy older sister. But that did not deter me from sneaking out to play when the neighbors were visiting, or when my mom was occupied with my baby sister, Jouliana. Aside from my gang of boys, I found two girls who preferred soccer and climbing trees to playing with dolls. But to please my mother, I played house with my sister.

When it came to me, my mom believed in corporal punishment. She was the disciplinarian from hell. I was just an annoyance to her since the day I was born; I could never please her. So I tried to measure the punishment with the amount of mischief I could get away with. I found ways to have fun despite my circumstances. I used to sneak around with my friends and go play with Henry, his brothers, and other boys in our neighborhood. One of our favorite ways to pass the time was climbing a giant fig tree overlooking the elementary boys school next to St. Joseph school. We hid in the thick leaves and branches and shelled passersby with green figs. We stifled our laughs as we watched people react to the pelting. Young kids cried, teenage girls and boys threatened to catch and beat us, and older women yelled, "We know who you are, we are going to tell your parents!" Since no one could see us, we were not worried about the consequences. Occasionally, someone would come to the tree and threaten to kick our asses. We hid in the branches, where it was hard to see us unless they climbed the tree.

We were like mountain goats, always climbing walls, trees, and monkey bars. For kicks, we hung upside down from tree branches or monkey bars and held our breath as someone counted to see how long we lasted. The winner of this game picked the next game or activity for the day. This dangerous game landed us at the local clinic several times, where Sister Leticia treated and scolded us at the same time. We loved living on the edge. The fig tree holds many beautiful memories.

We sat for hours telling each other scary stories of ghosts and dabaes (hyenas), who came in the middle of the night and stole little babies from their mothers. Sometimes, when we were bored with our daily routines or games, we created new games just to kill the monotony of the lazy, hot summer. One day, Henry suggested that we jump from the fig tree and walk home and knock on every house we passed and run. It was a great game until we knocked at Crazy George's house, and he came after us. We ran on adrenaline and fear, and we did not stop until we passed my grandfather's coffee house. We hid behind my stunned grandfather who was drinking coffee with his friends. After we caught our breath, we found out no one was chasing us. My grandfather was not amused when he heard what we did. He wanted us to apologize to poor George. I don't recall if we apologized, but we never went near George's home after that episode.

We also played hide and seek and spent hours finding places to hide. Sometimes we took the liberty of hiding in someone's yard or home, scaring the family who lived there. We used to sneak into the neighbors' homes through an open window and hide until someone found us. It was a happy summer. Rich kids went to the YMCA and summer camp; poor kids like us made the streets their summer camps.

The summer of 1965 was a dichotomy of many events. My sister's death brought bitter sadness to all, yet we continued to enjoy life with my grandfather. We celebrated the Assumption of the Blessed Virgin Mary when we went with him and my grandmother to Jerusalem. In memory of Hilda, we lit a candle in the Orthodox Church of Sittna Maryiam. My grandfather bought us cotton candy, popcorn, and hamleh (green roasted chickpeas). We spent the whole day with my grandparents and my aunts without my parents, who were still in mourning.

After my sister's death, my grandfather made every effort to comfort us and ensure Hilda's spirit stayed alive. One day before school began, we sat outside in the corner at my grandparents' home and looked up at the bright, blue sky. He smiled and pointed his index finger to where some mystical white cloud was forming. He touched his mustache and said, "Heaven is busy today, and everyone is celebrating." He pointed at the flaky and bulging clouds and began to talk slowly about the little angels who were gracing the clouds.

We followed his finger and marveled at the rolling clouds. I squinted to see the images he described to us. Each cloud was different than the other. Some were small and resembled animals and babies, others looked like angels and saints and were like the pictures the nuns gave us for good behavior. At one point in the story, he stood, strained to see and shouted with glee, "Look, look, Hilda is holding hands with my brother Shoukry." We all stood and watched what looked like a young man holding hands with my sister. She looked like she was wearing the dress she had on when she was in the coffin. From then on, we listened intently to all he said; we did not want to spoil the moment.

After we were silent for a while, Giovanni, Henry's younger brother, asked my grandfather, "Who is Shoukry?" For a second, my grandfather seemed to be at a loss for words. For the second time this summer I saw tears in his eyes. He collected himself and began to talk about Shoukry. I did not want to hear about Shoukry; I wanted to hear about where my sister was going with Shoukry. I did not have to worry; he told us to look again at the cloud and exclaimed with joy: "See, see, they are talking to Christ ... they are going to heaven together ... Shoukry must have waited for Hilda ... I can't wait to tell everyone about this!"

Then my grandfather began to talk to us about his identical twin, Shoukry, who did not leave Yaffa with the rest of the family in 1948. For two hours, Sido (my grandfather) told us about the joy of growing up with his twin brother, Shoukry, and the pain of their 1948 separation.

He talked about his school days when the priests and nuns would confuse the two boys and punish one for the infractions of the other. He spoke about how he and his brother used to go with their grandmother to pick oranges and play on the pig farm. He enthralled us with how they helped their grandfather plant orange and lemon trees in Yaffa. He laughed as he recited to us the names of every tree they planted. Each brother was responsible for ten trees. He told us that the first tree he planted was after their first communion.

At first, he and Shoukry did not like the gift; they would have rather been given candy or a toy. However, as they saw the trees mature over the years, they began to love tending to them and began to take ownership of them. Plus, tending to their trees gave them time to spend with their grandfather, a man they dearly loved.

My grandfather went on to tell us how the whole family had to leave Yaffa at a moment's notice. His twin brother and his wife and their adopted daughter stayed behind and hid until it was safe. My family was desperate and tried to reach them but could not for a long time.

The Israeli Hagana and Stern Gangs went on a rampage, terrorizing people and forcing them to leave town, with the consent of the British rulers, who looked the other way. The whole family was forced to flee on foot most of the way until they found and paid a high price for a rickety bus which took them to their destination.

They had no food nor water, only the clothes on their backs. More than forty-five members of my family marched along with 750,000 others who walked from their homes to unknown destinations, looking for safety. During their treacherous journey, my grandfather kept going back and forth to look for his brother.

He talked about their eviction from their home, but he spent the rest of the two hours telling us the story of all the mischievous trouble they got into. My grandfather's tale ranged from humorous to sad to witty, but most of all, he introduced us to his early life through the mosaic of clouds in the sky.

Our favorite story that day was about how he and Shoukry snuck into St. Anthony's Catholic Church and replaced the wine with vinegar just before Mass. He chuckled as he told the story.

"It was 6 a.m.; Shoukry and I were not allowed to serve as altar boys until my mother apologized to the priest she insulted two weeks earlier."

The Italian priest did not like that my grandmother was challenging him in front of her children about how they dressed for the Sunday mass. The priest decided to ban the boys from serving as altar boys until their mother (my grandmother) apologized.

"My stubborn mother," Sido went on to say, "refused to do so."

The boys, taking their mother's side, decided to trick the priest by replacing the wine with vinegar. He went on with the story. "After we had changed the wine into vinegar, we went to the 7 a.m. mass. We sat where we always sat with my mother and father. We kept our eyes on the ground we did not want to be caught "

The Latin Mass was the same as usual — the priest and the altar boys performed the ceremony, the nuns checked the pews for any kids misbehaving, and the attendees went through the ritual of kneeling, standing, and sitting. When it was time to give the wine and water to the priest, the altar boys brought the wine as was the ritual and poured the wine and water into the chalice without incident. Shoukry and Sido stifled a laugh. At that time, the priest performed the ceremony with his back to the multitude; therefore, it was difficult to see how much vinegar the priest poured into the cup. Since this priest was known for chugging lots of wine during mass, the boys knew that the priest was going to be furious.

Henry was making faces as if he tasted something sour. We were now hanging on every word my grandfather said! My face lit up as he described the moment the priest downed the vinegar at the altar. My grandfather was laughing, and we were laughing with him.

They got away with the prank. The priest almost choked on the vinegar but did not dare say anything during the mass. He kept clearing his throat during the service and the altar boys kept looking at the priest's face and stifling their laughter. When the priest turned to face the people, he looked like he was about to kill someone. The two boys sitting in the pew next to their parents, Sido and Shoukry, kneeled, cupped their faces in their hands and pretended to pray while laughing softly.

The priest accused the altar boys of the trick. The two were suspended from serving as altar boys as long as the priest served in town. I asked my Sido if he was ever caught, he replied "No," but, after the chaos died down and the priest stopped hunting for the children who participated in the hoax, my grandfather went to confession and told a young and benevolent priest about the trick. To my grandfather's relief, the priest laughed and told my grandfather not to repeat the trick again. For repentance, he told my Sido that he would have to work with him once a week for three months to aid the poor. At first, my grandfather and Uncle Shoukry did not like the sentence set by the priest, but after the first week, the boys looked forward to their time with him. The priest always tried to help the poor and introduce kids to serving the poor. This created a lifelong passion in my grandfather who always went around to help the poor in Ramallah.

As my Sido regaled us with this tale, we listened intently; we sat listening to him for more than two hours without fidgeting. We laughed, smiled and sometimes we had tears in our eyes as he told us about how much he missed his brother. I was so happy to know that my sister Hilda was taken care of by my dead Uncle Shoukry, who seemed to be such a fun guy.

Sido finished his story when the kaak vendor approached us with the delicious, freshly baked sesame bread with falafel. The young man was pushing the heavy cart up the hill, hoping not to lose his cargo or have some of the kids steal some kaak from him. As he approached us, Sido stopped him with a beautiful greeting, "Allah Maek (God be with you), Allah yerzeak (God grant you a profit). The young vendor, Ali, replied in kind "Allah Yukon maek (God also be with you)."

Sido bought us sesame kaak and told us to be on our way. As we left, Sido yelled to us not to tell Tete (my grandmother) about the kaak; he always wanted us to keep stuff from my grandma. We played until dinner, and then each of us went home for the day.

Besides playing with the boys and spending time with my grandfather, I was preparing for my first communion, which was going to be a year later. Although younger than the other kids, by the time I finished my catechism, I would be seven and a half years old. My mother insisted I have my first communion at the Melkite church instead of our regular church. I was not happy about it.

First communions in our neighborhood were a time for celebration. Every young child who went to Catholic school looked forward to his or her first communion, and I was no different. I remembered the beautiful white lace dress that my sister Ghada wore to her communion and was anxious to go through the ritual. I was extremely disappointed when I found out that my sister, Hilda, was buried in the dress and, because my mom was in mourning, I would have to wear an ugly dress given to me by the nuns from the Melkite Church. Also, instead of going with Henry to catechism, I was going with strange kids.

The Melkite nuns did not wear habits. They spoke French and were gentle, but they were not familiar to me. I went to catechism every Tuesday and learned my lessons but did not enjoy the experience. To top it all off, I picked fights with some of the boys who thought I was poor because the nuns had me wear a donated dress for my first communion.

What was supposed to be a memorable experience turned into a miserable event. The day of my first communion, my mother did not even bother to show up. The other girls wore beautiful gowns; I did not have that luxury.

I found myself with some misfits who were dressed like me in donated, ugly, borrowed, white, faded long dresses. After the wretched service, everyone had a photographer take their picture, except for a few kids from the more impoverished neighborhoods and me. I made every effort not to cry, but I could not help it. One of the nuns took pity on me and escorted me to breakfast. I sat with her because my parents were not in attendance.

As soon as the festivities were over, I ran home. I stopped at my grand-parents' home to see my grandfather. I was surprised he was not at my first communion. He was not home; he and my grandmother were visiting my great grandmother in Jifna.

I went home depressed. My mother pretended that nothing unusual had hap-pened. My father was working but when he came home, he apologized and explained to me why he could not attend.

We ate our usual Sunday dinner without fanfare. Around 4 p.m., my aunts and grandparents came to visit, and to my surprise, they gave me a twen-ty-one-karat gold crucifix with a delicate long chain. My aunt Salma gave me a kiss and put it around my neck. I forgot my earlier misery and was euphoric. My mom let me wear the crucifix to bed but the next day she took it from me and hid it. A few weeks later, she looked for it, but never found it. She blamed me for its loss.

During the summer, the neighborhood boys and I were inseparable when Sido was not with us. We played soccer, teamed up against other kids in marble games, climbed walls and ran around chasing butterflies, birds and other crit-ters. We would sometimes play a prank on the kaak vendor. As we got older, we began to steal kaak and falafel from the poor vendor. One day, one of us stopped the vendor to buy kaak, while the rest of us tried to grab a treat.

Of course, we confessed to stealing and were admonished by the priest. He ordered us to recite Hail Mary ten times plus. But that did not stop us; the poor peddler did not know that every time one of us stopped him to buy a kaak, Giovanni, Henry, my sister Stella, and I stole a kaak or falafel. It took a year before the vendor caught on to our prank! When our mothers learned about our trick from a neighbor who caught us in the act, they went berserk, especially my mom. That evening, I got the beating of my life. I was denied dinner and dessert and was not allowed to leave the house for three days.

By then, my mother began to repress her depression and anger. She was short on patience, especially with me; when she was not crying, she was screaming at me. I received the brunt of her hurt and anger. When I woke up with wet pajamas because I wet my bed, my mother went on a rampage. She was not diagnosed, but I swear she had a nervous breakdown. I feared her, but I stayed defiant.

On the six-month anniversary of my sister' death, my mother went over the edge. She scared me, but I stayed defiant. No one could console her. The only time she was at peace with herself was when my sister, Jouliana, was suckling at her breast. Our neighbors became concerned. They took pity on me and tried to shield me from my mother's rage. By the time school opened, I was relieved I would be away from her for at least eight hours.

By October, the sky was becoming gray and dark. It did not rain much, but with schoolwork and chores at home, we were not able to go outside as much. My mother was becoming less and less hostile toward me. She was still unhap-py, but my punishments were less severe. My grandfather talked to her and told her that if she continued with my abuse, he would take me to live with him. Of course, I was hoping he would do that. After all, I adored the man! Fearful of the shame of losing me, my mother stayed away from physically hurting me but began neglecting me instead. She became my mental tormentor.

At school, I excelled in sports, religion, history, Arabic and French. I hated math and science and made a mental effort not to learn them. I became a leader and a star in my class. During gym class, I was appointed a team leader. I loved religion and gym classes; they were my daily salvation. Until my mother returned to work, the school became my refuge.

In October, we began to prepare for the Christmas pageant. The annual Nativity Pageant at the Holy Family Catholic Church in Ramallah was a significant tradition. During that time, we had quite a few traditions in the Holy Family Catholic Church. On Palm Sunday, we had the parishioners compete for the best-decorated palm. We sang songs, especially the Hosanna song while waving our palms with zest. There were many memories, but the Christmas pageant was the biggie. We went to church every day to practice for it.

Henry and I wanted to be part of the Nativity portion of the pageant. We wanted to be angels; Sister Mary made us shepherds. The speaking parts went to the older kids. We got into character as the choir sang beautiful Christmas hymns. My role was to sit quietly next to Henry and pretend to be asleep until the Angel comes to announce the birth of Jesus. Although boys our age hated being with girls and vice versa, the boys did not puke when they saw me.

The role of shepherd was easy; all we had to do was walk onstage and sit by a marked place. Since Henry was the first shepherd onstage, he began to walk slowly, thinking it would be fun to have others bump into him. Also, during rehearsals, he started making fart noises to make everyone laugh. Although patient, Sister Mary would stop the rehearsal to tell us how disappointed baby Christ was in our behavior. We would stop laughing for a minute, and then another farting sound would come roaring from the back. When it was our time to perform in the real play, the priests and nuns all but threatened to ban us from any church activities if we didn't behave.

During the Nativity ceremony, we staggered on stage with our long garments, snorting silently toward the manger. When I came close to where baby Jesus was laid in the manger, I almost fell when I saw my little sister, Jouliana, lying in the wooden bed. I whispered to Henry, "Holy crap; baby Jesus is my sister!" Henry almost dropped his large stick on her. Lucky for us, he caught it just in time. The Three Kings almost dropped their gift on Mary's foot. When they looked at baby Jesus, they began to chuckle, and the baby was giggling along with them.

All the parents except mine attended. They were still mourning over my dead sister.

I was worried I was not going to have a visit from Papa Noel (Santa). I was wrong. Papa Noel came as usual, in his fake plastic mask, riding in the back of a red convertible Cadillac, ringing the bell, and shouting "Ho, ho, ho." It was exciting. He arrived at our house at 8 p.m. to deliver our gifts. I sat on his lap, barely containing my excitement while awaiting my gift. He patted my head and told me I should obey my mother and father and listen to them at all times or he would not visit us again next year. I nodded as he reached to give me my gift. It was wrapped in thin red paper with a blue ribbon. As he handed me the gift, I began to cry because I got a kitchen set instead of a ball.

I was devastated. I thought I did everything right, and I asked only for a soccer ball. My mother was ready to scream at me for being ungrateful, but before I said anything, my grandfather asked Santa if he had taken the other gifts to my grandparents' home. "Oh yes," replied Santa, "I even dropped a football off for this little girl. Shush, my dear. You did not want two footballs, did you?"

I jumped from Santa's lap so fast that I almost ran down my grandfather. Before my mother was able to react, I bolted out of the house and sprinted to my grandfather's home. But when I arrived, the door was locked because my grandparents were at our house with Santa. But that did not stop me. I went around to one of the windows and opened it without a problem. When I checked to see if there was a football under the tree, my eyes almost popped out of my face. Wrapped under the tree, I saw three round gifts. I was about to open them when I heard my grandma and Aunt Salma yell, "Stop! If you open any of the gifts, we will call Santa to take them away from you." I turned toward them pleading, but they would not budge. The gifts would not be opened until the next morning.

My aunt tussled my hair and told me to be patient, "You don't want Jesus and the Virgin Mary to be upset at you, do you?" I shook my head no. "Okay, go home before you get into more trouble with your mom." She gave me a kiss. My grandmother put a cigarette in her mouth and smiled, bemused at my antics. She gave me a peck on my forehead, patted my butt and told me to rush home before I got in more trouble.

I left their home anxious, but happy. When I got home, Santa was gone. My father had just arrived from work, and my sisters were talking all at once about Santa's visit. My grandfather was gone, and my mother was unusually calm, almost smiling. Since I had not wanted to upset her, I joined my sisters to talk about Santa. That night, we truly had a happy Christmas Eve. Instead of the usual light supper, we had stuffed cabbage and grape leaves. Dad opened a bottle of Ouzo and gave each one of us a sip. After dinner, we dressed and went to mass. Mom stayed home because she was still in mourning.

I was still too young to go to Bethlehem to midnight mass in Holy Nativity where Christ was born, but my Uncle Zouzou and my aunts took my older sister, as was the tradition of the Palestinian Christians. They joined our friends and neighbors in a pilgrimage to the mass. The rest of us went to our regular church. When I came back, we ran into the house only to see my mother sitting in the corner crying over a picture of my dead sister. My father consoled her and gave her a bear hug. The rest of us tippy toed to our side of the room, undressed, and went to sleep without saying anything. My mom often cried so we learned how to cope with her sadness by giving her privacy. Within two minutes I was asleep, but I was worried that if I did anything wrong, the gifts Santa left at my grandparents' home would disappear.

They say that time heals all wounds; that was not true in my mom's case. She succumbed to depression. At my age, I did not understand the concept of depression. I was a kid who only wanted to have fun. I tried to behave but was not successful. She always seemed to be disappointed in me. I wanted my world to revolve around playing with my friends, eating, hanging around my grandfather and going to school. I wanted the feeling of the holidays to last forever. Since not everyone in town had a visit from Santa, I always felt special because he chose to visit our home despite my mom's sadness.

4 / My Grandfather's Illness and Brother's Birth

For the most part, life was simple for kids in my neighborhood. Like a tumbleweed, my friends and I floated through life doing the same things — going to school, listening to my grandfather's stories, trying not to get caught when we were in trouble, and playing soccer and marbles. I was even selected to be in a school play and dance at school. I continued to run, jump, and climb trees.

Yes, life was simple... until my grandfather got ill. In 1966, he was diagnosed with heart problems a few months before my first communion. He was in the hospital for a couple of days. My mother and father were worried about him but refused to take us to visit him. I was worried because the last time someone I knew was in the hospital, she died.

During that time, I prayed to God, Jesus, and my favorite saint, St. Colette, to heal him. I did not know who St. Collette was, but I liked her name and wished I had a beautiful name like hers. After a week, my grandfather came home, but was in bed in a coma, dying. I went to visit him almost every day, or whenever my grandmother allowed us to see him. Friends, relatives, and neighbors were there constantly.

I saw my grandfather's doctor arriving in his Mercedes Benz, carrying his black leather briefcase. He looked like Humpty Dumpy — round with a pointy head, but he thought he was better than everyone else. Despite his lousy demeanor toward people who were not from his upper-class crust world, he loved my grandfather.

He came out of my grandfather's bedroom with a gloomy, sad face. My Uncle Zouzou was following him. They whispered so that Henry and I could not hear them, but we knew that my grandfather was not doing well. Our worst nightmares were realized when we saw tears creeping down my uncle's face. Before the doctor left, he put his hand gently on my uncle's shoulder and said, "You need to bring the priest fast; your dad has only days to live."

With these words, my world began to blur; I took off and started running aimlessly, and Henry followed me. I ran and ran to nowhere. I wanted to be with my grandfather, but I was afraid. After running for almost an hour, I climbed our favorite fig tree and went up to the highest branch and sat. Henry was with me but knew not to say anything. Because of my sister Hilda, I knew what death was.

I did not want my grandfather to go to heaven. I wanted him to stay with us on earth. He was the kindest person I knew. I loved his stories. I loved his touch and kisses. I loved that he loved us. I loved that he loved me. I sat fidgeting for some time and then decided that I wanted to be with my grandfather. I jumped down from the tree. Henry yelled at me to slow down. I pretended I did not hear him. Although the fig tree was only two blocks away from my grandfather's house, I ran for an hour.

As I approached the house, I saw that all my grandparents' furniture was set out. I saw relatives and neighbors converging on the house. I saw my Uncle Zouzou bidding Father Louis Favreau goodbye with tears in his eyes. My uncle had one of the neighbors call Father Louis as soon as the doctor left. Father Louis came and gave my grandfather his last rites. I went inside. Henry stayed outside and waited for me while he peered from the window.

My grandfather was sitting up on his bed smiling! My grandmother was between tears and smiles sitting next to his bed aligned with his head and pillow. Her sister, the nun, was sitting on the other side with a rosary in her hand. My mother, her sisters, and other aunts and uncles were watching in disbelief at what was happening. His younger brother, Mansour, looked at him and said with a high-pitched voice "Yelan Emik ...a curse on your mother," an endearing profanity used when someone is surprised about something. "Khouftna ... you scared us; don't ever do this again."

Everyone believed a miracle had happened in front of their eyes; however, they were still terrified that my grandfather's revival from the coma was momentary. They still thought he was dying. Someone told one of my mom's cousins to go get the doctor again. I was secretly hopeful. My grandfather asked me to approach him. He gave me a kiss on the forehead and began to tell everyone what happened to him. "When Father Louis administered the last rites, the Virgin Mary was standing next to him ... she was telling him what to do."

He stopped for a moment. His voice began to crack, but he continued to say "as Father Louis poured the oil and ointment on my head, eyes, and mouth, the Virgin Mary was holding his hand. A drop of oil got into my mouth, and here I am. I am no longer in pain, and I am not scared." When he finished his tale, my grandmother took her rosary and fell to the ground in a kneeling position. The rest of the family followed her, and they all began to recite the rosary feverishly. Those who arrived late to check on my grandfather entered the room, looked at my grandfather and knelt with the rest of my family and prayed.

In less than fifteen minutes, the word spread around town that my grandfather was doing well. Dr. Humpty Dumpty arrived at the house, ignored the people who were praying, and with his stethoscope, began to check my grandfather. Henry entered the room with the doctor and came and knelt by me. My curiosity got the best of me, so I got up from my kneeling position and went and stood by my grandfather.

My grandmother watched the doctor examining my grandfather while my grandfather was joking with him. Initially, Dr. Humpty Dumpty did not care about the hubbub and prayers going on all around him and my Sido, but after the first examination, he stood so perplexed about my grandfather's improved condition that he began to twitch. He murmured something to himself. He walked away and came back. He went back and forth, not sure what he was going to do next. Then, he yelled, "Get out, get out, get out, all of you, now, now, now! I don't want anyone here."

The kneelers stood up and began to evacuate the place. When my grandfather's brother, Mansour, and the nun hesitated, Dr. Humpty Dumpty yelled at them "You too, and take this child with you!" My grandfather, although still weak, sat up and asked the doctor not to yell. After half an hour of thorough examination, Dr. Humpty Dumpty came out of the room, shaking his head in disbelief. "He is going to be just fine. He needs a lot of rest, but all his vitals are okay." Upon hearing this, my grandmother turned and gave him an unexpected hug; Dr. Humpty Dumpty was a little taken aback. At the same time, one of our neighbors began a zagrouta, a salutation, as a sign of happiness for my family. It is a practice used on euphoric occasions. This ritual goes back hundreds of years. It is used to express strong emotion in Palestinian culture.

Everyone was clapping and laughing. My Uncle Mansour went to the store, bought two bottles of arak (ouzo), and began to pour shots for everyone. Tears of pain were replaced by tears of joy. My grandfather was not going to die. He was going to live.

After a month, my grandfather's heart had gotten stronger. Dr. Humpty Dumpty brought in another doctor to examine him. They both concurred that my grandfather was going to live. Soon, my grandfather began to venture out of the coffee house and to spend time with his grandchildren and friends. My grandmother went back to work. My Uncle Zouzou quit school and began to work in a tile factory across from our school. My aunts went back to work, and my mother's youngest sister was put in boarding school in Nablus. After a month, everything was back to normal; my family resumed life as before my grandfather's illness.

My father switched jobs and began to work more in Jerusalem and the surrounding areas. My mother continued working in the kitchen. She was still edgy and unpredictable, but for the most part, I learned how to avoid her wrath.

Like my grandfather, my Uncle Zouzou was always pleasant. Although he was not in school, he still hung around his cool buddies from his old school. On Friday, before he went out with his friends, he came to our house to give us treats or pennies. He spoiled us and used us to get closer to girls his age.

My two oldest uncles, Abrahim and Issa, were doing well in a place called Detroit, Michigan, in the United States of America. Every three months, my grandparents received a check for $100 and instructions to give some of the money to my mother. When the letter arrived, the mailman, a local and humorless man who thought highly of himself, delivered the letter to my grandfather, who was usually home while my grandmother was at work. Since neither my grandmother or my grandfather could read or write; they waited for my Uncle Zouzou to read the letter to them.

The anticipation of waiting for the letter to be read was exhilarating, not only for my family but for my neighbors who knew my uncles. The friends who did not understand the geography of the United States always hoped that news from my uncles would also include news about their relatives in the United

States. These letters were also the source of constant disagreements between my grandmother and my grandfather. Since the instructions were to give my mother some of the money from the check, my grandmother always insisted that my mom only get $5. My grandfather, on the other hand, always wanted to give my mom half the amount of the check. It never failed that with all the joy of hearing some fantastic news from my uncles, my grandmother and grandfather still ended up fighting. But grandfather won the argument every time.

Soon my Uncle Zouzou started getting restless. Like any teenage boy, he was preoccupied with girls. Once, to impress a girl, he accepted a challenge from her brother to go up on the roof of the radio building and remove the Jordanian flag. My uncle, who was not involved in politics, did not know that removing the flag was considered treason and punishable by imprisonment. No one in my family was involved in politics. People in our class stayed away from any controversy.

My uncle did not know the trouble he was in until he arrived home and saw my grandmother crying while my grandfather talked with a couple of elders in the community. My grandfather was upset; he did not bother to look at my uncle. The rumors of the flag removal had reached all corners of the city.

For a moment, Zouzou thought that someone had died, but before he could open his mouth to inquire, one of the elders looked at him in disdain and spit in Zouzou's baffled face while shouting "You brought shame on your father ya ghawad (you miserable shmuck)!"

Zouzou was not sure what was happening but attempted to ask, "What did I ..." But before he could finish the sentence, another man asked him why he removed the flag from the radio tower. Zouzou stood silent.

My grandfather and the men went back to putting a strategy together to help save Zouzou from trouble. The few hours of fun he had trying to impress a girl dissipated. From the grim faces around him, Zouzou realized the gravity of what he had done. "I did not mean anything by it; I swear," he said. "I just wanted to impress the girl."

"Meen hathy alshurmouta (Who is the whore that you want to impress?)," they all shouted together at Zouzou. My grandfather was still angry, silent, and ignoring Zouzou.

I was sitting next to my neighbor, who was listening without saying a word. As a Jehovah's Witness, he thought the whole commission was ridiculous and outrageous. He looked at me, patted my head and took out two pieces of candy. He gave me one and put the second one in his mouth and began sucking it and making funny noises without his teeth.

After an hour of back-and-forth conversations on what actions my grandfather and Zouzou would take to minimize the damage, it was agreed that my grandfather would purchase an ad on the radio and the local news proclaiming our family's allegiance to the king and the Hashemite Kingdom of Jordan. Luckily for my family, my uncles from Detroit had just sent $100 to my grandfather and the ads would cost only $25. With this public proclamation, my family averted any trouble. But this episode and the rumors of unrest of the intellectual class prompted my grandfather to ask my uncles living in the United States to bring my Uncle Zouzou to Detroit.

Within months, his brothers had sent him an airline ticket. My beloved Uncle Zouzou was preparing to leave behind everything he knew to live in Detroit. My two aunts took him shopping and bought him two new suits. My grandmother cooked him his favorite meals for a month. Two days before he left, he took my sisters and I to the central park in Ramallah, bought us ice cream and candy and spent half the day with us. He promised to send us candy and toys from Detroit. He gave us hugs and promised to write. The day before he left, my grandfather threw him a great party and invited all his friends and family. People came to bid him goodbye and promised to stay in touch. No one slept; we stayed up until the taxi came to take my uncle to the airport. We were not allowed to go with him, but all the adults in the family went to the airport situated on the way to Jerusalem and waited until the plane left. For good luck, my grandmother threw some English coins at the tarmac behind the aircraft. When they came back, they were all crying and talking about how they are going to miss Uncle Zouzou.

A year after my Uncle Zouzou left, my mother became pregnant again. With the death of my older sister, she now had six girls. As her stomach grew, everyone was wishing for a boy. Instead of greeting her with a good morning and or good afternoon, everyone greeted her with "Allah Yetamek waled (May God give you a boy)." My mother had always delivered her healthy baby girls at home. With this pregnancy, my aunt, who was a nurse at the army hospital, convinced her to have the new baby at the hospital. On August 13, 1966, my mother delivered a healthy baby boy.

The joy of this news seemed to reach the whole world. My uncles from Detroit called the nuns and arranged for a later call with my dad. People from throughout the country sent telegrams of congratulations to my parents. After a week in the hospital, my father, grandfather, grandmother, aunts, and uncles brought my mom and the new baby boy home. It was like the second coming, everyone was happy, including my mother. People were coming and going with boxes of chocolates to congratulate my mom and see the baby. Relatives came from Amman, Jordan, Jericho, and villages from throughout the region to visit us.

Our priest came to bless the child. The nuns from my school also came to see the new baby. While my mom held him, we were allowed to give him a kiss. They gave him the name Michael, after my paternal grandfather.

As was custom, the mother and baby stayed home for forty days. During that time, my grandfather came to visit three times a day. In the morning, he brought us small pastries; at noon, we got pieces of candy; and in the afternoon after our nap from the heat, he brought us ice cream.

After a week, my father went back to work. In the evening, my usually quiet father spent time with the well-wishers. Before we went to bed, he gathered all of us and told us fairy tales of a woman who lived in a cave and outsmarted an evil genie who took young, orphaned girls and boys and fed them to the wolves. As he told the story, we sat at the edge of the bed waiting to hear the heroic work of this brave woman who battled with the genie and won every time. At the end of the story, my father gave each of us a kiss on the forehead as we went to sleep.

The birth of my brother was a time of joy. On the fortieth day, my mom dressed my brother in a white outfit and took him to church. We walked with her and both our Christian and Muslim neighbors and friends joined us there. It was a festive tradition for the "First Baby" visit to the church. When we arrived at the church, the priest was waiting at the door. He gently took my brother from my mother, lifted the baby above his head, and began chanting and walking slowly toward the altar. Everyone walked behind the priest, and as he approached the altar, my mom and dad walked toward him and stood in front of the altar while the rest of us went to the pews. After a few minutes of mumbling, chanting, and lifting up my brother, the priest gently gave Michael back to my anxious mother.

My great-grandmother began a Zagrouta Ululation (high-pitched tongue trill) with the thrill and the joy of this special occasion. When my great-grandmother was done, my grandmother took over the ululation for more than ten minutes. Women were competing to outdo each other with the Zagrouta. The priest waited patiently, and after ample time given for this tradition, we continued with the daily prayers.

I had mixed feelings about this tradition. I was happy to be part of this great fun but wanted to go and play. As soon as church ended, I bolted out and ran to play marbles with the boys. Although I was dressed in my Sunday clothes, I joined my friends and some cousins from a different town.

By the time I got home, all the festivities were over. My dress was full of dirt. My shiny black shoes were beige from the dust. My hair was disheveled. Yet, I had a bag of more than 500 marbles! I was excellent at that game; I could aim from anywhere and score.

I was worried my mother was going to punish me for my appearance and for playing with the boys again, but she did not. She still had company visiting, including her aunt, the nun, who was staying at my grandparents.

When I arrived, my mother looked at me with amusement and told the sisters "I have two boys, Michael and her." She asked me to give one of the nuns a kiss and show her my marbles. I was astonished. I could not believe my luck. My mother, who couldn't stand me, was bragging about my ability to win! I apprehensively approached the nun, holding the bag of marbles as if I was holding a bag of diamonds. As I looked down at the bag, the sister kindly asked if I could show her the best marble. I knelt in front of her, reached inside the bag, and showed her my three favorites. "Why are they your favorites?" she asked with a smile. I looked at her as if she was a dummy and said, "Because they are winners." After discussing marbles with me, she patted me on my dirty behind and told me to wash up. I left my mom and the nuns talking about the new baby and sneaked around to the cabinet and stole a few pieces of chocolate. The sisters stayed for more than an hour. When they left, they promised my mom and Sido they would go to Bethlehem the day after Christmas and participate in my brother's baptism.

A couple of months after Michael's birth, two buses arrived in our neighborhood to take "the prince of our family" to be baptized in Bethlehem. It was a glorious moment that is etched in our hearts forever. Although there was chaos in the coordination of taking two buses and several private cars to Bethlehem, everyone we knew and loved who lived in Palestine and Jordan came to join in the happy occasion.

The year 1966 was a great one for our family. My father had a huge contract with the United Nations. He was hired to refurbish all the wood in all their offices in Palestine. My Sido was healthy again. And my mother had the boy she and the family had always wanted.

Michael was cute and adorable. Everyone wanted to be his godparent. After some deliberation, my aunt Salma, my mother's glamorous sister, and my Sido were chosen as godparents. Since his baptism was the day after Christmas, the kids, including me and my sisters, wore our beautiful Christmas outfits. My dress was a royal blue velvet with a small bow in the middle. My aunts helped dress us and put our hair in ponytails. I looked like a geek from the land of nerds, but I was careful not to complain since I was warned I would be left behind.

My brother was dressed in a white baptismal suit. My aunts from my dad's side of the family gave him a gold crucifix. My grandfather pinned an evil eye pendant on his suit to protect him from people who would envy us. In our culture, the evil eye is a magical curse that causes harm, illness and sometimes death. I did not know who would envy my baby brother, but my grandfather did not want to take chances.

When everyone was ready for the 20-mile bus trip to Bethlehem, my grandma (Tete) began her Zagrouta, and everyone started to clap and sing traditional songs. The trip to Bethlehem was memorable — my brother was getting baptized in the Church of the Nativity, at the site where it is believed Christ was born. I was on the same bus with my Sido. I knelt at the back of the bus with other kids my age, including Henry, and some of my cousins from Jaffna. We watched the traffic, our motorcade, and its wheels hit the semi-wet pavement as we cruised to our destination.

We could not measure our happiness that day. It was a day of ecstasy. Some of our Muslim neighbors were with us and were just as joyous. At one point the whole bus joined in a song: (Ya shouffair dous, dous Allah Yebathlak Arous; Y shouffair ala Mahalak, Allah Yakalilak Ahalack), a traditional rhyme people sang when they went on a field trip. It meant, "Speed, speed, Mr. Bus Driver, may God grant you a bride, and slow down Mr. Bus Driver, may God bless your family."

We sang, laughed, and danced all the way to St. Katrine Church, adjacent to the Church of the Nativity. Throughout this ruckus, my brother slept. Everyone gathered around the baptismal basin where the priest was chanting while my grandfather and aunt, as his godparents, held Michael. Henry and I climbed over the ledge to have a better view of the festivities. I had visited the Holy Nativity before, but never at Christmas. My turn to go to Bethlehem on Christmas was going to be in two years when I would have turned twelve years old.

With my grandfather leading the festivities, we returned to Ramallah the same way we went. However, this time the drivers were directed to blow their horns as we entered the city. People on the street stopped and cheered. It was like a beautiful parade for my family. We could not even count the number of gifts my brother received. We had enough chocolate for a whole year. We shared the sweets with some of our neighbors.

A few months later, we received news that my uncles in Detroit wanted my grandfather to come live with them. I was heartbroken. My grandfather, on the other hand, had been waiting for the invitation. What stopped him from going sooner was the hope for an opportunity to visit his twin brother, Shoukry, who hid in Yaffa and did not leave. Every day since their separation in 1948, my grandfather had petitioned the Israeli authorities to allow him to visit his brother, who lived only 30 miles away. His petitions were always denied. After his twin brother's death, my grandfather decided he did not want to miss any opportunity to be with his three sons in the United States. His wife and other children would follow.

We felt a variety of emotions the day my grandfather departed for America. We were sad because he was leaving us, but we were also happy because he would be joining his sons. We also knew that once he settled in the United States, he would be sending us more gifts and money. That was the last time I saw and hugged my grandfather. His generosity made an impact on my life. I live each day trying to emulate him. He died in 1971, a few months before we arrived in the United States to join him.

Life without my grandfather was normal but sad; we missed him. Gone were the enjoyable hours we spent with him as he amused us with his stories. Gone were the wonderful treats that awaited us each day and the silly jokes that entertained us. But most of all, we lost protection from my mother's anger since he was always our buffer. After he left, I tried to stay away from my grandmother's place. I also tried to avoid my mother at all costs. There was frequent news from my grandfather. He sent letters and money for my grandmother monthly with a directive to give money to my mom. The weekends were not the same without my grandfather; however, the church filled some of the gaps.

I turned ten in 1966. The Holy Family Catholic Church, run by Father Lewis Favro and a young associate priest, offered many programs to keep young children in the church busy. Aided by a couple of nuns from my school, the church offered summer camp, field trips, religious plays, Catholicism classes, sports, choir, and other programs. I loved taking part in these programs. I loved soccer and religious plays. To please the young associate priest, Henry and I began to memorize the New Testament so we could join the older kids in religious debates.

I began to spend more and more time at church and school. By the end of 1966, I had learned the Gospel according to Luke. Henry got bored and stopped after the second chapter, but I was determined. Before I went to bed, I snuck into the basement with a lantern and read and reread each chapter until I knew it by heart. I cried when they beat and crucified Christ and began to wonder about the horrible people who committed this ugly crucifixion. I remembered some of the stories my grandfather used to tell us about the crucifixion but did not know that Christ was so kind and that he forgave the people who killed him. I did not know what it meant to forgive, but I thought it was nice.

Impressed by my determination, the priest allowed me to be part of the debate team as long as I continued reading the Bible.

Like all Catholic Schools with nuns, emphasis on religion and catechism was essential. Although our school accepted kids from all Christian denominations and Muslims, we Catholics were expected to go to church every Sunday wearing a pleated navy-blue skirt, white shirt, and beret. And once we had our first Holy Communion, we were required to go to confession. I did not mind confession, especially if the young associate priest held it during French or math class. If our confession happened during a time when we had tests, I used to make up sins so the priest would give me longer penance.

Apparently, my classmates and I had the same idea. In fact, it seemed that we always confessed to committing the same sins. In fifth grade, the priest told us to stop using the same sins week after week. We must examine our conscience, he said, and think about God's commandments and confess if we violated any of them and then ask God and Christ for forgiveness. Since he did not specify what kind of sins applied to young kids, the majority of us decided to use adultery as one of the sins during Confession. After a month, he came to class and announced: "You should all know that adultery is not one of your sins." I know that when my friends and I were standing in line to go to Confession, we talked about adultery even though we did not know what the word meant. We just knew it was one of the Ten Commandments.

One time in the school chapel, my classmates and I became convinced that the Virgin Mary was crying. It started when I was kneeling in the front pew, where the nuns required us to go and pray or meditate at least twenty minutes a week. I mechanically recited the rosary but when I looked up and saw red tears rolling down the beautiful statue of the Virgin Mary, I nudged my friend Dianna and told her to look up. She gulped and nodded yes, affirming my belief that the Virgin Mary was crying. She elbowed our friend Najwa and pointed. Najwa opened her mouth wide in disbelief and shock. By the time the rosary ended, most of my classmates believed we had witnessed a miracle. We did not mention it to Sister Ida and Sister Gilbert, who were leading us in prayers, until we left the chapel. To our amazement, the nuns did not discount our story. They went into the church and witnessed "the Miracle" for themselves. They even used this vision to impart lessons to gullible students.

The word of the crying Virgin Mary spread throughout the school. For the first time in years, the students went to the chapel without being pushed and without complaining. Every child who went to see the Virgin Mary cry came out believing it was a miracle. Some of the nuns told us that the Virgin Mary was crying because we were misbehaving. For three days, the school was abuzz with this beautiful news. The older students did not dispel our miracle, they went along with us.

Some parents came to the school and talked to the nuns about the situation. Unlike us, they did not seem to make a fuss about it. Since the nuns told us that the Virgin Mary was crying because of our behavior, I tried to be good. I did my homework. I attended chapel without complaint. I did my chores, studied, and did not rip out the pages of my notebooks, which I often did. But then, I overheard one of the nuns telling my mom and grandmother about the hoax of the crying Virgin Mary.

They were sitting in the convent kitchen where my mother and grandmother worked, drinking strong Turkish coffee after dinner, and talking about the events of the day. They were laughing about "the Miracle." Since they did not see me approaching, they continued talking about how the nuns were duping the students. Sister Ludovica, laughing loudly, said, "Even the Muslim girls believe that the Virgin Mary is crying." I stopped moving; I did not want them to know I was there and listening. Then my grandmother, who had a cigarette in her mouth, chuckled and said, "Only if these children would look up at the ceiling, they will see that the tears are dripping from the leaky ceiling."

I was mad and devastated at the same time. The nuns had tricked us. I walked backward forgetting that I had come down to the kitchen to get my mom to meet with Sister Victoire, the principal. I ran to the chapel, looked up at the ceiling and saw the leak. This was my first disillusionment with religion.

My dad had steady work, thanks to his contract. My mother still worked at the school and was a little more patient with us. She worked with her mother at our school, while her youngest sister went to boarding school in Nablus, a city twenty miles away from Ramallah. Her divorced sister still worked as a nurse with the Jordanian Army and her other sister still worked at the St. Joseph hospital as a nurse. On the weekends, they all came to visit my grandmother for dinner. Also, my grandmother, my aunts, and my mom's cool cousins used to spend Sundays with us.

During the winter, we went to church in the morning and then had lunch with my grandmother. We were allowed to bring some friends as long as we did not make a mess. When it was really cold, we gathered around a gas heater and played cards, or listened to popular programs on the radio.

In March of 1967, our routine began to change. Sometimes, the radio programs were interrupted so King Hussein of Jordan could address his people with the latest news, some of which discussed Israel's aggressive actions toward the surrounding countries. He always ended his speech with assurances. Immediately after his speech, we listened to patriotic music praising the king, his leadership, and his hard work.

The adults would often discuss his speech. Everyone would talk at once, presenting their opinions but not listening to each other. Frequently, my grandmother's neighbors visited and joined in the conversation. They were all worried war was pending. Talks about my grandmother moving to America with my aunts had begun early in the year but my grandmother's worst worry was if a war began, she would not be able to leave and see her husband and children in America.

In March, my Uncle Zouzou called and told my grandmother that he and his brothers had started completing forms for her move to Detroit. In his brief phone call, he told her about the civil unrest in Detroit. The next few months, my grandmother was full of anxiety about the fate of her country and the problems in Detroit.

Early in June 1967, her anxiety about war became a reality.

5 / Catholic School

May and June were the best months and the worst months in young school-girls' lives, especially for those who attended Catholic schools. We had numerous festivities around the schools and the church. Our hometown of Ramallah celebrated May with gusto in honor of the Virgin Mary. These celebrations and traditions went back to medieval times.

Catholic school kids took part in these celebrations and customs. Each afternoon, we went to church after school and participated in processions and recited the Holy Rosary. What made the month of May more lovely was the growing gardens full of calla lilies, white and red roses and the nice whiffs of the fragrance of various other flowers. Unlike what Israel proclaimed, my homeland was not a desert.

In May 1967, instead of going home from school, we walked to church. Since the service started at 4 p.m., we took the opportunity to mill around the church grounds until the first bell rang to usher us to the service. My friends and I ran around like usual and joined the boys in pick-up soccer or marble game.

Even at a young age, we had a clique. Each clique gathered in their corner to plot their actions for the hour before church service. Sometimes, the young priest joined in on a soccer or marble game.

The hour between school and church always provided a respite from the daily grind of school, homework, and chores. It provided a much-needed rest from final exams and memorization of useless facts. The final tests, which took place in Palestine in May, were time-consuming and rigorous. In 1967, although, I was only ten, my courses included French, English, Arabic, algebra, geometry, science, religion, physical education, chemistry, and home economics. Failing these classes was not an option. Failing one subject guaranteed summer school. Failing two subjects ensured repeating the grade — a shame no one would dare bring on their family.

Teachers, parents, friends, and neighbors always monitored our progress and made sure to shame us into succeeding. We all remembered the alienation of children who did not pass their grades.

Playtime during the month of May was reduced to a few hours a week. The average student spent about three hours a day studying plus seven hours in a classroom. I loved school but struggled in math. I had to work harder than my schoolmates to achieve a decent grade.

I loved math until the fifth grade. The teacher spoke above my head and peppered my friend and me with her spit as she spoke. She loved standing by my desk. I concentrated more on her spit than her lessons. I was grossed out. Since no one at home could tutor me in math — my mom had a third-grade education, and my dad dropped out in sixth grade to support his family — I was doomed. I stumbled to passing grades by memorizing my books. I did not understand anything, but I managed to pass ... barely.

The hour between school and church was play time. The noise level on the playground was high and joyful. Some children played soccer; others jumped rope; some little girls played with their dolls. Young teenaged girls gathered together and giggled as they watched the boys. One time, I picked up a marble game in which I won one hundred marbles! A couple of nuns stood near the rectory to catch up on the latest news and gossip. The rector, Father Lewis, a middle-aged Italian priest, often stood near the church door and greeted people who trickled down to the church half an hour before the service began. The wealthy parishioners usually arrived in their German Volkswagens or Mercedes-Benzes.

The church was the equalizer in our town. Poor and rich men and women mingled together as regulars and talked, but in May 1967, their voices were a little more hushed.

The nuns and priests took the month very seriously, organizing plays, festivals, and parades to honor the Virgin Mary. They worked with the associate priest on many great festivities. The biggest honor was when our school was asked to participate in a national Catholic parade in Bethlehem. The nuns trained students from the two Catholic schools to march. Every student, including non-Catholic Christians over ten years old, was invited to join the parade. Muslim students were given the option to attend with their parents' approval. The only reason we would be prevented from going to the parade was when we had a failing grade.

Shaher Alwaardeya (the month of flowers) began like previous years. The church was decorated with all kinds of spring flowers, as was the custom. During the service, the celebrant priests wore white vestments with calla lilies embroidered on their robes. The weather was perfect; the sky was blue, and the women who came to church dressed in their summer dresses from the latest fashions.

On the last day of May 1967, we assembled early in the morning at the church dressed in our Sunday uniform, pleated navy-blue skirts, white shirts, clip-on tie, and beret. Although we had no classes that day, we arrived at the school in the early afternoon, as instructed by the nuns, and lined up as we normally did for classes. The sisters inspected our uniforms. As usual, mine needed some adjustment.

After a few minutes, the bell rang. The Mother Superior, Sister Victoire, stood on the ledge where we were lined up, crossed herself, and asked us to bow our heads. We recited some prayers. She asked Sisters Marie De L' Esperance, and Ida to guide us to church. Since we were the youngest, we marched first. We walked to the church where the buses were waiting to take us to Bethlehem for the parade.

We were ready to burst from excitement. We boarded our assigned buses with boys our age and began to have fun by chanting our favorite children's songs. It was the last time that year we experienced pure, innocent happiness. If the adults among us were at all concerned, they did not show it. We celebrated the end of the month of May with thousands of Christians, not knowing what was ahead. We returned home jubilant and tired from one of the greatest field trips of our young lives.

For me, the month of June was also special. It promised the beginning of a great summer and an end of final exams. The daily drudge of schoolwork and final tests took a toll on us. Like for students everywhere, summer meant freedom to play visit friends. In my case, summer meant more soccer and marble games, running after butterflies and climbing trees and walls and driving the old ladies in our neighborhood crazy. With both my mother and father working, summer meant I had at least four hours where I could sneak out and play. Unlike my older sister, I disobeyed my mom and faced the consequences ... I tolerated the corporal punishments and humiliations for a chance to have fun without supervision.

But June 1967 came. It shrouded our happiness with a life of hell we could not escape. The winds of war came to us with no warning (at least this is what I thought) and altered our free and simple life. It transformed it into a life of pain. The occupation brought brutal, strange, and unfriendly soldiers who took over our lives and imposed their hateful will on us. Our joy, innocence, and safety were forever stolen from us.

6 / The Occupation of My Home

I had been looking forward to a great summer. I'd just finished my final exams and was ready to shred my books to pieces, as was my tradition. I hated hand-me-down books, and as a middle child, I inherited my older sister's books; that irritated the hell out of me.

Every year, to no avail, I begged my parents for new books. But my older sister kept her books in excellent shape, and since the books didn't change from year to year, I got her books. My parents saved money this way; Catholic School was expensive. For me, the hand-me-down books were an insult and only added to my belief that my parents did not like me as much as my older sister.

For me, the end of a school year was a day of liberation from school, hand-me-down books, and nuns who believed that rules and studies were the only salvation. I knew that by September, I would be eager to get back to school, but for now — no more pencils, no more books, no more teachers' dirty looks!

Despite the punishment that awaited me at home, I relished the act of destroying my books. Even in fifth grade, I almost understood the value of standing up for a principle.

The last day of school was supposed to be joyous. I ran out of the schoolyard with my best friends and headed to the local candy store, which occupied a corner building on Main Street. Owned by a local shopkeeper and his family, it had extensive selections of delicious candy — from super sour candy to ones that melted in your mouth. For a few pennies, we could choose from a variety of candy from all over the country. A child can gorge on gummy bears, gum, and taffy. The store was like the old neighborhood dime store — the "everything" store. From cleaning supplies to stationery, from crafts to candles, from seasonal goods to Slinkys: you name it, they had it!

That day, as on all final school days, the place was jammed with kids from different schools. It was mayhem; kids were shouting with excitement. The clerks were trying to sell their goods while keeping an eye out for any mischief. Older kids typically bullied the younger kids, shoved them aside and went in front of the lines.

The friendly owner stood by the door and asked everyone entering about their exams. His wife ran the cash register and made sure everyone was served fast. One of the clerks roamed around checking for shoplifters. He yelled at a young boy trying to hide a piece of gum in his pocket without paying for it. "Come here you little prick," he yelled. The boy froze and dropped the gum to the floor. The clerk took the boy by the collar and ushered him outside. "Don't you ever come here again!" The store owner smiled and then rolled his eyes.

As the drama unfolded, I decided it was time to get the hell out before the crazy clerk lashed out at me or my friends. I looked for a few pennies deep down in my pocket. Finding them, I was able to buy a Twist, a favorite chocolate bar with nuts, and a pack of gum. I ran outside looking for the young boy. I knew his name. I called him. He did not respond; he just stood there with tears in his eyes. He was about seven years old. I called him again. He did not move. I heard a little-muffled sound and saw him wipe his eyes. I approached him and said, "Didn't you hear me; I called you?" The boy began to cry. I jerked him around and said, "Hey listen, I just wanted to give you your gum." The boy looked at me in disbelief and took the gum and shoved it in his mouth. I put my hand on his shoulder and warned him "Don't ever try to steal again. I will tell your parents." He nodded and said, "Thank you." I replied, "Now go tell your brother, Mahmoud, I will be over to your house at 3 p.m. to play marbles." The boy nodded and started to run toward his home.

I went back to my friends to retrieve my school bag. I still had to shred the books before I went home. I was happy and anxious at the same time. My friend Dianna asked me about my summer plans. "Don't know, probably hang around the house," I replied. Dianna asked if I wanted to spend time with her. "If I can sneak out, you know I will," I said.

I picked up my school bag and was about to put it on my shoulder but changed my mind. I sat on the curb and asked my friends to sit with me. I opened the bag, took the books out, and one by one began to tear the pages and crumble them into a ball. The only book I left untouched was my religion book; I tore the rest to pieces. My friends had their mouths open in disbelief. "Uh, oh, you're in trouble" yelled Lina, a close friend, "Your mom is going to kill you." "I don't care," I replied, "I just hate hand-me-downs." After I had ripped up the books, I got up and began kicking the torn paper like I was kicking a soccer ball. My mission was accomplished; my younger sister would be getting new books. Hooray to the savior!

Although I was not paying very close attention to the world around me, something was different the last day of school in 1967. If I had paid more attention that day, I would have seen people running in all different directions, trying to reach the grocery stores before they closed. I also would have noticed the presence of Jordanian soldiers on almost every street corner. If I were paying attention, I would have noticed that more parents than usual were picking their children up from school. But as a fifth-grade student, the only thing I paid attention to was my friends walking with me.

After tearing up the books, my school bag was lighter. I hauled it over my shoulder and resumed playing soccer with the rolled-up paper. I kicked it to my friend; she kicked it back to me, and within seconds we had a football game going with the crumbled books. Between kicks, I shoved some candy in my mouth.

Again, if I had paid attention, I would have seen that the carpenter store owned by my uncle was closing. I would also have seen the older peasant women with packages of rice and flour stacked on their heads walking quickly. I would also have seen the boys from the public high school rushing in all directions trying to get home. I was in a world of my own; I was just playing, eating candy and looking forward to a summer of fun.

All my dreams came to a halt three blocks away from home, when I saw my mother and several of our neighbors rushing toward us. "Come here, fast, yalla, yalla, yalla (with urgency)." The other mothers echoed the same tune: "Yalla, yalla, yalla." Men and women were rushing toward their children and rushing them to their homes.

A little confused, my friends and I ran toward our parents. My mother was unusually fearful. "Where is your sister, Stella?" Before I answered, she told me to run directly home. The anxiety in her voice gave me a chill I could not describe. I ran faster than I ever ran in my life. I was not the only one running; people were moving in all directions.

On my way home, I saw a Jordanian Army Jeep with my Aunt Samira in it. My divorced younger aunt worked as a nurse in a government hospital. An army Jeep picked her up every day for work. As I approached the vehicle, she asked the driver to stop. He obeyed since she outranked him. She waited until I approached the Jeep. She opened her arms and gave me a bear hug. She had tears in her eyes. "Listen," she said, "I want you to be good and brave. You're a big girl, you can't be afraid." She reached into her uniform pocket and handed me a dinar. I could not believe it. A Dinar (equivalent to five dollars) is more than I ever had in my whole life. My eyes and mouth opened wide in disbelief. I thought I was dreaming. Before I said thank you, my aunt gave me another hug and told me to be good. "When your mother says, it is okay, you and Beno (her son) buy candy with the money. I will see you in a few days. Tell everyone that I love them. Give Beno a kiss." Again confused, I nodded my head and waited. She patted me on my butt, and said, "Yalla, go run home and be safe."

I started running. I turned my head back and saw her climb into the Jeep. I did not see my aunt again until she defected from the army a year later.

When I arrived home, my older sister, Ghada, the twins, Sylvia and Esperance, my youngest sister, Jouliana, and my almost one-year-old brother, Michael, were sitting in the corner of the basement. My older sister was rocking my brother, who was crying and asking for mom. The twins were seated next to each other in silence. Espie's nose was running, and her cheeks were red, an indication that she was crying. Sylvia was trying to calm her. Jouliana was playing with a doll with a missing arm; she was combing the doll's hair. When I arrived, I threw my school bag by the front door as I always did and ran to the basement. Ghada, my oldest sister, asked me if I saw our mom. I said, "Yes. She is looking for Stella."

I asked her what was going on; she put her index finger to her lips and said, "Shush, I don't know." I asked about dad. She replied, "I think he is still at work in Jerusalem."

"When is he coming back?"

"I don't know."

She sounded frightened. She started to cry. Before I could say anything, our neighbor and her grandchildren came in. She was carrying pillows, blankets, a transistor radio, and scarves. One grandchild was carrying pots and pans full of food. Her youngest grandchild, Jamil, followed with bags of food. They put all the stuff they had with them in a corner at the far end of the basement.

She started counting the kids. "Where is Stella?" "My mom is looking for her," I answered." She looked at one of the Tawasha kids, who had just put all the food on the ground next to the blankets and told him to take care of the children. "I will be back in less than an hour. Make sure that no one leaves this basement." She collected her wallet from her purse. "I will be back, you hear, I don't want anyone to leave... I don't want anyone to be scared. Remember, the Samaan family will be coming soon. Make room for them in this corner." She pointed to the farthest side of the basement.

You could see the concern on her face; she tried to hide it, but it was evident. I was scared but I did not want to show it. I did not want anyone to think I was weak. For God's sake, I was a tomboy — "Sayed," the toughest kid in the neighborhood.

As soon as she left, one of the Tawasha boys started to make room for everyone. The 400-square-foot basement was very tight, but it would soon accommodate about 30 people. It was the only safe place in the neighborhood.

There was a lot of commotion outside. The Army loudspeakers were directing people to go to shelters. One of the Tawasha kids turned on the radio. He switched it from BBC to the Voice of America news. The radio announcer sounded very anxious. He announced that Israel had struck the Egyptian Air Force. One of the Tawasha kids listened to the radio with concern about what I understood to be a pending war between the Arabs and the Israelis. He was alarmed, but like the rest of us, he did not know what the war meant. Unlike our parents, kids my age lived in a relatively calm time, where soldiers were friendly and the only explosions we heard were in Indian movies — where the hero always wins.

After five minutes, he switched the radio to an Egyptian station. The dynamic and boisterous leader of Egypt was giving a loud and lengthy speech urging all Arabs to stand and defeat the immoral and wicked Israelis. Since I secretly had a crush on one of the Tawasha kids, I sat quietly next to him listening to the radio.

Within 15 minutes, most of the 30 people arrived and were crammed in our basement. Our neighbor George, his wife, and three children came in with their belongings. My uncle and his wife and children brought mattresses and black blankets and put them in the center of the room. My uncle immediately took charge and asked one of the Tawasha kids to help him. The women took charge of the food and children.

My uncle first re-arranged the cramped room, so everyone would be a little more comfortable. Then they tallied how many gallons of water were set aside in case the water was shut off. They also checked the number of pillows, blankets, candles, kerosene cans, and kerosene lights. I wanted to help but was told to go play with the other children, but the kids were not playing. They clung to their mothers; even the older kids were confused and did not want to move. I was frightened without my mom and dad and my sister Stella at home.

Almost an hour later, I was about to bolt out of the house to look for my mother without telling my uncle when she came in with Stella, who was sobbing. It turned out that Stella and two of her friends were so crippled with fright that they hid behind the wall of one of the neighbors. My mom and the other mothers searched for them for almost half an hour, yelling their names the entire time. They were just about to give up when they found them. My mom grabbed Stella and rushed to the store; she was carrying the food she bought while she was out. Everyone who was supposed to be in our basement (shelter) was there now ... except my dad.

We could still hear the commotion and loudspeakers outside, but inside, the only noise we heard was the muffled sounds of the children crying and the radio. Feelings of terror and anxiety, however, dominated the whole basement. The silence lasted less than a few minutes, but it felt like hours. My uncle was the first to speak. "God Almighty saves us from this hell." In unison, we echoed, "Amen."

My mother, in her commanding voice, told all the young kids to move to the farthest section of the basement; she did this as she and one of the other women rearranged the room again for more comfort. They were trying to maintain some kind of normalcy for the kids at a time when their lives were being turned upside down.

Although hosting about 24 more people in her home, my mom was anxious about my dad, who had not returned from Jerusalem. She was also worried about her mother, sisters, and her nephew, who were staying at the convent a few blocks away. Her sister Salma had to work at the French Hospital, while her sister Samira had been evacuated by the Jordanian Army.

My mother, more than anyone else, knew the consequences of war; she been had driven out of her home at age twelve in 1948. They left everything behind, including their roast beef dinner. Like 750,000 other Palestinians, they became refugees. She vowed that no one would drive her from her home again. But she was not in control. She did not know what would become of her and her family if the enemy came marching in. She resolved to die in the basement with her kids and neighbors before she would leave her humble home.

The small portable clock was ticking, but it seemed like everything was moving in slow motion. Aside from the radio and some muted conversations between the adults, everything was eerily calm. As soon as Egyptian President Gamal Abdel Nasser finished his speech, the adults sighed in unison, "Allah Yinjena. (God saves us)."

My uncle switched the transistor radio to the Jordanian station, which was playing patriotic songs paying homage to the king for his bravery and resolve in standing tall in front of the demonic enemy. Personally, I loved these songs; I used to march to them with my friends, pretending we were brave soldiers. The adults were not amused by these songs; they wanted to hear the hard news.

A half an hour later, we began to hear jets flying overhead and "Boom! Boom! Boom!" Even I was frightened. We all started to cry and scream. The adults tried to comfort us, but with no success. Several times the basement shook. The radio continued to play in the background. My uncle and one of the Tawasha kids inspected all the windows for damage then they covered them with black blankets.

My mom and neighbors tended to the children. Besides trying to comfort us, my mother was worried about my Baba's whereabouts. It was about five p.m. and we had not heard from him. We did not have a telephone, so there was no way for him to reach us. What made matters worse, the Jordanian radio announced several times that their jets had attacked Jewish areas near Jerusalem. More frightening, the Voice of America news announced that the Israeli army was trying to occupy Jerusalem.

Sitting next to my mother and feeling a little safer, I listened carefully to the radio. I did not understand what the word "occupy" meant; however, I knew my Baba was working in Jerusalem. I also knew that the Israelis were the bad people who kicked my mom out of her home and killed some of her neighbors. I began to scream "I want my Baba! I want my Baba!" With tears in her eyes, my mom tried to shush me. "He will be here soon. Shush! Don't scare your little sisters … be a good girl."

The other children began to cry when more jets flew louder over our heads — "Boom! Boom! Boom!" My older sister peed in her pants. One neighbor began to curse her luck, "I should have left for the United States when my son asked me to go." My unlce shushed her by putting his finger on his lips.

Although it was summer, the basement was darker because it had no windows, and the house windows were covered with black blankets. Normally, our basement was used for storage. It was sectioned into areas. The back of the basement, where my mom kept her homemade jelly, pickles, and other canned goods. Since my family had olive groves, we stored olive oils in big five-gallon cans. We also stored goat cheese. In another section of the basement, we stored old furniture, including mattresses and blankets.

Last year, my father and his friend installed a light in the central section of the cellar. As children, we used to be afraid to go in the basement after certain hours. Although I was terrified of ghosts and believed that evil spirits lived in the basement, I conjured up courage about two years ago and began to venture down into the cellar to hide my marbles. I found a haven among the blankets for the marbles I won from the neighborhood boys.

A few weeks earlier, I had counted my stash and found that I had more than 300 of all colors and sizes. During the bombardment, however, I did not think about my stockpile of marbles at all. I just sat frozen in the central section of the basement with everyone else. My Baba was still out there and with every noise, my mother either murmured, "God, lift your anger from us," or she gently prayed for my Baba to return home safely.

By six o'clock that evening, we became hungry. My mom nursed my brother Michael and the other women made sandwiches for everyone. My uncle warned the women to conserve food and water. "Feed the children," he said, "make sure to give them enough not to be hungry, but don't overdo it." Most of the adults nodded in agreement.

Our old neighbor began to recount her past experiences in 1948. "I remember," she said, "We ate lentils for six months, every day. We left without food, and money and we did not know where we were going. If it was not for the mercy of the church, God knows what would have happened to us. God, we beseech you; save us from this misery."

Still scared, the children ate their food in silence. I wanted to go to the bathroom, but my mom asked me to wait. The closest bathroom to the basement was outside in the neighbor's yard. Our bathroom was upstairs, and my mom did not want us to take a chance on turning the lights on. She thought that going to the yard was safer but still wanted me to wait. For once, I did not protest. I was anxious but thought I could hold it; I did not want to wet my pants like my sister. I began to play with the three marbles I found in my pocket and soon forgot that I had to go.

After half an hour, my mother and our next-door neighbor took all the children to the bathroom. One by one, all twelve children went to the toilet and then prepared for sleep. But every time we thought the danger was over, the loud deafening noise of the jets flying over, followed by the booming sound of the bombs, terrified children and adults alike. There was no doubt we were under siege and in the middle of a war.

My brother, Michael, who was usually asleep by 5:30, could not go to bed. He was now howling, and my mother was frustrated she could not calm him. Both the women and men, including one of the Tawasha boys, tried to rock him to sleep. Finally, after an hour and a half, Michael cried himself to sleep.

Before the rest of the kids were sent to bed, one of the Tawasha boys' grandmothers began to recite the rosary. Everyone, including Uncle Foaud, who regularly made fun of religious people, including our family, recited the rosary with us. We then recited the Litany for the Virgin Mary:

> Holy Mary, pray for us.
> Holy Mother of God, pray for us.
> Holy Virgin of virgins, pray for us.
> Mother of Christ, pray for us.
> Mother of divine grace, pray for us.
> Mother most pure, pray for us.
> Mother most chaste, pray for us.
> Mother inviolate, pray for us.
> Mother undefiled, pray for us.
> Mother most amiable, pray for us.
> Mother most admirable, pray for us.
> The Mother of good counsel, pray for us.

Not all our neighbors were Catholic; some were Orthodox and Protestant. Still, they recited the rosary with us. After we finished, my mother laid next to my twin sisters. I slept on the same mattress as my other three sisters. My mom, brother and sisters and I managed to fit on two mattresses. The men moved to one side of the room where there were mattresses set up for them. The other women helped their children prepare for bed.

I closed my eyes but was not able to go to sleep. I wanted my Baba to come home. I began to count backward from 100 so I could fall asleep, but before I reached 80, a bomb hit, and the force shook our home. We all jumped and began to scream again, including my sleeping brother. My mother yelled "Allah Youstrana. (God save us)." Once again, shock, fear, tears, and panic took over everyone. Showing his bravado, Uncle shouted, "If these sons of bitches don't stop it, I am going to bomb them." His wife smirked and said, "Tell them, big boy, tell them." In the midst of panic, the adults started to laugh uncontrollably. I don't know if her remark was divine intervention or not, but for more than an hour, everything was calm. Once again, the adults tried to put us to bed; this time they succeeded.

Though exhausted, I still wanted to stay up and wait for my Baba. It was too early for us to go to bed, but everyone convinced us that if we went to sleep, the bombing would stop. I dozed while listening to the adults talk in hushed voices. They turned off the radio to save the batteries.

It was hard to sleep in a room full of people who were not our family. Besides one of the Tawasha kids and his brother and grandmother, we had our neighbors, the Samaan family from a block away. Although they lived several houses south of ours, I did not play with their girls because they went to public school and were always inside doing homework. They were beautiful and shy. Their mother, Aida, was a seamstress and always made beautiful dresses for them. Even though I didn't like dresses, I always thought the two girls looked pretty in their ruffled dresses. The first night in the basement, they sat between their mom and dad in silence. Even when they cried like the rest of the kids, they did not make any noise.

One of our neighbors was talking to my uncle about money matters and how everyone in the basement could pool their money together if worst came to worst. He told my uncle about an underground market he could walk to if we ran out of food. His wife gave him a dirty look and told him to stop yapping about things that did not make sense. Their three boys were talking among themselves in hushed voices that I could not hear.

By 8 p.m., everything was quiet. My uncle turned the radio back on. The Voice of America news detailed what was going on in Jerusalem. I was too tired and too afraid to listen. I closed my eyes and began to say my prayers. My real nightmare finally gave way to sleep.

Despite the terror befallen us, I slept well. I did not wet my pants during the night. The adults took turns sleeping, not that any of them could. I woke up the next morning to the noise of jets overhead. The radio was on, but I did not pay attention. I was looking for one of Tawasha kids; he was not in the corner. My mother had a worried look on her face. My uncle was telling her that if she did not hear from my father in the next two days, he would go out to look for him. My mom and my aunt opened their mouths at the same time and said: "No you will not." My mother went on to say, "I don't want to lose a husband and a cousin in one day; no you will not." Listening to the conversation, Stella asked my mom about how we lost my Baba. Aware of the problem she and my aunt caused, my mother, said "Your Baba is fine. He is not lost; he is at work."

The morning after was no better than the day before. We had a cramped basement, but since we were conserving water, no one dared to take a shower. We did not even brush our teeth. My father was still not home.

My uncle drank Arabic coffee and talked quietly with my mom. I wanted to go to the bathroom, so I asked my mom if I could go. She told me to wait a few minutes. She resumed whispering to my uncle. Her voice was too low; I could not understand her, even though I was almost sitting in her lap. My uncle turned and tousled my hair, and looked at my mom and assured her, "If Jabra does not come home by the next day, I will go and look for him." My mom stayed silent this time. Our neighbors were listening in silence.

The radio was barely audible; they did not want to wake the rest of the kids. The jet noise from the night before had subsided and for a couple of hours, everyone thought the worst was over. I tugged at my mom's blouse, "I need to go." She nodded and told me to go upstairs "Go, now, but come back fast." I ran to the bathroom. I finished peeing and was pooping when a loud boom shook and rattled the whole house. I did not know what to do. I was not done, but I was so terrified, I was paralyzed. I wanted to scream, but like in a nightmare, I had no voice.

I was still sitting on the toilet when another loud boom exploded. I stood up and went to the corner, screaming in panic. My mother came rushing in; she snatched me from the corner, with my underpants and pajamas hanging below my knees, and rushed me out of the bathroom and into the basement. By then, the loud noise had awakened everyone. The children were all screaming and crying, they sounded like a symphony gone haywire.

The adults were trying to show courage, but fear overcame their bravery. Although not screaming like the children, they sat still for some time ... scared shitless. One of the Tawasha kids broke the tension by saying," I am going to get the sons of bitches if they God damn." With this remark, everyone was quiet. It was an unusual outburst from this kid. He never swore before. The adults all looked at him in disbelief. Although his grandmother frowned at his choice of words, all the adults started to laugh. It was nervous laughters, but it gave respite from the overwhelming distress in that basement.

One neighbor reached for the radio and turned the sound up. The news was devastating; the Voice of America confirmed that bombs from jets were dropping nearby. The announcer urged everyone in "Ramallah, "Albireh, and Jerusalem to stay in shelters and take cover; Israeli jets are hovering over the Jordanian Army hospital at the north end of the city of Albireh."

The bomb strikes were coming fast and furious, "Boom! Boom! Boom!" Although paint chips were falling on our heads, no one moved.

The men fiddled with and around the radio in silence. The women began to prepare the morning meal. Nazha Tawasha started to move toward the door but stopped and turned around. Even over the sound of terrorized adults and crying children, she spoke firmly and with confidence. "I need you all to listen." She began "You know I am older than all of you in this room, and although you lived through the first war; you were young, and you don't remember what happened as I do."

Before she continued, a jet flew over. My brother started to scream in terror and my mother began to rock him. At the same time, my other neighbors held their children tightly and started to rock them. One of the Tawasha kids was helping with the twins and my younger sister. I was just sitting on my mattress in terror.

Nazha put her index finger to her lips and said, "Shush; let me continue. We may have to think about another place for safety." She went on, "If this continues after a week, we need to find a safer shelter. We can go to the Holy Family Catholic Church; Hannah, you know the priest, we can stay in the basement under the social hall."

My mom shook her head, and, in a calm, purposeful tone said, "Everyone is free to do what they want; my children and I will stay in our home until my husband comes back." The room erupted with everyone talking at once and giving their opinions. A loud boom interrupted the conversation and sent everyone to their corners. The children, especially the younger ones, began to howl. There was more … another Boom! Boom! Boom! and loud jets overhead.

I started to cry like all the other children. I tried to muffle my voice, but I could not. I wanted the noise to stop, and I wanted my father to come back. I began to wail and heave. "I want my Baba, Baaaaaaaaba, Baaaaaaaaaaaba." No one was paying attention to me or the children, they were all in the middle of a debate on whether they should stay or go to the church. The noise was deafening.

One of Tawasha kids and his brother were sitting silently nearby. You could see the terror in their eyes, but you could also see their determination. They did not want anyone to see them afraid. In a sudden move, one of Tawasha kids came and sat next to me. Carefully and lovingly, he tightly embraced me. "Hush, habibty, we are all going to be okay ... hush habibty (hush my love, we are going to be okay)." He winked at me with a smile, showing his beautiful white teeth. "I won't let them hurt you, okay?" He was speaking in a low, soothing voice, "Your Baba will be here soon." He caressed and gently stroked my tangled hair "Shhh, shhh, you are going to be okay."

His voice appeared to calm everyone; my sister, Stella came and sat next to us. One of the Tawasha kids was whispering to both of us at the same time, calmly and gently, "Shhh, we are going to be okay. Everything is going to be alright." Somehow, while writing this, I remembered everything as if it were yesterday.

As the sounds of shelling continued, we huddled closer to him. I continued to cry, my right hand rubbing my swollen, red eyes. I could hear the conversation in the room, but I was not listening; it was just too much noise. Someone turned the radio off.

My mom was breastfeeding the baby. The other women were tending to their children and making sandwiches. My uncle was tense but was trying to stay calm. He was usually an easy-going guy, but the shelling made him anxious. He got up to stretch but could not stand long. It was very awkward; all eyes were staring at him. He moved toward the door and stood for a moment. He was contemplating whether to go out or stay. Before he reached for the door lever, his wife shouted: "Don't go! Please don't go; I don't want to worry about you."

He looked around the room. Everyone was quiet, including me. He cautiously opened the door and peeked outside. He was listening intently for any movement; he did not hear any. He took a step forward and just before he took another step we heard "Boom!" He shut the door fast and jumped over two of the kids and sat on one of the mattresses. In unison, the adults shouted "Ya Adra! (Holy Virgin Mother!)" After the boom, there was silence.

For two days, we lived in terror and despair. The only thing that sustained us was our belief in God and his mercy.

The adults settled into a routine of listening to the radio, comforting crying children, whispering and praying. I continued to wait anxiously for my father to return; the adults kept their hopes up. Besides my dad, my mom still worried about her mom and sisters. Her mom and youngest sister were at the shelter in St. Joseph's convent with the nuns, and her two sisters were on duty as nurses. One was in Jerusalem and the other was with the Jordanian Army.

On the second day, we heard a loud knock at the door, and my father's voice screaming, "Open, open for God's sake!" One of the Tawasha kids jumped over my sisters and opened the door. My father barged in, exhausted. He maneuvered toward my mom and my brother and sat in silence for a few minutes. He smoked a cigarette and slowly said to no one in particular, "I thought that I will never make it."

It was eight in the morning. Everyone was anxious to hear about what was going on outside. My Baba asked if he could eat before he talked. "I have not eaten in two days, he said. My neighbor handed him one of the sandwiches she had prepared for the day. He took a bite and smiled "Shukran (Thank you)." My mother was subdued and quietly breastfeeding my brother. My father surveyed the room while chewing and said hello to each person. Everyone thanked him for the use of his home. My dad nodded, "Of course, we are family. God saves us." After he had finished his sandwich, he began to recount his two-day ordeal trying to get home.

He began to describe the destruction he saw. At one point he stopped talking and looked at us and began to whisper to the adults, "Let's stop talking until the kids sleep tonight." He did not want to scare us.

He turned on the radio and began to listen. He said, "Don't believe what you hear." After that, the only voice we heard was the one on the radio. Jet noises still hovered over our heads; but unlike the day before, we did not hear as many blasts.

Four of the children were running light fevers. I was becoming restless. At first, I was afraid to bring my marbles out from their hiding place, but after my father arrived, I mustered the courage to get them. I looked at my mom, fearing her wrath, but surprisingly, she encouraged me to play with the marbles as long as I shared them with the other kids. I sat in the corner near some of the kids who were doing their own things to occupy their time when the bombs were not going off over our heads.

For two hours, we played without fighting. My aunt began to prepare lunch. As she stood, a loud deafening boom rocked our home. A moment of silence passed, and everyone began to scream. We were terrified. I dropped my marbles and ran to a corner and started to cry.

The next hour passed in chaos, children and adults wailing, and then pure rage, and then everyone fell silent. It seemed we sat in terror for hours without moving. My aunt, who stopped cooking when the blasts started, got up slowly and began to make preparations again.

The stench of urine now hits the room. One of the older ladies began to complain about the smell. One of the Tawasha kids was embarrassed and told her to stop. My dad interrupted and asked if he could talk to the adults after lunch. The food was ready, and we ate in silence.

The kids were then directed to take a nap, and everyone did! I pretended to sleep but was listening to the low voice of my dad. "I don't want to scare you, but things are not looking good for anyone ... we need to think about leaving for safety," he said.

He began to recount the horror he saw during his crossing home from Jerusalem. He talked about the Jordanian soldiers who were killed, and how their bodies were left in the middle of the streets. He talked about soldiers' uniforms being abandoned as the soldiers left their posts and ran for their lives. He named a couple of buildings that had been bombed on the main road from Jerusalem to Ramallah. He also talked about some gangs who were looting the souk (market) and the bus station. He spoke of the car that was bombed near the boys' school.

His voice was low and shaky as he recounted what he saw. No one interrupted him, holding on to every word. Anticipating what my mom was going to ask, he told her that St. Joseph Hospital, where her sister worked, was okay, and the Catholic church and our school were intact.

After Dad finished, My uncle asked, "Where should we go?" My old neighbor, who sat silent most of the time, cleared his throat and said with force. "Let's wait for a day, and if the bombing continues, we can start moving through the back road to my small rooming house in the mountain in the Khalah (the rural area)." This one-room home was about six miles away in the wadi (valley) on the outskirts of Ramallah.

He was not the only person who owned land there; my father and uncle also owned a few acres. However, we did not have any structures in which to hide. After the discussion of further evacuation, we all sat in silence for what seemed a long time. The tension and anguish were so high that you could feel it. Just when we were on the brink of a catastrophic breakdown, someone farted. The fart was so loud and so smelly, everyone moved back and started to laugh hysterically. For a moment, we forgot our nightmare. We were a group of people taking delight in the mundane.

The laughter quickly subsided with a sound of Boom! Boom! Boom! and turned into sobbing and wailing. I sat still afraid to move and wet my pants. I was scared my mom would find out and punish me. I did not need to worry; I was not the only one. Besides not having space to move, the mattresses where we sat were now saturated with urine. The stench of urine, sweat, food and various body orders began irritating the women.

For six days and nights, we experienced boredom, fear, irritation, tension, uncertainty, sickness, and some hope for an end to the war. What we did not know was that those days in our basement were only the beginning of a nightmare. On the sixth day, we began to hear cars and tanks outside. On the loudspeakers, we heard soldiers in perfect Arabic directing anyone who was inside a shelter to come out with a white sheet. They also ordered the men to come out first, with their hands up in the air.

At first, everyone was happy because they thought the soldiers they heard were Iraqis who had come to help the Jordanian Army. The chatter of the adults was giddy and loud. My uncle proclaimed victory and was preparing to celebrate. My dad told him to take it easy and wait until they went outside.

Slowly, it became noisier outside as people emerged from their shelters and homes as told — men first with a white sheet and their hands in the air. My mom ordered us to stay put. As they opened the door, we looked outside for the first time in six days. It was sunny. The old man went out first, followed by my uncle, Baba, and the Tawasha boys. My mother and the other women fluffed their wrinkled clothes and patted their hair and followed the men. Although I was told to stay inside, I followed the last woman outside.

I squinted at seeing the sun for the first time in a week. I saw the first tank, the second and the third as they rolled by just a few feet from our house. Soldiers jumped from their tanks and began barking orders. In perfect Arabic, they ordered the men to line up and began to push them while pointing guns at their heads. I hid behind one of the old ladies and held on to her dress.

A soldier spotted me and came toward me. I was intrigued by his gun but was afraid to look up. He patted my head and gave me a piece of candy. I was about to put it in my mouth when out of nowhere someone knocked the candy from my hand! I could not believe my eyes; my mouth was watering for the taste of the candy. The person yelled, "He is Jewish, and he wants to poison you!" The soldier heard her and with his fierce eyes staring at her, he said in perfect Arabic, "Do you think I am evil?" The lady lowered her eyes and did not say a thing.

The day was quite pleasant. The sun was shining, and the sky was blue. There were no clouds, not even the beautiful clouds from my grandfather's stories. After a few minutes, the soldiers, guns drawn, directed the men to move to one side of the street, with their eyes forward and their hands up. Slowly the men and boys, including the Tawasha kids, moved to the other side. Surprisingly, everyone was calm, including the soldiers, who were talking in a different language and smiling and laughing. The men and boys kept their eyes on the ground. The women stood and watched timidly.

One by one, the men were searched. After an hour, everyone was told to go back to their homes except one neighbor who was forced to go with the soldiers. I came face to face with the neighbor. He had a look of terror on his face. His wife began to sob. One of the soldiers came toward her and with a mock smile said, "Don't worry. We will bring him back." She did not hear him. She continued to sob and call his name, "Mohamad, Mohamad." Her husband did not say a word. My mom and the others went to comfort her, but the soldiers yelled at them to return to their homes and wait for an announcement.

The six-day war was over, but the terror began. Although the soldiers directed us to go back to our homes, everyone went back to the basement. As soon as we closed the door, the adults began to babble all at once with fear and anxiety. They were petrified of what was coming; some, including my mom, recalled what happened to them in 1948. After the initial commotion subsided, they began to talk about what they needed to do to survive. The old man began by saying "I am staying here; I am not leaving. If they want to kill me, they can kill me in my home."

At the beginning of the six-day war, we entered our basement shelter as neighbors, and we left as family. Despite the horrendous circumstances that put us together in a small, windowless basement, the beginning of the war brought us together as a unit of people who would take care of each other.

After six days of bombardment, the soldiers and the radio announced that Ramallah was now under the rules of the Israelis. The occupation of my hometown had now officially begun.

Part II
Life Under Occupation

7 / Introduction to Hell

No one can describe the horror, pain and apprehension that gripped everyone in that room, but the adults saved face by trying to be defiant. At 6 p.m.,
the women began to prepare a light supper. My uncle began to hum a song by
Abdul Halim, a famous Egyptian singer, "Zay Al Hawe." It was a song about
love. My dad began to whistle the tune and the women joined in by humming.
By 6:30, we sat and ate in silence. No one dared to ask the obvious question —
what was going to happen next?

After dinner, the men played cards, and the women talked about what they
were going to prepare for tomorrow's dinner ... as if everything was normal.
Although aware of the reality, they were afraid to acknowledge it. They were
afraid if they spoke about what happened, Israel's occupation would become a
reality. Anxious and afraid, I willed myself to stay up until 9 p.m., just before
my dad turned the lantern lights out.

The next day, we were all awakened by the sound of the loudspeaker, "Come
out from your home with your hands up. If you have weapons, bring them out
with you. Do not do anything stupid and you will not be harmed."

We got up in a hurry; some of the kids began to cry. As directed, the men
went out first. The women followed with the children. When I mustered the
courage to look at the soldiers; they did not look any different than people I
knew. Some had dark skin like mine; others were light skinned like my cousins. They were younger than my father. Most were the same age as the older
Tawasha boys. They had guns pointed at us, but I could tell they were afraid.
Initially, I was not afraid, just curious. I pretended not to watch, but I followed
their every move. The men were asked to go to the front and put their hands up.
They did as they were told, except for our crazy neighbor George.

George lived down the block from us in a gated single-family home with a
lovely garden. Our family always warned us that George was crazy and to stay
away from him. If provoked, he could be dangerous. Years later, I found out
that George was a harmless paranoid schizophrenic.

As the soldiers approached him, he became hyper, waving his hands and
talking gibberish. He was ordered to stop. One of the soldiers yelled at him to
"shut his mouth." He did not hear them because he was agitated. One of our
neighbors attempted to calm him while trying to explain George's condition to
the soldiers. A soldier with a kippah (Jewish skullcap or yarmulke) on his head
screamed at my neighbor. Before he could finish his explanation, another sol-

dier ran over and hit George square in his ribs with the butt of his gun. George fell to the ground in pain. When I saw this, I attempted to scream, but no words or sounds came out. The neighbor who tried to explain George's behavior was dragged in front of everyone by two soldiers who proceeded to kick him. By then everyone was petrified, including the soldiers. Panic set in. We stood still. No one dared move or say anything; new sheriffs were in town, and they were not friendly. One by one, the soldiers searched the men. After they had completed their search, they barked at them to go for further inspections.

My relatives and neighbors who had stayed with us in the basement left and went home, leaving all their belongings behind. When we returned to our home, my parents told us to go to the main section of the house, not the basement. We went to the upper level. We were still not sure how safe we were. The jets continued to fly over, but we stopped hearing the bombs. My parents were tense and weary but tried to put up a good front. They sat in the corner and whispered to each other. A couple of times, my mom mustered up the courage to lift the black blanket from the window to see what was going on outside. She reported to my scared Baba that Saleh, the baker who lived three blocks away, was blindfolded and kneeling on the asphalt with other people. They were surrounded by soldiers with guns pointed at them. She muttered words of sympathy and besieged God to help them.

It was getting dark, hunger set in, but no one wanted to eat. My parents told us to huddle together in their bed. To ease our terror, my Baba recited the story of Ginny, who fought the ruthless army and saved the children. I don't remember if he finished the story, but my family and I got up to the sound of loudspeakers telling us of a pending curfew. "You have two hours to shop before a curfew is imposed." It was agreed that it was safer for Mom to do the shopping. Baba handed her the money and told her to come back as fast as possible.

My mom left wearing the same clothes she had on for the past five days. She ran off with tears in her eyes but refused to look back at us. We waited an hour, but my mom was not back. My dad was pacing back and forth and jumping at every sound he heard. He held my brother who cried non-stop. We became restless. I asked my dad if I should go look for my mother, but he said no.

Time stood still. Anxiety overwhelmed us. I kept looking at my dad; he was preoccupied with my brother, who was still crying. I convinced my older sister to go with me to look for my mother. My other sisters were taking a nap. Terrified that my mom was not coming back, we agreed to sneak out as soon as my dad's back was turned. When he turned away looking for a bottle to give my brother, we quietly opened the door and bolted out toward the market. The streets were full of people running in all directions.

I saw Henry's neighbor running with a bag of groceries in one hand and a gallon of gasoline in another. As we approached him, he asked us what we were doing in the street. My sister said, "We are looking for my mother." He yelled at us to go back home.

Fueled by adrenaline, we searched everywhere, but could not find her. We noticed that many strangers were roaming the streets. Many of the villagers had left their small towns to come shop in Ramallah. At first, we did not see the soldiers watching us from the roofs. After we had crossed the main road toward the St. Joseph convent, we looked at Henry's home. Soldiers were there with their big machine guns pointing at the people below. The door to Henry's house was open, but I did not see Henry or his family. I almost started to cry, but my sister told me that Henry had left with my grandmother and the rest of the neighbors for shelter at the convent. We did not know where else to go, but since we knew my grandma was at the convent, we headed in that direction in the hope we could find someone who knew where my mother was.

The trees in the blooming garden sheltered us. The garden was lined with a variety of trees including pomegranate, clementine, lemon, almond, and white berries. We took comfort, knowing the soldiers would not be able to see us under the trees. We peeked in the window of the convent, where students took piano lessons from old Sister Antoinette. We then knocked on the door several times, hoping someone would open it. No one did. We decided to run to another door where the sisters, my grandmother, and mom often cooked for the students during school. Just as we were about to knock, a powerful jet flew over our head. We bolted and dived under a small branch of the pomegranate tree. The roar of the fighter plane almost crippled us; I thought I lost my hearing, so did my sister. We could not hear each other, our eardrums nearly ruptured from the loud noise.

We thought we were dead for sure. I peed in my pants and so did my sister. We were wet and crippled by terror. We sat under the pomegranate tree motion-less. We huddled together crying and paralyzed by fear. Eventually my mom and Sister Ludovica found us in the garden, frozen and crying.

When my mom saw us, she almost had a heart attack. Sister Ludovica yelled, "What are you doing here? Why aren't you home? How did you get here? Is your dad okay?" She kept asking questions, but did not give us a chance to answer.

My mom recovered her senses and asked us how we got to the convent with-out detection. Crying, my sister told her that we came looking for her because we did not want her to die without us. She dropped the groceries she had in her hands and came rushing toward us. She hugged us like she never hugged us before. She cried as she whispered reassuring words that we were going to be okay. She bid the sisters goodbye, talked to her mother and sister, and gave Bernard, our young cousin, a hug and a kiss. A porter from the school carried the groceries for my mom as we went back.

I thought we were going to get in trouble with my dad when we got home, but he was so relieved to see my mom and us, he did not bother to admonish us until later. My father wished the young man a safe trip back to his village. As the young man left our house, the loudspeaker announced that the curfew would begin in half an hour. Anyone roaming the streets would be jailed or shot. My parent locked the door. The blankets were put back on the windows and we began to prepare for the night, even though it was early afternoon.

My mom recounted some of the stories she heard on the streets. She also told us about the people who fled town to Jordan. She heard that some people from the outskirts of the city put up a fight against the Israelis with no help from others. According to the grocer, some young men from the nearest refugee camps were murdered in cold blood. She could not authenticate the rumors; she was just repeating what she had heard. After every story, my father said: "God save us."

We went to bed uncertain that the war had ended. We awoke to the endless nightmare that still haunts us to this day.

8 / Soldiers from Hell

June 10, 1967, was the birth of our nightmare. Our lives now belonged to our Israeli oppressors. They wanted our land, but they did not want the people on it; they only wished us ill. My peaceful neighborhood transformed into an eternal hell from which there was no escape.

Words cannot describe the vile Israeli occupation and its impact on our lives. They tore our world without batting an eye. Cruelty and violence became the new norm. No one was spared, not even children. Too many Israeli soldiers took pleasure in intimidating and scaring people.

At first, they engaged in diabolical psychological games. They pitted us against one another. They excelled in the divide-and-conquer game. They held fathers hostage and forced kids to squeal on their neighbors. They had access to our homes at all hours, even in the middle of the night. Few, if any, saw us as fellow humans.

Our days began with the Israeli Defense Forces (IDF) screaming out orders on loudspeakers. Curfews and house imprisonment became our norm. Our windows continued to be covered with black blankets. Following their rules did not spare us from their punishments. In the early part of the occupation, they allowed us two hours of freedom. The directive came on the loudspeaker daily. They ordered men and boys to stand in the hot sun for hours. They entered our homes in the middle of the night shining their flashlights in our faces.

As they punished our fathers and brothers, they offered us candy. They rounded kids up while letting some go and detaining others. One time when I was walking with one of my schoolmates to a nearby shop, a soldier patrolling the street stopped us and asked us in sign language if we were Christian or Muslim. Innocently, we told the truth. Since I am Christian, they let me go but detained my friend for hours. I did not know what to do; I did not want to leave her, but I had no choice. I ran and told her mother. That created the seed of suspicion between friends and families.

Almost daily, the IDF picked on one or two randomly chosen families. There was no set time for their arrival; they came in convoys of Jeeps and tanks. They ordered everyone out of their homes and then arbitrarily picked a house, most of the time a home of a Muslim family and proceeded to search it. They used kids as human shields as they barged into our neighbors' homes, and then kicked the kids aside.

They caged us in our homes, releasing us for only an hour or two a day. They put us on edge because we did not know when the IDF was going to arrive or whose home they would ransack next. It could be during the day or in the middle of the night. They belittled the elders, disrespected the women, kicked and shoved the children, abused fathers in front of their children. To inflict terror, they yelled and screamed at us to show us who was in charge. They ruled us with hate and an iron fist.

With black blankets covering our windows, everything was always dark. Occasionally, we peeked outside only to see men, boys and some women handcuffed with a piece of rope, blindfolded, and kneeling on the hot asphalt while the sun beat down on their uncovered heads. We started conserving food and water in case that they would put us under curfew without notice. We skipped meals and did not wash as much to save food and water.

Immediately after the end of the bombardments, my mom connected with her mother, sister, and nephew at the convent. My grandmother was worried about her daughters, who were working in the field, and her only living brother, who was serving in the local, national Jordanian guard. My father connected with his brother, sisters and their families. Like us, they were so afraid that they stayed home in their basement.

After two weeks without any news from my Aunt Salma, who worked at a French Catholic hospital in Jerusalem, the Counsel General of France brought her home to visit her mom. The two-hour reunion was full of tears and joy. My aunt was happy, petrified, and sad at the same time. She had heard many horror stories about what happened to our family; the stories were wrong.

She recounted tales of injured soldiers and how they sought help at the hospital where she worked. Many of the wounded died without a chance to say goodbye to their families. She held their hands as they took their last breaths. She described young soldiers who lost their limbs during the six days of fighting.

She did not want to leave, but she had no choice but to go back and help these young men and little kids who lost their families. Like the rest of us, she had nightmares. She told my grandmother that she woke up screaming. It simply broke her heart that some of the people died at the hospital alone with only the nuns and the kind nurses and doctors to love them. The Israelis scoured the hospitals and took some of the injured to prison.

The invasion of our country created unspeakable horror, even to those who lived through the 1948 war. War is hell, and my grandmother knew it. She had no hope for a better future. As a devout Catholic, she had great faith, but the misery of war overpowered her senses. She was lost without her husband, who had left less than a year earlier for the United States. And with her daughters, sons, brothers, and family scattered everywhere, she was often overwhelmed. She always smoked, but she became a chain smoker. She refused to eat and opted for tobacco when she could find it.

Ten days after the invasion, when the Israelis lifted the curfew for more than six hours, my grandma talked my mother into going with her to the Army hospital about three miles away from Ramallah to look for my aunt and uncle.

My grandmother put on her traditional long Palestinian dress and made sure her crucifix was visible. In her mind, the Israelis did not harass the Christians as much as they harassed the Muslims. My mother, as usual, wore her western clothes. No one knew about their excursion except my father. Although he protested, he was no match for the will of two strong women on a mission.

When they returned, they described their gruesome encounters to my dad and the neighbors. They walked a few hours among the homes, looking for anyone who saw a glimpse of the Jordanian army. They came across some Israeli soldiers who harassed them and spat at my grandmother despite her cross. They also met some decent Israeli soldiers who told them what road to avoid and what route they should take to their destination. In some wooded areas near the hospital, they saw stray dogs and cats eating the flesh of a couple of dead soldiers.

At one point, my grandmother sat next to the bloated dead body of a young man who was shot while running in the woods. He had been left for days without burial. She and my mother paid their respects by chanting traditional funeral wails. They searched for some identification but found none. They wept and wailed and beat their chests, as is customary at a young man's funeral. They caressed his swollen cold face. Before leaving, my grandmother took off her headdress and covered the body of the young dead soldier and then gave him a kiss on his cheek.

With no place to go, we sat and listened to my grandmother and mother recount their day's search. They did not find any useful news about my aunt or uncle.

Like everyone else, my life changed. I became a prisoner of nervous and overly cautious parents. I was only allowed to go to the bakery with supervision. After my close call with the jets flying overhead in the garden of St Joseph's convent, I did not protest.

Henry was away at his grandmother's home and was not coming back until they believed it was safe. Most days, I stayed close to my parents and the neighbors next door. Tanks, army Jeeps, and soldiers replaced the noisy neighbors who kept an eye on us while my parents worked. The neighbors no longer visited each other to pass the time. The hustle and bustle of a jovial neighborhood was replaced with hateful soldiers who took pleasure in harassing people.

At first, no one went to church to avoid the risk of being stopped by soldiers. But when my parents felt it was a safe place, my sisters and I began to go. At first, the church was mostly empty; but after a couple of weeks, people began to return just to stay connected. The church service was a respite from the dreadful new routine imposed on us. Few, if any people, went back to work.

Grocery store shelves were empty. Fruit and vegetable vendors from nearby villages brought their goods and sold them at inflated prices. People stopped gathering in coffee houses and on street corners. Kids no longer played in the streets; their parents kept them home for their own safety.

We craved normalcy but found none. Sometimes we found solace in the few hours of freedom when the soldiers lifted the curfew and allowed us to go places. Even then, we had to be home by 6 p.m. with the doors closed and the windows covered with black blankets.

9 / Strangers in Our Homes

We did not know what to expect. Soldiers ruled our lives. Most were brutal and callous. They also looked scared despite their automatic weapons and tanks. They barked orders at us in a different language. Sometimes they yelled at people in foul, vulgar Arabic. They wanted us to know who was in charge. One could count the kind soldiers on one hand. Even the polite soldiers participated in the abuse committed against the people. Throughout the first month of the occupation, we did not see any civilian Israelis. Everyone was in fatigues and carrying guns.

One day, safeguarded by soldiers, thousands of Israelis descended on our city. They began milling around our neighborhoods. They entered our homes without permission and inspected our belongings. They walked our streets as if they owned them. They ignored us like we did not exist.

Most were obnoxious and rude, walking around like victors hungry for power. A few were friendly and jovial. They came early in the morning and stayed all day. They went to the bakery and bought bread. We did not know what to do; we tried to stay out of their way.

Some spoke English, others French, but the majority spoke a language we did not understand. My dad said it was Hebrew. We tried to be invisible so as not to get in trouble. We couldn't even protest their presence for fear of punishment from the soldiers who walked and mingled with them. We were keenly aware of the soldiers; they were always in sight.

My mother ordered us to stay in one corner of the house and remain quiet. She held my brother and always kept her eyes on the people. They examined us like you would examine a display or an animal in a zoo. Some smiled, others growled at us for fun. We were afraid to cry.

One or two people who spoke English tried to give us candy. Scared, my mom let out a muffled scream "Please don't." Taken aback, the stranger mumbled something and gave my mom the candy and left. My mother threw the candy in the garbage. "I don't trust the Jews; they want to poison us."

By noon we were exhausted and hungry. My mother decided to close the door, risking punishment. None came. We continued to hear the strange voices outside, but for a couple of hours, we enjoyed the privacy in our home.

My mom and older sister attempted to clean the house and make sandwiches. We ate Spam sandwiches with homemade pita bread. Since it was hot, we took a nap while my parents kept an eye on the door and windows. With all the noise outside, I could not sleep. I waited until my mom and dad were distracted and snuck out through the side windows. The soldiers did not order a curfew until after 7 p.m.

I walked the two blocks toward my grandmother's. I was nearly crushed by the visitors who continued to mill around the neighborhood. Middle-aged women with bizarre hats walked around with shirtless white men. Young women wearing miniskirts and halter tops walked with an air of arrogance. Some of our neighbors tried to sell them trinkets and trash from their home. Peddlers from nearby villages tried to sell them fruits and vegetables.

Teenaged boys and girls checked out the clothes the strangers wore. Silly boys full of testosterone ogled over the young blond girls walking the streets. One boy tried to untie a girl's halter but was stopped with the butt of a gun from a soldier walking by. Blood gushed out of his nose. He attempted to run, but someone tripped him. I saw the soldiers scuffling with him as I tried to hide.

The other boys ran away. Some of the strangers stood and watched, others moved away pretending nothing of importance was happening. Dreading the collective punishment, my neighbors swiftly moved away. I hid behind the wall as I watched the boy being dragged away and put in a Jeep. Afraid that might happen to me, I ran into the small, isolated street between our neighbor's homes. I went back to my house without being detected.

Even as a kid, I was struck with the cruelty of the situation. Instead of being out playing with my friends, I was now sneaking out, while my family was locked down at home and while strangers roamed freely around my neighborhood. They viewed us as an oddity. Even the strangers who attempted to be nice did not see us as individuals. They did not know that the boy in trouble was a typical mischievous fourteen-year-old boy full of testosterone who loved to tease beautiful young women to impress his friends. They saw the abuse but did not act. They did not know that we were just as curious as they were about the situation. Our lives were in their hands. We were fucked but did not know it; our lives had descended into hell.

With dark covered windows, it was hard to tell the time, so we often fell asleep very early in the evening. A few weeks into the occupation, we awoke to a loud commotion. Startled, my sisters and I woke up to see my terrified parents standing by the door with their hands above their heads while soldiers shined their flashlights into their faces. A young, redheaded soldier stood between my parents and us with his gun pointing at my dad's head. We began to cry. One of the twins attempted to run toward my parents; her sudden movement startled one of the soldiers. He cocked his gun; my mom screamed. Ghada wet her underpants and I began to wail. The soldier in charge yelled at my mom to stop and told her that they would not hurt us. "We are just looking to see if you are hiding a Fedai freedom fighter."

My dad, like the rest of the men, tried to remain quiet. With a jittery voice, my mom explained that we do not participate in politics or fighting. The soldier tersely told her to shut up. They ransacked the house, flipped the mattresses and then walked out. As soon as they left, my dad locked the door and put chairs behind it to thwart any further intrusion.

This was the beginning of our home invasions. Not a week went by that we did not have to suffer through a surprise inspection or raid. It was always the same; The Israelis announced a curfew around 6 p.m. and came knocking right after. The loud knock could come in the middle of the night or immediately after the beginning of the curfew. After a couple of weeks, we stopped locking our doors. First, the Israeli soldiers roughed up my parents, especially my dad, and then searched the house. Our cries and protests did not bother them. Some even took pleasure in scaring us. Our parents were vulnerable and could not protect us.

The disruption of our sleep took a toll on us. We became cranky and tired. Fear engulfed our lives. We were not safe even in our own beds. Like all the other parents in our neighborhood, mine tried to keep us safe, but they were not in control. We started to sleep with my parents in their beds. They were overwhelmed with what was happening, but very determined to stay home. They refused to leave because the Palestinians knew the consequences of leaving the safety of their home. My mom lost her home at age twelve and was resolute. "If we are going to die, we will die in our own home," she always said.

Between home invasions, we stayed inside the house or very close by. We kept to ourselves. My mom left every few days to get food and check on her mother. My sisters and I played together inside the house. We took turns helping with chores and played with my brother, who by now was walking all over the house. We missed my grandma and aunts. We fluctuated between horror and sadness. With all the sleep deprivation, we began wetting our beds. One of us ran a fever. When they had a chance to check with the neighbors, my parents discovered that their children were suffering the same malaise.

We also began to hear about the disappearance of our teenaged friends. Once or twice, boys from the neighborhood sought shelter in our basement. Everyone was concerned.

We began to listen more to the news on the radio about the Israeli occupation. When we had the courage to lift the black blanket covering the windows, we saw young men lined up in the streets kneeling in the hot sun. It was easier for my mom to go out to talk to the neighbors and report back to my dad.

We woke up daily to the sound of the loudspeaker. Our new normal was home imprisonment. We could not establish a routine since the soldiers came into our home whenever they wanted to. We passed time in fear and trepidation. My father lived in the danger zone; he and all the men under the new regime were a target for abuse. My mom and dad put a schedule in place to keep us occupied. My mother gave me, Ghada, and Stella house cleaning assignments. In some ways, this was a good thing; I was not in trouble tearing up the neighborhood as I had before the war. Since we were poor, we had few books. My sisters had their schoolbooks, but I had destroyed mine at the end of the school year. My dad read and helped my mom with the younger kids.

Since we were going to bed as early as 6 p.m., my mom snuck out to visit her mother and sister and check on the status of others in the neighborhood. My dad did not dare leave the house. Low on food, my mom persuaded my father to let her buy us fresh fruits and vegetables if she could find any.

Immediately afterward, I slipped out of the house undetected by my father and sisters. My cousin caught me, and almost sent me back, but I lied to her and told her that my mom had sent me to buy bread. She shook her head and mumbled something I did not hear. She sternly told me to stay out of trouble. I promised her I would, and continued walking.

I saw soldiers milling around on the roof of some homes in the neighborhood. I walked past one of my classmate's homes. I peered through the flower bed and bushes but quickly hid behind a bush when I saw a soldier approaching.

I was looking directly at my aunt's house when I saw a big, camouflaged tank moving slowly through the streets, with soldiers walking behind it with guns drawn. In front of them, I saw several boys I recognized blindfolded, with their hands tied behind their backs. I panicked but stayed put. I wanted to cry but could not cry. I wanted to scream but could not scream. The tank and soldiers moved toward my house. As soon as they turned on the street before our street, I bolted back to my house.

When I returned, my dad was furious. He was always gentle and soft, but this time, he was pissed! He shook me and told me that he was very disappointed and "wait until I tell your mother." I began to cry nonstop. Between my muffled cries, I told my dad about the boys with the blindfolds. He caressed my hair and promised not to tell my mom. My older sister, who usually could not wait to tell my mother whenever I misbehaved, gave me her favorite doll and a kiss on my cheek.

The hour and a half went by fast. My mom came back on time. She gave the money to my dad and told him everything was okay with the family, but the soldiers were rounding up people, primarily young Muslim men from the city.

That night I went to bed hungry; I did not want to eat. Although the soldiers invaded our house again that night, I did not wake up to the noise and the flashlights in my face.

We were not allowed to leave the house without supervision. My dad took a job in a nearby carpenter's shop owned by his friend. Dread, mistrust, and lack of information about our future created a threatening atmosphere for all. Any movement from someone triggered panic by the soldiers, who were always roaming the streets with their guns.

Our summer of paradise, endless hours of play, and picnics was replaced by a hellish summer of endless curfews, mean soldiers, and blackouts. The friendly Jordanian troops were swapped for young foreign soldiers who were afraid of us, despite having guns and power over our lives. Our water supply dwindled. We spent days at a time without electricity. To cook and wash, we relied on oil and a small single gas burner.

The most shattering part of the war and the occupation was that we stopped being kids. Those carefree days of milling around with Henry and the other boys were gone. Like me, Henry, who stayed with his grandmother, was not allowed to go out and play. We felt buried in our own homes.

The constant presence of abusive soldiers had begun to psychologically affect us. Our nerves got the better of us and we began to have nightmares even when the soldiers were not invading our home. We felt like animals trapped in a cage.

10 / My Aunt Samira

In the meantime, we kept vigil that my Aunt Samira and Uncle Farid would return home safely. With the nuns' help, my grandma reached out to the British and French embassies for assistance. They did not find them. But in less than two months, our prayers were answered. MyAunt Samira came home, having defected from the Jordanian Army.

One day, she just stumbled in and collapsed into her stunned mother's arms. When we heard the news, we went to my grandma's and joined the celebration. We laughed and cried, all at the same time. For a few minutes, we forgot we were under Israeli occupation. Her four-year-old son, Bernard, was jumping with excitement.

She was flabbergasted to find us alive and unharmed. She had heard the horror stories and saw people killed during her flight and had prepared herself for the worst. Someone along the way told her that her hometown had suffered a lot of damage. She saw dead bodies scattered on the side roads. But that did not stop her from going home to see her son. Although exhausted, she could not stop talking and hugging her son and mother.

She recounted the story of her defection and escape. After a few weeks of leaving with the Jordanian Army to Amman, and experiencing trauma in the war field, she decided to defect. One day she left the army compound very early in the morning, when there was less security. She took nothing with her so she would not attract attention. She wore her work shoes, the only comfortable shoes she had. From memory, she began to walk toward Jericho. She kept her head down. Although afraid, she was safe in the Jordanian territories.

As she approached the border to the West Bank of the Jordan River, she saw Israeli tanks and soldiers rounding up people. She turned around without being seen and hid. When it was safe, she started walking aimlessly. A young, good-looking man who resembled her brother Issa approached and asked if he could help her. She was terrified. He assured her that he did not mean harm. He told her to follow him. Her heart was beating fast, she worried that he was going to rape or rob her. She had no alternative. She was not going back.

He started talking to her to ease her anxiety. It was hot. He introduced himself. She did not respond but walked in the same direction. He continued talking as she kept her head to the ground. She tried to peek at him when he was not looking. She decided that he may be sincere. Without saying anything, she followed him on dirt roads. She was not used to the desert terrain and the harsh and uneven roadway. She had to jump in and out of the ditches. He reached out to help her. At first, she was reluctant.

He assured her that he was like her brother. "Eitebrini zye akhee … think of me as your brother." She was still afraid but followed him. After a couple of hours, he told her she was on her own, as he had to go back to his family. He gave her directions for the rest of the way. He told her what she needed to do to arrive in Jericho safely. He advised her to go to the center of the city. He told her what to do when approaching the center. He told her she would have to cross the river, but to not be afraid. She carried with her only two shillings. She hid the money in her bra in case someone tried to rob her. After giving her instructions and directions, the young man asked if she had money. She lied and told him no. She still did not trust him. He reached into his pocket and gave her ten eurash, the equivalent of two shillings, in case she needed food and a ride. She began to cry. He soothed her without touching her with words of encouragement. He bid her goodbye as he watched her walk into the desolate desert. They waved at each other, he shouted some encouraging words, "Don't be afraid, keep going. Cross the water; it is not too deep."

She walked alone for hours, afraid of the environment. She was also afraid she would be jumped by thieves. Her fear, adrenaline and prayers helped move her forward. Her feet and legs ached. She was hungry. She saw dead bodies scattered around and left behind. Some of the dead looked like they had tried to escape their fate by removing their uniforms. She did not dare to look closely. She intensified her walk. She was parched. Her lips were chapped. Blisters developed on the bottoms of her feet. She moved forward thinking of her son.

She wanted to stop and rest but was afraid that if she stopped, she would not start again. She refused to give up. She wanted to go to Bernard, her only son. She willed herself to walk. She sped. She began to devise strategies in case someone wanted to harm her. She gave herself a pep talk. "Walk! your son needs you." She did not want to look back. She checked on the money tucked in her bra. It was safe. She recited the rosary as she walked. Aching, she began to think "what if?" She silenced her mind and kept moving. The seconds turned into hours in this dreadful uneven desert land. She felt dehydrated and cursed herself for not bringing a bottle of water.

After what seemed an eternity, she reached the outskirts of Jericho. Relieved as she left the desert behind, she was unsure where to go. She squinted to see what was ahead. She was relieved there was no one walking on the dirt street where she stood. There was a stench that almost made her gag. But she walked on to a desolate dirt road, lined with date and banana trees. It looked like God had forsaken this place. Neither the banana nor date fruit were ripe. She was afraid that thugs or soldiers were hidden behind the trees. A part of her wanted to rest, but she could not. She felt a little faint and wished she could find a stream to take a sip of water. At least she did not have to go to the bathroom. Cautiously she moved forward.

She saw a house from a distance and walked toward it. She knew the people would open the door for her. She knocked. A friendly woman opened the door and stood behind it. She greeted my aunt with a sad smile and her what she wanted.

My aunt began to recount her story, but the woman stopped her, apologized, and said she could not help. She had people knocking on her door daily for help. "It is too dangerous." She was not willing to put her family in jeopardy. The woman gave her a glass of water, directed her to the center of the city, and told her to be careful. "Deery-balak-ahalek. (Take care of yourself)." My aunt thanked her and began to walk again. She did not want to be on the street in the dark.

A slender and tall woman, my aunt felt the sun beating on her. She wished she had a scarf to cover her head. Every noise or movement made her jump. She kept looking for someone to ask for directions, but no one was out. After more than an hour, she approached the city. She saw a young black boy roaming around. She thought that if the boy was a scammer, she would harm him if she had to. She looked disheveled. Sweat poured from her face. Her hair was wet. Her white shoes were dusty and looked brown. Her manicured nails indicated she was not a peasant or a street person. She looked lost.

The boy approached her carefully, but without fear. He asked if she needed help. He addressed her with respect, calling her aunty. She was reluctant to answer. He pointed to a nearby building and told her he could take her to his house for safety, if that was okay with her.

"It is dangerous in the center of the city," he said. "Elyahoud betjawlou fee Alshare'e. The Jews are roaming the streets. You will be safe with my family." She hesitated, wondering if he was a thief or a decoy for gang members. "I don't have money" she told him.

"That is okay, you don't need money," he replied She did not move. He pointed to the building again. "This is where I live with my family, it is not safe for you to be out." As she began to walk, she saw Israeli soldiers rounding up people. She decided to take a chance and follow the boy.

He pointed to his house again, "we are almost there." She was too tired to care and thought that if he attempted to harm her, she could kill him. She was not thinking rationally. He told her his name. She followed him. As he approached his home, he called for his mother and father, who came out to greet him. They saw my aunt and hurriedly invited her inside. She began to cry. Their welcome affected her. They comforted her and told her that she was safe in their home. The mother approached and hugged her. "Think of us like your family," she said. "You will be okay." After introducing himself, the father directed his daughters to give my aunt food and water. "We don't have much, but we can share what we have," he said.

My aunt, hiccupping her words, thanked them. The boy, 9, told how he found her wandering the dangerous street and was worried about her. They smiled and congratulated him for his kindness. They invited her to take a shower and relax and told her to stay over until the next day for safety. Including the boy, the family had ten children. They apologized and told my aunt she would sleep on the roof. They did not want chance soldiers coming to their home searching for strangers. She was grateful. "Don't worry," the father said, "my three girls will sleep with you on the roof."

They sat in a small living room, the windows covered with black blankets. They did not want any light to attract soldiers. Before they went to sleep, the family told my aunt about their lives. The family lived for over 500 years in the Jericho region. They had land and worked as farmers. All their children attended school, but, because of the war, they were uncertain about the future. One son was in his last year of high school. They were worried about him. They told her they weren't sure what was going on but feared the worst. They did not have a TV or telephone and relied on news from the BBC and the Jordanian News.

My aunt walked to the roof, where the girls took folded mattresses from under the stairs and made up beds. The teenage girls told her she was lucky their brother encountered her before "Ewalad Alharam … harmful people" they said the family had sent the boy to get bread because he could easily hide without being seen.

The next day, my aunt, who usually dressed in the latest fashions from Paris, wore the same outfit she wore the day before. She washed her face and combed her hair with a comb one of the girls gave her. She went to the living room where the family waited. They greeted her with kindness, gave her something to eat and told her to hurry and go so she could take the first bus out of Jericho.

"One never knows, if there will be another bus," the father said. They apologized but said she needed to leave by herself. They did not want their children out and about. They gave her a couple of bananas for the road and told her to tell the bus driver that they sent her to him. If the driver was not on the bus, "come back and you will try later."

Before she thanked them again, they asked if she had money. She told them she had enough to go home. As they wished her goodbye, the girls, the mother and my aunt were all crying. They hugged her and kissed her on both cheeks as if she was a member of their family. "Allah youtoun maaki, God be with you." the father said. With tears in her eyes, my aunt told them that she would never forget their kindness and left for the bus station.

It was very early in the morning, the best time to catch a bus before the Israeli soldiers began to round up people and interrogate or detain them. Even at a very early hour the sun made eerie shapes on the brown landscape. By 6 a.m., my aunt could feel the heat beneath her feet. Even though she was wearing her comfortable work shoes, the blisters on her feet ached. But she did not let the pain bother her. She was worried she would never make it to the next city and ran to the bus station like a mad woman. She took the advice of her host family who told her not to speak to anyone but the bus driver.

There were a few people trying to catch the bus. She saw some military tanks from afar. Sweat poured from her brows, but she did not care. The bus station was not far from the house where she slept. She made a mental note that if everything went well, she would go back to visit the family once it was safe. She never did. She remembered the young boy, Hussain. Also, she remembered that the oldest child was named Mohamad. As for the parents, they introduced themselves as Em Mohamad and Abou Mohamad. But she could not recall the names of the girls who slept with her on the roof. In fear and exhaustion, she had not asked the family's last name.

***

Jericho, one of the oldest cities in Palestine, is near the northwest shore of the Dead Sea and was always known for its scorching sun. It is said to be the land where Jesus was tested by the devil. One of the oldest cities in the world, it sits in the Dead Sea valley. Part of it is an oasis in the desert. They grow oranges, lemons, and other citrus. My family used to go there during the winter for picnics. Wealthy Palestinians wintered there. Christ fasted and was tested by the devil on the Mount of Temptation, located two and half miles outside of Jericho.

In the best of times the road to Jericho was dangerous. Before the war, we used to hear about bandits who robbed people and left them for dead. When we went to Jericho, we saw remnants of cars in the valley by the road. Jericho is situated about 26 miles from Ramallah. My aunt knew that the journey would not be easy. Without money and other options, she had no choice but to board the bus with many strangers, manly men who were anxious to go back to their homes. Like her, they were stranded out of town when the Six Days war started.

She reluctantly approached the bus; the driver was confident and cautious at the same time. He had a few passengers heading to the Ramallah region. My aunt asked him when he was leaving. He said as soon as possible. He asked her why she was out and about in this dangerous situation. She told him she was trying to go to Ramallah to be with her son. She gave him the greeting from Abou Mohamad and pointed to the house where she stayed. The driver changed his demeanor and smiled at her.

"Abou Mohamad is a good man. The family is the jewel of the city," he told her. She agreed. She asked about the cost. "Don't worry about it," he said, "Abou Mohamed is like my brother, if he sent you, you don't have to worry about paying." He told her to sit two seats behind him. She thanked him and went to her seat. A young boy and his sister sat next to her.

Although she grew up as a refugee and had a difficult childhood, she got accustomed to private cabs and being picked up by an Army Jeep for work daily. She was not used to boarding buses by herself. She had horrific memories of being on a bus when her family was forced to flee their home in Yaffa. At that time, she sat on the bus floor because Jewish terrorists shot at the bus. Her memory of that bus ride was dim and terrifying.

The kids who sat next to her were apprehensive. Like her, they were returning to their home. She stared out the window trying to avoid everyone. Before the driver shut the door, he stood and told everyone that he wanted to deliver them safely. He pleaded with people not to start any trouble. Except for a few nods, everyone remained silent.

My aunt was born in Yaffa and became a refugee at a very young age. She lived in Ramallah most of her life. Although barely middle class, she grew up in urban Ramallah and Jerusalem. She was exposed to the latest and greatest of French, Lebanese and Egyptian style and culture. She modeled her life after the wife of Omar Sharif and Bridgette Bardot, the French actress, a trendsetter in the '60s. She was not used to riding buses with strangers. She and her friends were city folks who looked down on peasants, Bedouins, black, people from refugee camps.

On the bus, she found herself beholden to strangers trying to help. The irony of the moment almost made her smile, but there was nothing to laugh about.

Ramallah was under curfew and surrounded by her enemies. She did not want to imagine, and refused to believe, that her son, mother, and sisters were in danger, and her adopted city was destroyed. She forced herself to focus on survival. She wanted to close her eyes, but her fear, and the boy and girl constantly moving made her uncomfortable. She had no choice but to think forward. She reminded herself not to panic. She thought of her father and brothers who lived in the United States and wished they would be in Ramallah to greet her.

As the bus trekked forward, she saw Bedouin tents near the road. She saw a few camels, goats, and lambs roaming and eating the dry bushes. In the distance, she saw a man approaching the bus. The driver did not want to stop, but some of the passengers begged him to let the man approach. He was dressed in a white galabia, an ankle-length loose-fitting garment. A passenger recognized the man and told the driver; "he is a good man." My aunt stiffened; she did not want the bus to stop. The driver stopped and the man hopped on the bus and was greeted by two people who knew him. "Yelaan abouk khouftney. (Damn your father, you scared me)," said the driver. "What are you doing out and about? Ya zalemeh betoukhouk (Man, they will shoot you)." The man smirked and without hesitation said: "No one is going to stop me from being on my streets."

They arrived in a village south of Ramallah, where the driver stopped to drop off and pick up people. A trip that should have taken half an hour took three hours because they took back roads to avoid soldiers and stopped to pick and drop people who needed rides. They saw bombed buildings. Except for one or two store fronts everything was closed. She worried life would never be the same. She was right. Our lives changed forever. A foreign power took over our towns, streets, and life. She worried that without a job, her life was going to get harder. She put her anxiety aside and prayed for mercy.

As they approached Ramallah, all the familiar stores and roads were closed. She saw charred cars, remnants of bombs. She did not dare cry. The boy and the girl next to her woke up and moved by their parents. Everyone was quiet. It was eerie. The bus passed the center of the city and continued to the bus station near her house. It passed by the church and her house. Everything was the same, except no one was on the street.

My aunt's return to Ramallah is indelibly seared into my mind and heart. The anxiety and depression of war and its uncertainty caused distress in our lives. Every time my cousin Bernard cried for his mom, our hearts ached. The war scattered our close-knit family. When my aunt came home, we forgot the war and celebrated her arrival. Although, apart for weeks, it seemed like a century. With her return, our family again became concerned about my Uncle Farid, my grandmother's younger brother. But within weeks, we got word from a cousin in Amman, Jordan, that Uncle Farid was safe in Jordan.

My aunt's homecoming and the news of my uncle's safety gave us hope. We rejoiced in those moments, but our happiness was temporary. The ever-present sound of the loudspeakers continued to remind us that we were under Israeli occupation. The hell of occupation never ceases to destroy any semblance of normalcy.

11 / Our Lives Changed Forever

The Israeli occupation turned our homes and neighborhoods into prisons. Our health and safety depended on the benevolence of soldiers, the majority of whom did not see us as human. The uncertainty and confusion of war touched every Palestinian's soul. We stopped wishing and dreaming of a future. Our dreams were temporary, such as not having soldiers visit us in the middle of the night. Most nights, my baby brother cried himself to sleep; the soundtrack on the radio my parents usually played to soothe him no longer worked. There was no more music. Instead, my family became addicted to the news.

Even when a curfew was not imposed, we stayed home. We felt safer behind closed doors. We missed the blue sky and the bright summer sun. We went to bed at 6 or 7 p.m. Children no longer filled the streets. The kaak and ice cream vendors became a thing of the past. The old ladies in the neighborhood were now prisoners behind the dark, black blankets on the windows of their homes.

My parents stayed home and did not go out unless it was necessary. My dad still had his job in Jerusalem, but was unable to go to work. The Israeli military authority shut down all public transportation, so few people could get to their jobs. My parents worried about money. After a month, my mother went back to work part-time with the nuns at St. Joseph. We had food on the table, but we rationed it. Before the war, we ate meat or chicken every Sunday. This custom changed to every other Sunday or whenever we found someone who sold fresh meat.

What we ate or how we changed our habits were the least of our problems. Within months, the occupation reared its ugly head. The soldiers became crueler and less tolerant, determined to show us who was boss. Their cruelty extended to rounding up our neighbors in the middle of the day and requiring the men, including young boys who had not reached puberty, to kneel in the hot sun for hours. They also demanded the women stand and watch. Anyone who protested this mistreatment found themselves hit in the head with the butt of a soldier's gun or in the spine by a soldier's boot. They ridiculed old people, like my neighbor Jamil, and spit at them. When one of our courageous young teenagers protested the humiliation of an older respected gentleman, the soldiers kicked and beat him until he was unconscious.

Stories of beatings and humiliation began to emerge from all corners. Everyone began to fear the soldiers and worry about what was coming. Who would be the next victim was anybody's guess. No one was safe. No one was spared an ugly intrusion on our lives. The invasion of our homes became more routine and more brutal. They crashed in on us during breakfast, lunch, and supper. They sometimes made us get up from our dinner table while they milled around our house doing nothing. They invaded our homes during the night and interrupted our sleep.

Men and boys became the target of vicious and inhumane violence and beatings. Soldiers used children as human shields when it suited them. As a game, soldiers patrolling the streets often scooped up a young child of seven or eight and hoisted them on the hood of the Jeep and drove them around in the neighborhood.

In the early weeks of the occupation, there was little or no resistance by the Palestinian people, especially in our area. I knew this to be true because I continually disobeyed my parents and snuck out to see what was going on outside. I was scared but fascinated with the new normal. Once, I saw Jamal's brother sobbing while being driven around on top of a Jeep; he had wet his pants. He was less than ten years old. When I saw him, I froze right where I was. I was worried I would be spotted, but I hid well that day. After a while, I scurried home. I did not tell anyone of what I witnessed. I was afraid of being punished for leaving the house without permission.

That night, I could not sleep. Every time I closed my eyes, I saw soldiers coming after me and putting me on the hood of a Jeep. I tossed and turned and cried. My parents tried to calm me, not knowing what I witnessed, but to no avail. After a couple of hours, they gave me a bit of ouzo and I fell asleep.

One morning around 7, we awoke to the sound of loud knocking at our door. It was one of my cousins. He anxiously told my parents the soldiers had arrested two of my other cousins. Khalil and Ibrahim were fifteen and fourteen and were asleep when the soldiers came to their home at 4 a.m. and took them. My cousin asked my mother if she could help them by asking the nuns or the Catholic priest to go with their grandmother to look for the boys at the local police station, where the military authority had set up a command post.

My mother immediately changed clothes and went back with my cousin to fetch his grandmother. Since there was no curfew, the soldiers were not patrolling the side streets. The distressed grandmother, Auntie Hilway, went with my mom to the convent to seek help. The sisters were eager to help but did not know how. With the support of the other nuns, Mother Superior made several calls. While on the phone, she asked Auntie Hilway for vital information about the boys, since she did not know them well. After several calls, the nuns told Auntie Hilway that the British Consulate in Jerusalem would check on the situation and get back to them.

After assurances from the Mother Superior, my mother, aunt, and Sister Pia, a self-assured Irish nun, went with them to seek information and file a complaint at the local police station. It was in Almanarah, about a ten-minute walk from the convent. On the way, they saw young men kneeling, blindfolded, with young soldiers guarding them. They noticed that few of the shops were open. They saw women with bundles on their head moving toward one of the refugee camps in the area. They had young children following them. Some were crying;

they looked like they had been walking for some time. As they passed, some of the women asked my mother for money. Since my mom had no money with her, she apologized and kept walking. These women were not regular beggars; they were just being evicted from their homes.

When they reached the police station, they found more than a hundred people standing in line. There were no men in the line. When they inquired about what was going on, they discovered that everyone was looking for their sons, brothers or husbands who were also rounded up by the Israeli Armed Forces during the night.

The line was not moving. My mom, Auntie Hilway and Sister Pia knew most of the people in line. Ramallah was a big city, but everybody knew everybody. It was a close-knit community. Armed with her French and Irish passport, Sister Pia walked to the front of the line and demanded to speak with someone in charge. As she passed by, people thanked her for her support. She stopped at the front of the line and asked the soldier if he spoke English or French. The soldier responded to her in an Australian accent. She asked if she could speak with his superior; he was reluctant, but he soon succumbed to her charm. He radioed someone on his walkie-talkie, speaking in Hebrew. He told her to wait. They both made small talk. She asked him, "Why are the Israeli soldiers being cruel?" He shrugged his shoulder and said, "I don't know. Security?" She did not want to antagonize him, so she let it go.

After this brief conversation, they waited in the familiar police station. The structure used to be the Jordanian local police station. It was the first building commandeered when Israel occupied Ramallah. They replaced the Jordanian flag with the Israeli flag. The chief of police was arrested, and the commanders who did not flee to Jordan were detained.

After fifteen minutes, Sister Pia was ushered inside. She met with the person in charge who told her to tell everyone that all their relatives would be discharged in a few days, and they should all go home and not worry. She politely demanded to know the reason why all those men were being detained. He responded that they were all being held for security reasons. He then said to her, "Tell them not to worry; everyone will be released unless they are part of the resistance."

Sister Pia was politically astute; she did want to build a good relationship with the person in charge, so she did not react to his remarks. As she was leaving, he told her to tell the people who were standing in line to leave before the soldiers forced them to.

She urged the people to leave for own their good while trying to assure them that everything would be alright. Drained by the humiliation and feeling dejected, the people began to disperse. Sister Pia walked around and talked to almost everyone and told them that their family members were safe. She also promised them that the nuns would seek the help of the French, British and the Italian consulates, if necessary.

Humiliation, misery, defeat, and brutality became the norm for us. The land where we were born and where our ancestors had lived for generations was no longer ours. These new rulers who came crashing in on us did not know our families, friends, or neighbors. They did not know that my cousins were not involved in politics. The Israeli troopers just came to their home at 4 a.m. and dragged them off in front of their grandmother, father, mother, and sisters, without cause and without any consideration for their well-being.

After leaving the police station, the three women returned to my uncle's home to give them the news. My aunt was inconsolable. Everyone in the family was in shock about that morning's events. After hearing that the boys would not return home immediately, their mother fainted. My uncle recounted how the boys were rudely arrested while sleeping. The soldiers arrived at my uncle's house and ordered everyone to stand in the corner. The boys and their father stood on one side, while the girls, their grandmother, and their mother stood in another corner. After a brief search of the house, they dragged Ibrahim and Khalil out of the house and put them in their Jeeps. The boys were in a trance; they were half-awake. As the soldiers led them out of the door, they began to scream "Baba, Mama" "Mom, Dad." The family kept repeating the boy's cry "Mama, Baba." And, with that, the nightmare began. The family was still crying when Sister Pia and my mom left.

True to her word, Sister Pia checked with the British and the French embassies, who helped track the boys whereabouts. With her help, the French consul general worked with the United Nations and the Red Cross to seek the release of all who had been taken prisoner. After three days, and after having endured extensive and brutal interrogations, beatings, sleep deprivation, and torture, the boys were released. My cousins were a target because they belonged to the Boy Scouts and went to public school.

Those early morning raids were carried out by the Israeli Defense Forces to gather information on a resistance movement and to stop potential opposition to the occupation. No one was ever charged with a crime. My cousins' horrifying ordeal was just the beginning of what was coming next.

12 / Witness to an Assassination

In 1967, Frank Sinatra won a Grammy for his song "Strangers in the Night." Meanwhile, our lives were filled with strangers in our homes at night who did not care about the children they terrified. We were helpless; our parents could not protect us. Soldiers were at our doors at all hours. Our lives were transformed from a subdued and ordinary existence to a life of torture, panic, and mistrust. We lived in an abyss that included an unstoppable avalanche of routine persecution and cruelty.

Our persecutors came with a racist power who believed our homes were given to Israel, not us, by a racist God who believed they were the chosen according to the Old Testament. Their goal was to banish us from the land like Israel expelled our families in 1948.

But this time, the conqueror underestimated the will of the people to stay put and live in their own homeland. At first, the people were scared, but after a couple of months, they became enraged. Without guns or weapons, they stood up to the soldiers and became fearless. The oppressors came with their menacing weapons, tanks, and Jeeps, yet they were afraid of indigenous children who, by their very presence, created an alternative truth. They invaded our land and wanted to evict us by any means possible. We were the obstacle to their grand plans of conquering our homeland. Some of their leaders admitted as much.

In fact, many mainstream Zionist leaders, including David Ben-Gurion, the first prime minister of Israel, endorsed the expulsion of Palestinians, according to Israeli historian Barry Morris "The entire (Israeli) leadership understands that this is the idea. The officer corps understands what is required of them. Under Ben-Gurion, a consensus of transfer is created."[7]

In 1948, six months after the War of Independence ended, Ben-Gurion sought to expel more than 10,000 Palestinians, mostly Christian, from the north for unspecified "security reasons." This expulsion was not carried out, reportedly due to anticipated negative pushback from abroad. But in the years that followed, several attempts were made to transfer tens of thousands of Christian Arabs from Galilee to Argentina and Brazil.[8]

---

7 "On Ethnic Cleansing: Israeli Zionist Historian Benny Morris Speaks Out! An Interview" *Chicago Independent Media Center*, January 11, 2005.
8 "The Secret Letter Detailing Israel's Plan to Expel Arabs, 'Without Unnecessary Brutality'" by Adam Raz, *Haaretz*, December 21, 2018.

In his review of Tom Segev's book, *A State at Any Cost. The Life of David Ben-Gurion*, Samuel Farber states that examining Ben-Gurion's life shows "how the creation of Israel was from its beginnings incompatible with the creation of a democratic binational state composed of Jews and Palestinians, and the project of Israeli state-building was always doomed to turn Israel into an oppressor nation."

As far back as 1937, Ben-Gurion declared at a Zionist congress in Zurich that "our right to Palestine, all of it, is unassailable and eternal," Segev said. "Most Palestinians were forcefully expelled by the Haganah (Jewish Israeli Army) or ran away terrorized and in fear for their lives due to the threats and actions of the Jewish forces, and Segev shows that Ben-Gurion generally approved these actions, and that he also insisted, during a truce in the 1948 war, on restarting the hostilities as an opportunity to 'clean' Galilee of the 100,000 Palestinians who had sought refuge there."[9]

In many cases, senior commanders of the Israel Defense Forces ordered Palestinians to be expelled and their homes blown up. The Israeli military not only updated Ben-Gurion about these events, but also apparently received his prior authorization, in written or oral form. [10]

Within a few months of the end of the initial war, we began to go back to our churches or our mosques. Our markets slowly opened, although the vendors had little to sell. We did not have the mobility to travel to different towns, but we stayed connected and supported each other. We remained committed to staying in our land regardless of the cruelty inflicted upon us. Unlike 1948, most of us faced the torture with our heads held high. After all, we are people who love to live; we did not want to die. We cautiously obeyed their ominous rules but began to regain our balance by living life. Their collective punishment did not deter us from helping and working with each other.

The Israelis tried every avenue to expel the local Palestinian population. They took a surprise survey to determine how many people lived in each home. They then evicted any individual found in their homes who were not present during the survey. They skewed this census to their benefit.

Some of our neighbors who were not counted in the census had to plead for their right to move back to their homes. This was the beginning of an "ethnically cleansing" Palestine of its indigenous people. This also affected many people who lived in Jerusalem. Staying put became a priority. However, my grandmother and aunts already had plans to join my grandfather and uncles in the United States.

The United States encouraged Palestinians to leave if they had relatives in the US. My grandmother and aunts got their visas and immigration papers approved faster than anyone had anticipated. Within months, my grandmother, my three aunts and my cousin Bernard left to join mxy grandfather in Detroit, Michigan.

---

9 "A Zionist State at Any Cost," a review by Samuel Farber of *A State at Any Cost: The Life of David Ben-Gurion*, translated by Haim Watzman (New York: Farrar, Straus and Giroux, 2019).
10 "Catastrophic Thinking: Did Ben-Gurion Try to Rewrite History?" by Shay Hazkani, *Haaretz*, May 16, 2013

Since my grandmother's house was bigger than ours, we moved there. We were now next door to my best friend, Henry, and his brothers, who had returned home after being away for two months. They had lived with their grandmother in a different town.

The future was still uncertain. The new school year was approaching, but no one knew if the schools were going to reopen. We still stayed inside the house. Henry and Giovanni came over, but rarely did we venture outside. Being me, however, I began to explore the outside world when my mom and dad left to run errands, and when my mom went to work. Sometimes I went with Henry, other times I went by myself. Despite all the cautionary directives my parents gave us, I still wanted to get out of the house.

I ventured out one day to buy candy at a nearby store. It was scalding hot, even for Palestine. Few soldiers were on the street. I passed the bus station, which was a block away from our house. Most of the people there were villagers and strangers and were mostly women. There were a few old men and three or four young men. I was happy and surprised that there were very few soldiers.

As I approached the store, I saw a neighbor heading in my direction. I tried to avoid him because I was worried he would tell my parents, but it was too late. He stopped me and asked me what I was doing on the streets. I said I was buying some candy and my father knew I was out. He shook his head and told me to buy the candy and rush home. I went to the store, owned by a shabby-looking old man named Khara Alousha's "shitty lover." I did not understand the nickname, even though we all made fun of it.

I bought several pieces of candy and left to go home. Since I saw no patrols, I reverted to my old habits of climbing walls and collecting a few butterflies that were fluttering around. I felt normal and happy.

I skipped over the wall next to the store across the street from the bus station. There were several buses parked there and people were boarding them. Suddenly, all hell broke loose!

Four or five men with hoods and face masks jumped from two cars and approached one of the buses, called a man by his name and shot him at very close range. As the shooters began to flee in their vehicles, they continued shooting in all directions. People tried to scatter; others just stood there, screaming in shock. A few people, including Khara Alousha's and his daughter, were injured by flying bullets.

When I heard and saw the gunfire, I squatted and hid behind a wall where I could see but would not be seen. The man who had been shot lay face down by the front door of the bus. The other people who had been wounded were all over the bus station. People were still screaming. Some women shouted, "Allah WA Akbar (God is Great)." I was terrified, mesmerized, and paralyzed by fear, all at the same time.

People were running in all directions. A couple of men came running in my direction. They jumped over the wall and hid next to me. They were startled for a minute when they saw me and ready to fight, thinking I was with the shooters. When they realized I was just a young girl hiding, they took a breath and began to whisper. They spoke Arabic, like the peasants. They asked me if I saw the shooting. I nodded yes, without saying a word. We sat there for about ten minutes. Still, there was no sight of the Israeli patrols.

One of the men tried to reassure me by telling me everything would be okay. He turned to his friend and said, "I bet you that the shooters were Israelis undercover."

"How do you know," his buddy asked

"The cars have a different license plate than our cars."

His friend said, "Ya bayee, (Oh, my!); we need to get out of here!"

The second man said to the first one. "Yalla, let's go."

They both looked at me, "Are you going to be okay? Go home now!"

I did not let them finish talking, I ran back so fast! I did not notice that several army patrols were approaching the scene.

Israeli Jeeps finally arrived at the bus station about fifteen minutes later and started rounding up people indiscriminately. By then, everyone had quickly dispersed for fear of being implicated in the shooting — like the two men who jumped the wall and hid with me.

My father was anxiously waiting for me when I arrived home. He yelled at me and smacked me with the back of his hand. "What if you get shot down! This is not a play; you could have been killed!" I cried, not from the pain (his smack didn't hurt) but because I had disappointed him. Within half an hour, my mom was back home. She asked my dad if he had heard about the shooting, he told her that he had. My father did not say anything about me being around the area of the shooting; I was grateful. He asked her if anyone they knew was hurt; she was not certain. I wanted to say something but kept quiet for fear of punishment. It turned out I had witnessed the assassination of a local activist by the Israeli Mossad (the national intelligence agency).

Within an hour of the shooting, the Israeli Defense Forces imposed a curfew until further notice. We turned our focus on securing the blankets at the windows and locking the doors. Since it was summer, we did not have to do any homework, but my mom expected her four eldest girls, including me, to finish some chores, like washing the dishes, folding and ironing the clothes and practicing the embroidery.

I hated these chores; I only did them to escape punishment. No sooner had we finished our tasks when we heard a loud knock on the door. My mother opened it to a crew of soldiers who pushed her aside and began ransacking our house. After they had destroyed everything, they left without saying a word.

After every invasion of our home, we developed new ways to cope. The first time they burst in, we cried with panic. The second time, we looked at the soldiers with terror, but after the fourth or fifth time, we looked at the soldiers with disdain and hope. We always hoped that one of the soldiers would be merciful and not touch our father. We also prayed that they would quickly leave so we could resume our "new" routine. After the soldiers left, we cleaned up the mess they made, ate supper and went to bed.

Although I witnessed the murder at the bus station, I kept it a secret. I went to bed that night without uttering a word about what I had seen. I had a horrific nightmare that night. I woke up screaming, "Don't shoot; don't shoot!" and began to howl. My mother ran to me and held me, and with a soothing voice said, "They are gone; they will not hurt you." At that moment, I wanted to tell her but decided I'd better not. I went back to sleep.

The next day, everyone was talking about the shooting. I told Henry about it; I trusted him. I had him promise not to tell anyone else, but he went and told his mother. When his mother saw me, she asked me about what I saw. I blabbed to her about what I had witnessed, described to her what happened, and asked her not to tell my parents. As a former nun, she was understanding but was worried that I might be in danger. As she listened, she implored God for mercy, then she admonished me for going out without telling my parents. She had me promise not to disobey my parents again, or she would not let me play with Henry and Giovanni.

My nightmares continued. Every time I fell into deep sleep, I woke screaming, "Don't shoot; don't shoot!"

Things went back to normal when a curfew was not imposed. The stores began to stay open a little longer, my father found a local carpenter who needed help, and my mother continued to work at the school. We were ordered to stay at home and not go beyond our front door. Henry's mom and the other neighbors, including the nuns who lived across the street, kept an eye on us. Whenever they saw us stray from the area, they chastised us. They did not have to worry; after the killing I witnessed, I attempted to stay close to home.

For almost a week, I kept hearing about the shooting but still managed to keep the secret to myself. Soon after, my mom found out from one of the neighbors about my experience. At first, I did not admit to what I saw, but she told me that if I lied, she would drag me to the priest to confess. Sobbing, I told her the whole story, even about the two men who hid with me. I was waiting for her to slap me on my head for disobeying her orders, but instead she said, "You have been punished enough; no child should ever witness a cold-blooded murder. I hope you learned your lesson." I did not know what to do, I escaped punishment. I felt relieved after confessing to my mother. That night, I did not pee in my pajamas.

Before the war, August was the month when my family took time off to visit relatives in various cities. We always used to visit my great-grandmother in Jifna. My mom used to hire a taxi, that stayed with us all day while we visited and played in the apricot and almond groves. Although apricots were harvested in July, our family still gathered to sample some of the delicious preserves my great-grandmother made. As city slickers for grandchildren, my great-grandmother spoiled us. I played soccer with my mom's younger cousins and was able to run around gathering butterflies.

This was not the case in August 1967. Although my Uncle Farid was no longer missing, he was not able to return to his family in Jifna. Our family decided it was best to stay home and skip the annual trip. Besides, we could not find transportation to take us back and forth. Only a hand full of people dared to go to their fields to harvest the apricots and almonds. Most of the crops either spoiled or were looted by passersby who needed food.

August was a month when both Catholic and Orthodox Christians celebrated one of the major feasts in Christianity, the Dormition and Assumption of the

Virgin Mary. Before 1967, the celebration began with fourteen days of fasting and ended with religious services and grand festivals where everyone, including our Muslim brothers and sisters, celebrated the joyous holiday. The Church blessed the newly harvested grapes and people shared their crops with their neighbors.

In 1967, everyone stayed home. We neither celebrated nor went to church because of the curfew. The sound of soldiers' boots replaced the sound of bells ringing, ushering people to join the festivities.

Our lives were now constantly filled with terror, boredom, denial, fear, deprivation, illegal searches and seizures, beatings, curfews, and most of all uncertainty and insecurity. We were caught tangled in a calamity controlled by outsiders who did not know us and didn't care if we lived or died. Our days were dreadful, and our nights were frightful. The news on the radio was all about us, but the media did not understand us or our plight. It is still this way today.

Our oppressors didn't care that the Feast of the Assumption of the Blessed Virgin Mary, where everybody went to picnics and cookouts in Jerusalem and where my family attended this festival at the foothills of the Mount of Olives to celebrate the summer, was canceled. Before this tragedy, Christians and Muslims spent days celebrating this great holiday. Families cooked fresh mahshi (stuffed zucchini) and grape leaves, and brought fresh grapes, lush figs, watermelons, and cantaloupes and spent hours on rickety rides. We all played until we all fell asleep.

Before 1967, the faithful dressed their young girls in gowns resembling the Virgin Mary's robes. In Jerusalem, where we went to celebrate this feast, men and women descended, on their knees, the 47 steps of the church where it is believed Mary ascended to heaven, and lit candles on behalf of their families. During the festivities, many made promises to the Virgin Mary so that Christ could grant them their wishes. Except for the year my sister died, my family either went to Jerusalem to celebrate or took part in the festivities in Ramallah. But in August 1967, no one celebrated.

Back-to-school preparation always took place in August. Each year, my mom dressed us up and took us to school to register, where they always had a mini orientation for students and parents. It was fun being measured for new uniforms. In August 1967, my parents received a note that school was delayed until further notice.

After I had witnessed the assassination at the bus station, I tried to stay near home and play with Henry, Giovanni, my sister Stella, and a few other neighborhood children. We played marbles, soccer and a game called Tugga We-Agra. The game resembled cricket or American baseball. There were four bases built with small rocks; four players who played defense; a pitcher who threw a small tennis ball; and a batter who attempted to hit the ball with a long piece of wood. Like baseball, the batter hit the ball and rounded the bases. The defensive players tried to tag the batter. The batter was ousted with a tag. Like baseball, the winning team was the one with the most points. We sought to be kids again; we played when we could.

In the middle of playing Tugga We-Agra one day, we saw some soldiers around the corner. We pretended not to pay attention, but we saw the soldiers drag young boys, men, and women in blindfolds and put them in waiting Jeeps. Most of the people we saw appeared to be Muslims because they wore traditional clothing. We stopped playing and went inside our homes.

Within days, rumors began to circulate that the Israelis targeted only Muslims. Of course, that was not accurate, but it was this episode and many others that began to create a rift among the people in the community. The Israelis tried and sometimes succeeded in stoking that tension and anxiety between Palestinian Muslims and Christians. To feel safe and to avoid being hassled, our Muslim brothers and sisters began to buy a cheap crucifix to wear when going to the market. The dime store owner reported a spike in the sale of Christian religious icons and crosses. Wearing a cross, however, did not stop the Israeli Armed Forces' collective punishment of all Palestinians. Recognizing the deviousness of the Israelis' practice and policies inspired the Christians and Muslims to band together to help anyone in trouble with the Israelis.

13 / The Sealing of Our Neighbor's Home

One day, while sitting with Henry and Giovanni after winning a marble game, we saw a convoy of soldiers in trucks and Jeeps speeding toward an alley not far away from where we sat. We also saw people running toward the convoy, which stopped in the next neighborhood. I knew that we would be in trouble if we went to see what was going on, but being kids, we decided to investigate.

Hearing the sirens, Henry's mom directed him to come inside. I, on the other hand, saw an older lady from our neighborhood rushing to the scene, so I decided to tag along with her.

People were gathered around Saleh's house. Saleh was a seventeen-year-old boy who excelled in school and worked as an assistant baker to help support his family. On a bullhorn, the soldiers yelled at the family and told them they had only five minutes to clear everything out of their house. They then proceeded to seal the home, presumably as a punishment for something Saleh had done. I saw Saleh's mom and sisters crying while hauling out mattresses and pillows and other belongings. Some courageous neighbors tried to help, but the majority stood in disbelief.

The house was on the second floor above the shoe repair store. Someone murmured that Saleh had been arrested and accused of being a terrorist. Everyone knew and loved Saleh; he was nerdy, but a polite young man who was never in trouble. Saleh was in prison and his family was on its way to being homeless. It appeared some of the soldiers enjoyed punishing Saleh and his family and creating anxiety and panic in the community. I was, again, surprised that some of the soldiers spoke perfect Arabic. In my mind, the enemy did not speak my language. One of them piped up on the loudspeaker: "This is what happens to you if you don't tell the truth."

The despair I saw that day was unimaginable. Even as a child, I knew that I was a witness to injustice.

True to their word, after the five-minute warning, the soldiers welded Saleh's home shut while the family watched in anguish. The orange sparks of fire that splashed from the welder created a lasting impression on everyone's heart. Women began to wail, and men put their heads down for fear of someone seeing them cry. Um Saleh (Saleh's Mom) wailed, "Saleh, my boy; he is innocent. He is only a child."

His sisters quietly sobbed. Before they sealed the house, the soldiers went in and looked for evidence of Saleh's role as a terrorist but found nothing.

Nevertheless, Saleh and his family were condemned without due process. After a few days, Saleh was released without being charged with a crime. Since he and his family were now homeless, they moved in with his uncle in a cramped apartment in the same neighborhood.

I returned home with my head bowed, not sure how to process what had happened. No one in my family knew that I witnessed the sealing of Saleh's home. The news soon reached everyone. My family whispered about it and wondered what injustice was coming next.

14 / Tony's Beating

As the sun beat down and the pavement burned the soles of our feet, we daily witnessed events that were out of our control, giving us a mixture of emotions — fear, defiance, stress, anxiety and hostility. Although our parents still strove to avoid all risky situations and tightly control our movements for everyone's safety, they knew we lived among destructible forces. We took solace in the fact that our lives were not in as much jeopardy as the lives of our Muslim neighbors.

Our Israeli oppressors did not see us as Christians or Muslims. They did not view us as good or bad. They considered us the enemy — cockroaches who needed to be crushed. No one was safe in our neighborhood. Our Italian friend Tony was their next prey.

A few days after the house sealing, Tony Melani went to the bakery to buy bread. He was eleven. Tony was Henry and Giovanni's older and gentle brother. In the neighborhood, Tony was known as the kind, artistic and obedient kid who never got into trouble. During the summers, when Henry, Giovanni and I were creating all sorts of havoc, Tony helped his father at the corner store.

He was a kind-hearted boy who loved art and was good at it. Whenever I had an art assignment, I gave it to Tony to do. Since the boys' school did not have an art program, Tony reveled at the prospect of working on our assignments. He never disappointed us with his skills. The only time my art projects were displayed at school was when Tony worked on them. The nuns knew that someone helped us with our art homework but did not object because the work was magnificent. Tony helped me with my embroidery, mosaics, and making baskets from raffia paper.

Tony's skills were not confined to art. He also excelled at solving puzzles. At a very young age, Tony participated in solving word puzzles in the local newspapers. When not busy in the store, he either was working on an art project or pouring over the latest riddles. Older people also sought his help. Tony won several competitions and was known as an artistic genius. He kept a supply of stamps ready so he could mail in his puzzle solutions.

Tony's kindness and talent did not stop an Israeli patrol from smashing his skull, breaking his arm and battering his young body. While walking home from the bakery, he dropped a key near the main street, a block away from his home. When he bent down to pick up the key, a patrol car of IDF soldiers approached him. Several soldiers jumped out and without warning began to beat and kick him.

One of the neighbors witnessed the whole episode and began to scream. "For the love of God; leave Tony alone!" She was horrified. She started to scream again, "For God's sake, he is only a child!" She continued to cry "Where did the love of God go; how can you beat this child?" They continued beating him for several minutes. Blood gushed from his mouth and head. When the other neighbors heard her, they went out to investigate. As the people began to assemble, a soldier shot his gun in their direction. Some soldiers laughed as if what they were doing qualified as entertainment.

By then, Tony lay motionless; everyone thought that he was dead. And, just like nothing had happened, the soldiers in the Jeep drove away and left Tony bleeding in the street.

A neighbor mustered her courage and picked Tony up and rushed him to her home. His mother, a former nun, fainted at the sight of him. By then, another neighbor, risking retaliation from the Israelis, went to get a doctor. By the time the doctor arrived, Tony had lost a lot of blood, but he was still alive. His father went with him while the neighbors tended to his unconscious mother.

Tony stayed in the hospital for more than a month. He had a concussion; a severe gash on his skull which required more than sixty stitches; broken arms; no front teeth, several bruised ribs, and stitches on his face, arms, and legs. His body was so badly beaten and bruised it was a miracle he survived. No one expected him to.

His parents took turns tending to him at the hospital while the neighbors pitched in to help the family. Henry and Giovanni were worried that Tony still might die. We went to church and lit candles and prayed the rosary for him. Since Tony's father was Italian, he filed a complaint about the beating with the Italian Embassy.

Tony's torture, in the middle of the day without provocation, sent chills through everyone in town. We became paranoid. Tony's beating was a reminder for all of us that no one was safe, not even the Christian children. More talks of people leaving and immigrating to the United States began to circulate around the neighborhood.

I began to have nightmares about soldiers running after me. These nightmares still occur today. They were frequent, and I was not the only one having them.

After months of rehabilitation, Tony returned to a semi-normal life. He developed a twitch that continues today. Everyone, including Henry, still talked about the beating, but Tony never said a word about it. He could not remember what had happened to him. If there was a response to the beating by the Italian Embassy, it did not trickle down to his family. After Tony had fully recovered, his family moved to a different section of town. It was hard for me to lose Henry and Giovanni as friends.

It appeared the abuse by Israel was systematic. Soldiers who committed the acts and were identified were not punished. In fact, some commanders encouraged the use of violence as a routine part of the punishment and as a deterrent to any disobedience.

Israel viewed every Palestinian, regardless of age, as a security risk. When caught, the IDF used this defense as justification for their inhumane treatment of the Palestinians. How can an eleven-year-old even know what the occupation was all about? Tony was a child who cared about art, school and helping his dad at the store. Neither Tony nor anyone else in our neighborhood had participated in any resistance movement. If there was one; no one knew about it or the identity of its members. These facts did not matter to the Israelis. No Israeli was ever held accountable for Tony's beating and torture or for the thousands of other unarmed civilians the soldiers tortured. Every now and then, we ran into a soldier who was kind, but that was a rarity. The subjugation of the people living under the Israeli occupation became the norm.

After Tony's torture, I became more attentive to what topics the grown-ups discussed. To pass the time, neighbors got together and played cards and drank dark Arabic coffee and smoked cigarettes. Men sat in one room, and the women gathered in another to catch-up on the latest rumors, news, and gossip. Since the adults restricted our movements, we sometimes listened to them to find out what was happening in town. Before the war, the gossip was about marriage, food, shopping, church, and the economy. They also chatted about the weather and their children. They always bragged about their kids' achievements and their after-school activities. The men talked about work, the Jordanian government, the king, the elected mayor, and the city council. After the war, they talked about two subjects: the Israelis and the pathetic Palestinian resistance.

The first time I heard about a Palestinian resistance movement and its members was after Tony's beating. A friend of my dad's mocked a man named Alshukari who had fled the country wearing a woman's dress. My parents and their friends took pleasure as they mocked the hapless Palestinian resistance.

No one in the resistance movement, or Fedayeen as we called them, came from our neighborhood. My parents and their friends were mostly illiterate and worked either in skilled labor jobs, like my dad, or in unskilled labor jobs. They kept to themselves and rarely talked about politics.

Immediately after the war, the men talked about Egyptian President Gamal Abdul Nasser. One group adored Abdul Nasser and viewed him as the savior of the Arab world. Another group, that my dad belonged to, found President Nasser to be a bombastic loudmouth with long-winded, empty speeches. No one had heard of Yasser Arafat. He did not emerge on the scene until 1968. During their card games, the men argued about King Hussien of Jordan or Gamal Abdul Nasser of Egypt. My father liked King Hussien. To my knowledge, it never occurred to my dad or his friends to ever fight or arm themselves. They just hoped that the Arab leaders would save them from the Israelis.

The occupation chipped away at us, mentally and physically. We stopped being the happy-go-lucky kids who just wanted to win marble games and play soccer. Palestinians, young and old, became the target of young Israeli soldiers. who intended to harm or kill them. If it were not for my sisters and a few neighborhood friends who endured the occupation with me, life would have been more dreadful.

15 / Dismantling Civil Society

As soon as the Israeli Occupation began, all Palestinian civil, judicial and police agencies ceased to function. The Israeli Defense Forces took charge of every facet of our lives. They decided how we lived, moved, traveled, and conducted our daily lives. What we experienced in our daily lives depended on how the Israelis felt about their security that day, and regardless of how little resistance we put up, Israel felt insecure. Therefore, when they felt particularly threatened, they led us with a tourniquet that they twisted and turned to suffocate our movement when they felt threatened.

The Israelis had an unrestricted power over our lives, so no one was safe, not even innocent, harmless kids like Tony. They had all the guns and the power, yet they feared us. No one knew who remained of our Palestinian leaders. Every now and then, we found leaflets urging people to rise and rebel against the Israeli injustice.

Our neighbors were not the kind of people who got involved in politics. Besides kitchen knives, no one possessed weapons. Before the occupation, we had limited petty crimes.

We had a decent police department. The police officers worked under the Jordanian regimes and made sure the community was safe. After the war, the police force was dismantled and months later the Israeli Defense Forces put in untrained people like police officers to take care of civil infractions. They recruited people like my cousin, who was known to be an alcoholic. He patrolled the town riding a horse. By the end of the day, he and his horse stumbled around drunk.

We always counted on two events in September, the Feast of the Exaltation of the Holy Cross and the first day of school. By early September 1967, we learned that the celebration of the feast was cancelled. The church opted for a regular mass only. The festivities became another casualty of the war.

Before the war, we celebrated the lifting of the Holy Cross. Various marching bands competed against each other and marched until midnight, when everyone joined in building a great bonfire. This Christian, Catholic and Orthodox holiday commemorated the finding of the True Cross by St. Helen, the mother of Emperor Constantine, the dedication of the Holy Sepulcher, and the restoration of the True Cross to Jerusalem. But in a deeper sense, the feast also celebrated the Holy Cross as the instrument of our salvation. Our Muslim brothers and sisters also engaged in the celebrations.

My sisters and I were heartsick. The cancellation of all summer festivities and the delay in school added to the melancholy we felt since the war began. For more than two months, we had gotten up every morning before dawn to sit idle — seeing nothing but darkness, since all the windows were covered with black blankets. We prayed that school would open so we could have somewhere to go. By the beginning of October, our prayers were answered. The Sisters of St. Joseph deemed the situation stabilized and opened the school at the end of September.

The day the school opened, we woke up in darkness, washed, ate breakfast and off we went. Unlike past years, we did not dilly-dally on our way to school. Our parents went with us and delivered us directly to the anxiously waiting nuns.

I was in sixth grade; I was no longer in the elementary branch of the school. Few students who lived at the boarding school returned that year. Only three students lived at the school in 1967 — Sarah and her sister Aida, and Josephine, a Syrian orphan who could not return home.

There were twenty-four young girls in my sixth grade. Every student had returned except a talented girl named Lina. The nuns said she would join us later in the month. Her father had been killed in action while fleeing in the war. The first day of school was surreal. The nuns and teachers were nervous. When the bell rang, we stood in line as we always had; shorter girls in the front, taller girls in the back. Each class had its own line. It was a habit for the nuns to change the uniform every few years, but in 1967, the uniforms stayed the same.

Soeur Cyril, the short but lovable Mother Superior, greeted us and blew the whistle to signal silence. Most parents stayed to hear her directives for the new school year. She started the speech with a short prayer and then outlined the new rules all the students had to abide by for their own safety:

1. No one could participate in any resistance movement; anyone caught talking about politics or the occupation would be expelled.

2. When a curfew was called, the nuns would determine whether the students would be dismissed to go home.

3. Students who lived more than a mile away must have an adult accompany them to school every day.

4. All extracurricular activities, including field trips, were suspended until further notice.

Before the war, our first day of school was exciting. The nuns and teachers milled around the school grounds welcoming back students and introducing themselves to the new students. Only parents of new students stayed after the bell rang. The directives the Mother Superior gave back then covered topics about the expectation for excellence in studies, cleanliness, and proper behavior.

After her speech, Mother Superior blew her whistle and off we went to our assigned classroom. Sixth grade was on the second floor with the older students. I was assigned a front seat next to Eman Marcus. Our windows overlooked the boys' public school. The windows were opened for fresh air; although it was October, it was still warm.

In the classroom, everything was the same. Our French teacher Soeur Antoine, an older French nun who was not known to waste time, started where we left off the year before.

The first day of school went off without any problems. The nuns and teachers were a little more cautious but proceeded like there was nothing unusual happening outside of the school's walls. During recess, we we noticed additional monitors watching the students. Since the school was surrounded by massive walls, we could not see what was going on outside. Rumors began to circulate about older students joining demonstrations. As soon as Mother Superior got wind of the stories, she sent letters to the older students' parents requesting a meeting to nip the issue in the bud. That was the last time anyone mentioned resistance.

Before the war, the upper-class students talked about fashion and boys. Almost every day, my group confiscated letters the girls had written to the boys and had hidden in the cracks of the walls. We read them to each other and gave them to the hall monitor, Sister Toufeel. She took the letters and was amused by our ability to confiscate them.

The students to whom the letters were directed were rarely in trouble. This changed when Sister Noel took over as a recess monitor; she was not as nice as Sister Toufeel. She punished the girls and ordered the holes in the walls sealed. She tried to put a stop to the letter exchange. She was so mean she reprimanded us for giving her the letters!

After the war, few love letters were exchanged; they were replaced by leaflets about demonstrations and talks about resisting the occupation. At ten years old, I wanted to counter the abuses inflicted on our daily lives with some form of action. I wanted to resist and stand up for what was right, although I was afraid. So instead of giving the leaflets we found to the nuns, we gave them to some of our favorite students.

The sisters tried to keep everything normal. We started school at the same time as before, for the most part, and we stayed at school until 3 p.m. But every time something erupted in the streets, the nuns scrambled to send us home. Most times, our parents were already aware of what was going on and arrived at school to pick us up before we could be dismissed. The first few months of school, the nuns managed to keep them out.

The public school next door was less fortunate. Since we could see everything from our window, we watched as the Israeli army entered the school several times and dragged students and respected teachers down the stairs and to the streets, forcing them to kneel for hours. The Army arrived daily to arrest a teacher, student or administrator.

We had to pretend that life was ordinary. We had to concentrate on reading, writing, math, religion, French, English, gym, home economics, and other subjects. We began to describe events as "before the war" and "after the war." Before the war, we looked forward to going on picnics to Jericho on the weekend and visiting my great-grandmother in Jifna. After the war, we stayed home. We worried about who was going to be hurt next. We stopped thinking of the future. We existed in a state of helplessness and fear.

Several weeks after school started, Lina, our classmate whose father died during the war, joined the class. It was awkward to see her; we did not know what to say. Sister Ida, a young, compassionate nun who taught us Arabic grammar, changed the dynamic by immediately giving Lina a hug. She asked us to do the same. Lina cried quietly. Since Sister Ida removed the awkwardness, it was easier to continue with our classes. Lina later told us that her father was killed right in front of her. We all agreed that he died a martyr for his country.

While school life gradually returned to normal, anger brewed in the streets. Soldiers continued to patrol daily, dramatically screeching their cars to a halt, so they could harass and beat students who were on their way home from school. They took pleasure in intimidating people. Some lucky students received only a whack on the head, while more unfortunate students suffered a real beating and were then forced to kneel for hours on the ground before being released. Warned by their parents not to confront the soldiers, the boys endured the humiliation. After several more incidents of young boys being beaten, the public-school kids took to demonstrations. It was not an uprising or anything like that, it's just that the boys and girls had had enough.

The anger boiled over when one of the favorite teachers at the boys' school was kicked, smacked, and dragged in front of the schoolyard by young soldiers. All hell broke loose; a demonstration spontaneously erupted. At first, the soldiers watched the demonstration from their Jeeps, tanks and their makeshift stations on street corners or from roofs, but after an hour they declared a curfew and brought in reinforcements. The nuns did not have time to mobilize the parents, but some parents had heard about what was happening at the school and were already headed there to bring their kids home. The sisters took a calculated risk and released some students who lived nearby.

They instructed us to run as fast as possible. There were two routes to my house from school. I ran with two of my friends to the main street. When we arrived, we saw Army trucks spraying colored water on some public-school students. The rush and the force of the water from the hoses hurled some students to the ground; some were knocked unconscious. Those who had fallen were picked up by other soldiers and thrown into army trucks. We saw blood everywhere. The soldiers' use of the water hose was purposeful.

Shopkeepers tried to shut their doors to avoid trouble. Some were brave enough to hide students. My friends and I stopped running and started to walk as close to walls as possible to avoid detection. Some of my friends began to cry. I was halfway to my house, but we did not have any more places to hide. A foot soldier saw us huddling together terrified and helpless. He approached us and declared. "Don't worry; you will be fine. You are from the Catholic school, right?"

We nodded our heads. He continued, "Your uniform will save you. Go home, but don't run. Stay inside." Since my house was closer to the main street, my friends stayed with us. My parents found ways to send messages to their parents to tell them everyone was safe. We sat in the living room barely moving; we cried and tried not to remember what we had seen. My parents tried to soothe us by saying a prayer to the Virgin Mary to save us. My mom gave us some fruit, but no one ate. Our next-door neighbor came over with sweets, but we rejected them. We were shell-shocked. The curfew lasted about four hours.

My friends' parents came and picked them up, schools were closed for the next few days. Rumors of who was hurt and who had been arrested circulated all over the city. Most of the kids who were hurt were children from the refugee camps or from villages next to Ramallah or from Al-Bireh, a city adjacent to Ramallah. Some children sustained lifelong injuries, some who had been arrested were detained in jails for years. They were school kids my age; others were high school students. They did not have any weapons; they did not pose a threat to anyone.

During that period, there were no Israeli casualties resulting from Palestinian violence. Israel was going on a rampage against an unarmed civilian population. They inflicted pain and suffering on every civilian. They did not care that sweet kids who went to public school were just like me. Their only crime was the uniform they wore.

Something happened to me that day. Some powerful force stirred my inner soul. Though scared, I felt a sense of rebellion or nationalism. I did not know what it was, but I knew that what the Israelis were doing was against God's law. I wanted to fight them. I did not feel hate, I felt rage.

As a result of this incident, the nuns took further precautions to guarantee their students remained safe. No one from our school was involved in the demonstration, but many students, especially the upperclassmen, were talking with pride about the students who demonstrated against the soldiers. Some had friends, neighbors or relatives who took part in the demonstrations. The nuns heard about of these discussions and promptly sent notices to the parents warning them about the consequences if any of their children took part in any protest. The school administration and the parents worked together to keep the children safe.

The weeks and months began to blur. Our social life was completely non-existent. The only pleasant surprise was the news that the nuns had canceled Le Certificate and the Brevet des Collèges, the international test sixth- and ninth-graders took to pass French. It was not a hard test, but it required memorization of French grammar. It was postponed for a year.

Besides academics, the sisters found ingenious ways to keep us busy. Knowing that we talked about the occupation during recess, the sisters required us to speak only French or English during that time. They punished anyone caught speaking Arabic by giving them extra homework. We memorized poetry and prayers. To avoid the extra work, we took it upon ourselves to recite French or English prayers. When we saw a nun approaching, we mumbled a prayer. We divided the prayers by line. Each one of us had a line, and when a nun came to stand by us, we loudly and discreetly exchanged our lines. One person said, "Notre Pere qui Es aux cieux" and another person responded, "Que ton nom soit sanctifie." And so on. We perfected our lines.

When we got bored with the prayers, we recounted lines from children's rhymes "Mon petit oiseau," the next person responded "Apris sa vole." And so on. Sometimes we conjugated verbs in English and French. We believed we were being clever until I heard my mom and some of her friends laughing at our antics.

The more pressure the nuns put on us to stop talking about events outside the school walls, the more we wanted to express ourselves. We secretly talked about what the soldiers had done. Seeing kids my age drenched with colored water and dragged and beaten by soldiers stunned and awakened my sense of patriotism, even though I did not know what patriotism meant. My friends and I began to listen to patriotic songs about the liberation of Palestine.

Before 1967, while living under the Jordanian rule, we amused ourselves by listening to modern English, French and Arabic music. We took pride in being Palestinians; no one tried to kill us for being Palestinians. It never occurred to us then to join a resistance group or listen to patriotic songs. Politics was never on our minds.

As I got older, I tried imitating the cool older girls who listened to American, British, Lebanese and Egyptian music. They snuck a small transistor radio to school and danced to the latest music. Before the dreaded 1967, when I could, I brought my mom's radio to the playground. We swooned to the famous songs sung by Abdel-Alhalim Hafez, a popular Egyptian singer, and Fayrouz, the greatest Lebanese singer. We kept up with the latest in pop music. We also daydreamed to songs from The Sound of Music, the Beatles and, of course, our favorite French/Arabic song, "Ya Mustapha," sung by Bob Azzam. We knew every song by heart. Tom Jones captured the hearts of the older girls, who listened to his songs with dreamy eyes as they sang along. Although I loved that music and wanted to listen to it, whenever possible I opted to play and run around competing for the fastest runner title in school. My classmates and I followed some of the older students and made fun of them and their music.

Again, this all changed after the war; our beautiful music became part of a lovely past. Instead, Radio Egypt or Jordan broadcast continuous news, speeches by the king or the president of Egypt, or patriotic songs. At first, I was irritated because the radio had carried our imaginations to a distant land and to a beautiful state of bliss. We were transformed by the music.

However, as we adjusted, we began to like the patriotic songs. We were pumped up by the beat and the words of songs or ballads like the American song "Ballad of the Green Berets." "Marha Lam-Daratana" was one of these songs I adored. The song is about the great Jordanian soldiers and their tanks and how they beat the horrible enemy. Most songs were about our victory and valor during the war. The reality was we were not the victor, and many of the soldiers who were brave died in the battle.

To hear the music and the politicians of that era, one would think we had won the war. Some of the speeches on the radio lasted for more than two hours. The bluster and bragging of the Arab leaders was empty rhetoric. While the Arab leaders gave a heroic talk about how they were going to defeat Israel, Israel waged a preemptive war and demolished the Egyptian Air Force, took the Golan Heights and the rest of Palestine. As a result of that defeat, we became hostages under an ugly, brutal occupation.

As months passed, the summer haze and its warmth disappeared, and the colder winter and the wretched war became joint companions in our misery. Major saintly holidays came and went without celebration. The only enjoyment we mustered was the new beats and rhythm of the Palestinian patriotic songs. The resistance movement began to produce song after song that stirred the heart of every Palestinian. Despite the fact Israel punished anyone who listened to these songs, many young kids like me could not resist the beat or the lyrics. The songs glorified the martyrs and the liberation of Palestine from the horrible enemy. These songs invoked a sense of patriotism that once was missing in our lives.

Since we lived close to the main street, soldiers often sought out the corridor between our home and the home of an elderly Jehovah's Witness neighbor and camped there overnight. They looked for resistors in our house, but never found anyone. As children, we watched the daily humiliation of my helpless father and mother. They ransacked our home at all hours and terrified us to no end, always checking under our beds for young boys who might be hiding in our house.

Despite the terror, our parents and the nuns were determined that we continue our education. They tried to maintain a natural learning environment whenever it was possible. Sometimes, the Irish, French and English sisters appealed to the British and French embassies for support and relief. For the most part, they succeeded, as soldiers stayed away from our school. Inside our school walls, we had a safety net; but not for long.

At age ten, I knew something was wrong during these first years of the Israeli occupation. I wanted my parents to fight the soldiers who invaded our home daily. I wanted the soldiers to hurt as we hurt. But since I had no power, I resolved to learn patriotic songs. We sang the songs with gusto. Despite the unrest and the uncertainty of the occupation, whenever I could, I continued with my routine of racing and playing marbles with the boys, climbing trees, scaling walls, and catching butterflies.

It is remarkable how children cope with war. On the one hand, we stressed about being safe and staying away from the soldiers. On the other hand, we continued to be reckless kids. Growing up in this ugly environment did not prevent us from misbehaving and exploring new adventures.

For example, my classmates and I became obsessed with seeing the nuns' hair. By then, the Sisters of St. Joseph changed their dress from traditional habits to a modest gray dress with a white shirt, and a small veil.

Every day before recess, we talked about which sister we should target, and what was the best way to accomplish our goal. We thought their heads were shaved, but we were still dying to get a glimpse of their hair. Even when my aunt, a nun in the same order, came to visit, I tried to sneak a peek, but I was never successful. She locked the door from inside, and we did not see her until she was dressed. Concentrating on the nuns' hair gave us respite from the stresses of the occupation. It took three years to achieve our goal of seeing a nun's hair. It was not worth all the work we put into it. But for children like us, our wretched lives had some semblance of normalcy.

Several holidays came between June and October; Eid IL-Barbara, or Saint Barbara's Day, came with little or no festivities. St. Barbara was revered by Catholics and Orthodox alike. It is believed that St. Barbara was a martyr who eluded the Romans who persecuted her. At St. Barbara's Feast, families made bowls of boiled wheat, pomegranate seeds, raisins, anise, and sugar, and offered the dish to children and neighbors who ran from house to house. I hated the food but loved the tradition. I never realized how much I missed it until the Israeli soldiers imposed a curfew preventing people from celebrating the event.

The ban on this holiday paled next to how the Israelis punished our Muslim brothers and sisters, especially those who lived in the refugee camps. We thought we were spared because we were Christians; we were wrong, and Musa's killing gave us a rude awakening.

16 / The Killing of Musa Al-Tawashae

I come from there, and I have memories
Born as mortals are, I have a mother
And a house with many windows,
I have brothers, friends, ...
I walked this land before the swords
Turned its living body into a laden table.
I come from there. I render the sky unto her mother
When the sky weeps for her mother.
And I weep to make myself known
To a returning cloud.
I learned all the words and broke them up
To make a single word: Homeland...

—Mahmoud Darwish

We did not choose our homeland, it chose us. There was nothing special about us except we were born on a land coveted by many with might. Some claimed that God Almighty gave it to them, others found my birthplace a strategic place from which to rule the world. The dreams of the powerful did not mesh with the simplicity of our lives. Like all mortals, we just wanted to live safely in our homes, tend to our land and olive trees, make an honest living with our sweat and blood, raise a family, and live as decent human beings.

I was lucky to be born into a community that knew its history. Our oral and written history gave me comfort that I belonged to a family, community, and people, who although harmed by many, lived on for centuries on their own land without ever harming others. They lived by kindness and not by the sword.

My family is descended from one of the seven brothers who moved to Ramallah in 1500. My forefather is Yousif, the son of Rashid El Haddadin, the patriarch of a Christian clan that resided in Ramallah in peace for centuries under different rulers. I grew up with an innate sense of belonging to a vast family who looked after each other. Today, the thousands of descendants of Yousif are mostly successful professionals, who live not only in Palestine but throughout the world, including in the United States.

I grew up knowing I have a big family with many extended cousins. The Tawasha and Kaabni families were part of the Yousif clan; we lived near each other. Musa Al Tawasha was a young married truck driver raised by his widowed mother. He was an easy-going young man with a kind demeanor. His mom worked to support him his wife and children. I saw him from time to time, but never talked to him when he came to visit his first cousin Azzizeh, who lived a block from us. I went to school with Azzizeh's kids. Sanaa was my classmate, and her brother Shuckri was my playmate. When Henry and Giovanni moved to another part of town, Sanaa, Shuckri, and I became inseparable.

The day Musa disappeared, Sanaa, Shuckri, my sisters Stella and Sylvia, and I played for hours, until Sanaa's mom ordered us home in a panic. We played in a field near their house and away from the main road. We played hopscotch, climbed the large fig tree, and played hide and seek. When Azzizeh yelled at her kids to go home and stay home, she told me to fetch my mom and dad but to stay home myself. Azzizeh lagged behind me and my sisters as we ran to get my mom. She was anxious and on the verge of tears.

By then, my mom had heard the news and was waiting for Azzizeh. She looked grieved. They told our neighbors to keep an eye on us, then left. They told the neighbors that Musa Al Tawasha had been missing for two days. Our neighbors told them not to worry. As we went inside our house, we heard the neighbor tell my mom to "be safe and don't worry about the kids." She added, "Ya Adra Ya Oum Allah Ehme Musa and Najima (Oh Mariam, the mother of God, protect Musa and save us.)"

As soon as my dad arrived home, we told him about Musa. He waited for hours for my mom to return, which she did just before the curfew. She said no one could find Musa. He had left for work two days ago with his partner and neither of them returned home. They also never arrived at their work destination. His wife, his mother, and relatives were worried.

At nightfall, the IDF posted soldiers behind our homes and in the streets. No one left the neighborhood. Azzizeh had not returned. We went to bed not knowing what had happened to Musa and his partner. After a restless night, my mom and dad waited until the curfew was lifted and went to see if there was any word on Musa's whereabouts.

Concerned about foul play, the family went to the Israeli authorities to file a missing person report. The callous police did not help. They gave the family a hard time and told them their son may have gone underground. By then, everyone knew that Musa and his partner were missing. Most everyone who knew Musa stopped what they were doing to help search for him and his partner.

After more futile searches, panic gripped the town. Our neighbors kept an eye on us, Sanaa and her brothers and sisters while our mothers and fathers continued the search. Even with soldiers lurking in the shadows, the people in the neighborhood kept looking. No one dared to think of the worst.

Musa's family again appealed to the authorities. His uncles were on their way to the military civil authority when they heard that someone had news about Musa. One of the searchers brought a young, frightened "kissya," peasant woman, accompanied by her parents, to see Musa's mom. As soon as they saw Musa's mother and wife, the kissya and her mom began to wail "Allah Yerhamou, Allah, Yerhamou, Allah Yesabrikum. (God has mercy on him, God has mercy on him, God gives you patience)." The people assembled at Musa's home did not need to ask what happened; they knew. Musa's mother fainted. Musa's wife began to hit her face and tear her hair. All the women present screamed; the men, as well. No one uttered the word "killed" or "dead," but the words of condolence offered by the young kissya and her family confirmed Musa's family's worst fears.

After the initial shock subsided, an older, respected man from our clan asked everyone to quiet down so the kissya could tell what she knew. When they were able to revive Musa's mom, she wailed, hit her face, shrieked, and fainted again.

The kissya recited her eyewitness story. As people listened, they wept, cried and screamed in horror as they heard how Musa and his partner had had been killed by soldiers in a field between his hometown and the village where he worked.

"I was tending to my sheep early in the morning when an Israeli patrol with six soldiers stopped Musa and his partner," she said. "When I saw the patrol, I hid behind the wall between my house and our olive orchard. I lifted my head to see what was going on but was very careful not to be seen."

She was young and frail and spoke like an uneducated peasant. As they listened to her story, everyone tried to muffle their cries.

Her parents urged her to continue "Ehki ma Takhafi (Speak and don't be afraid)." The girl quivered as she spoke: "They began by beating them with the butts of their guns; they kept hitting them and cursing at them."

She went on, "It did not seem that Musa and his partner were resisting. They pleaded with the soldiers to stop." She heard one of the victims beg "Don't hurt me; I have young children."

With these words, his mom screamed in agony, "Yamma Musa, Yamma."

The girl stopped to collect herself. She said the soldiers took part in kicking, beating, mocking and yelling … then the horror began. The soldiers dragged Musa and his partner next to the olive trees on the young kissya's land.

"They doused them with gas and burned them. When I saw this, I fainted; they were both alive when the soldiers lit them on fire. I woke up and saw the soldiers standing there and watching the burning as one watched a bonfire. I wanted to scream, but nothing came out of my mouth. The soldiers left, and I began to scream. We tried to save them, but it was too late. After a while, the boys stopped moving. Wallah Ya Khality Loa shaffouni loa qatalouni. (In God's name, Auntie, if they saw me, they would have killed me)." Musa's mom fainted again; his wife sobbed uncontrollably. The men and women began to cry.

One of the family elders thanked the young kissya and her family and asked them where they could find the bodies. Several people went to retrieve them from a nearby village, about six miles from Musa's home. They were greeted by the Muktar, the "unofficial leader" of the village, who gave his condolences to the family and helped put the bodies in a car. The family of Musa's business partners reclaimed their son's body and took it to their village for burial. Ramallah and its inhabitants were devastated by the news of the killing.

The Israelis sensed the anger of the people and imposed a curfew until nine in the morning. Musa's uncles ordered a coffin from a carpenter who specialized in making coffins. The children were ordered to stay home as the adults went to pay their condolences to Musa's family.

The funeral would be the next day at the Greek Orthodox Church. When someone died, it was custom for the funeral procession to pass on the main street, near our house. In the past, I had avoided funerals. I was terrified of the Orthodox priests with the long, unkempt beards. Their bushy eyebrows and beards reminded me of unknown monsters. But this time, a significant force within me gave me the courage to watch the funeral procession as it passed through the main street. I tried to persuade my sister Stella and my friend Sanaa to come with me, but they refused. I persuaded Sanaa's brother, Shukri, to come with me.

Seeing no soldiers near us, we climbed on top of a roof, which gave us a clear view of the main street. We could see for a half mile, north, and south. We watched the neighbors going to the funeral procession.

We saw soldiers stationed at every intersection, although they had not declared a curfew. They stood with their guns, ready to intimidate people. When the ceremony and prayer chants started, the shopkeepers began to close their front doors as a sign of respect for the dead, as was customary. Shukri, I, and a few other curious kids leaned over the side of the roof and squinted to see better. We heard muffled voices and smelled incense burning.

The members of the funeral procession came from Ein Musbah, the neighborhood where Musa's family lived. They walked behind several bushy-bearded priests, dressed in black vestments trimmed with amber, to the center of town. Two men with heavy metal canes walked ahead of ten altar boys, who carried various icons and crucifixes. They were followed by priests. They marched, chanting in front of men who carried the closed coffin on their shoulders. The rest of the people walked solemnly behind the coffin. Some wailed, other sobbed. I could hear and see everything. My heart was beating fast. I watched as my parents passed behind the coffin. My mom held on to the arm of someone I did not recognize.

As they passed, the women chanted "Ya arabiyat Katalou Musa; Hiddo A'Israel rayitha Khirbeh Mara'a lilHamir and Markab Laliklab." (Yee, Arab women, they killed Musa; Pray that Israel becomes a stable for donkeys and a place for wild dogs)." The women in the front of the procession led the chant. There were other chants, but this tune always stayed with me. This sobering, rhythmic song was spiked with screaming and weeping and the voices of priests chanting Greek and Arabic prayers for the dead.

I heard Musa's mother scream in agony as she walked, supported by two people on each side, "Yamma Musa Kataou Qalbi- Habibi Qum (Musa, my son; they broke my heart. Wake up!)" Musa's wife walked in a daze behind the coffin, anchored by her sister and mother. Unknowingly, I began to tear up and so did Shukri.

There were hundreds of people in the procession. Despite Israel's threat to impose a curfew, the people did not care. They heard what happened to Musa

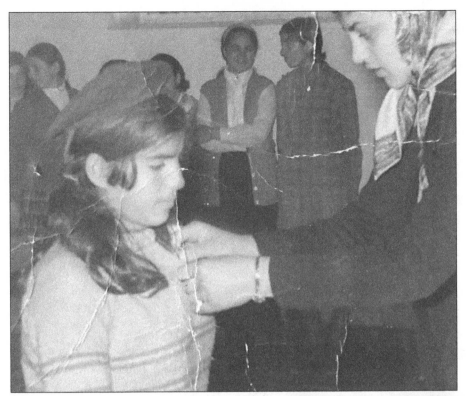

My initiation in the Jeunesse Étudiante Chrétienne, a worldwide group of young Christian students. Created 1929 in France, as part of the Catholic social movement, the JEC was formed by students from the Association Catholique de la Jeunesse Française wishing to minister to other catholic students.

From left: fromt row: My sisters Hilda and Ghada, me. Back row: Stella.

My parents, Jabra Ahwal and Hannah Ahwal, on their wedding day.

Here we are wearing our church school uniforms in a play. I am third from the right.

I am playing a maid in a school play.

Fully armed Israeli soldiers harassing Palestinians in Hebron, a city in the southern West Bank, 19 miles south of Jerusalem.

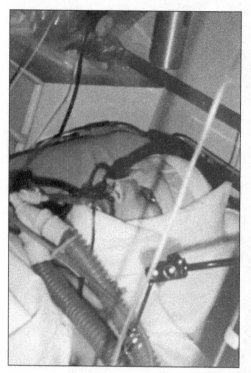

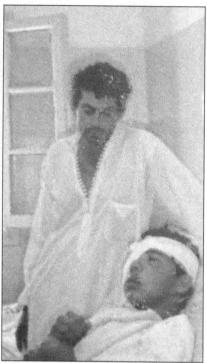

Clockwise from top left: I took this photo in 1988. The boy was shot in the head, and his parents were not allowed to visit him. He died shortly thereafter. The next little boy was shot in the eye by an Israeli rubber bullet. And this young man was shot in the leg by Israeli soldier, 1988.

From left, front row: My father; brother-in-law, Simon; Sylvia; Julie; my mother; Stella; me. Back: My brother, Mike.

Kneeling: My Aunt Nawal. Back row, from left: Samira, Zouzou, Salma, and my mom before 1967.

Bob and I on our wedding day.

129

Terry Ahwal

Participants of Project Hope with Palestinian President Yasser Arafat. I am to the right of Arafat.

On my trip to Palestine with Senator Carl Levin, we visited the Latin Patriarch Michel Sabah (middle). Levin is to his left and I am to his right.

and decided they wanted to pay their respects to him, his business partner, and his family. I don't know what kind of funeral his business partner had, but I am sure his village buried him with pride and dignity.

The news of Musa's killing dominated our conversation for a while. We began to speculate if the killers would be punished. To this day, no one has ever been tried for Musa's and his business partner's murders. He was not the first or the last civilian to be murdered by Israeli soldiers.

In 1977, the (London) *Sunday Times* conducted a five-month investigation on the use of torture in Israeli prisons. The torture documented occurred "through the ten years of Israeli occupation since 1967." The study presented the cases of forty-four Palestinians who were tortured. "The investigation resulted in concrete conclusions: Israeli interrogators routinely ill-treat and torture Arab prisoners. Prisoners are hooded or blindfolded and are hung by their wrists for long periods. Most are struck in the genitals or in other ways sexually abused. Many are sexually assaulted. Others are administered electric shock."[11]

A new era of terror brought poignant grief and acute depression to all, including children. We were condemned to constant curfews and disruption of our daily lives. We felt exasperated by the conditions imposed upon us. We sought refuge in the smallest activities at school or church.

But that changed when soldiers started to target the public-school teachers and students. The punishments were arbitrary. Soldiers would pick on one person and let another go. Some would be ordered to kneel for hours on the hard asphalt while others were hauled into a Jeep and driven to God knows where. Old men, and young men, including boys as young as ten, were picked on for no reason.

If someone cast a glance at a soldier by mistake, he would face a beating or jail time. We stayed home as much as possible for fear of being caught in the net of horror. By 6 p.m., we were at home with the lights off. We continued to keep the black blankets on all the windows to avoid attracting the attention of the soldiers. Even with the dark blankets, some light crept in during the summer. With the electricity shut off most of the time, we were usually in bed no later than 7 p.m. My dad continued to weave fairytale stories for us, as we sat and listened with my mom.

It was hard for my parents to keep seven children cooped up at home without ordinary childhood activities. If we slept through the night without any home invasions by the soldiers, we roused at 6 or 7 a.m., depending on whether we had school or not. Our schedule always depended on the imposed curfew; making regular plans was difficult.

---

11 *The Hidden History of Zionism* (Socialist Action Press) by Ralph Schoenman, 1994

17 / The Wedding

Hardly a day went by without news of someone being hurt, imprisoned, or killed. However, everyone, including the children, learned to adjust to the new circumstances. Sometimes, we pretended everything was well, throwing caution to the wind. This is a story about one of those times.

One hot summer day, Henry, I, and three other friends went to the store to buy candy. Although Henry's father had a store next to our house, we decided to go to a candy store that had more variety, about two blocks away. We passed my uncle's house on the other side of the street by the main road. No one saw us. When we turned the corner, the baker Abu Jebreel stopped to talk to us. He wore clean pants and a shirt. Since he worked at the bakery, we rarely saw him without his stained apron or with flour all over his clothes. After a few awkward pleasantries, he invited us to his relative's wedding. We immediately accepted. It is not unusual in our culture, in fact, it is protocol, to extend an invitation to someone you know. Without checking with our family, we followed Abu Jebreel to the wedding. We giggled as we went on to experience the best time of our lives!

It was to be our first Muslim wedding and the first without our parents. We arrived at the house where the wedding was to be held. We entered a small dark hallway leading to the main room where they would hold the reception. In a smaller room, void of regular furniture, but lined with white plastic chairs and a table in the middle, women with traditional Palestinian dresses from the Khalil region greeted us with joy.

They treated us like the guests of honor. They served us food, gave us sweets, and invited us to participate in the dancing and singing. We witnessed different, yet beautiful, wedding traditions and customs. For five hours, we did not think about any of our parents' rules.

We watched men in another room serenade the groom as he dressed for the ceremony. They sang songs we had never heard before. Every twenty minutes, the bride changed from one lovely shiny dress to another. We watched as old women with wrinkled faces applied makeup to the bride's face. We watched the bride and groom as they sat together on two chairs on top of a table.

It was as if heaven opened and welcomed us in. No one bothered to ask us if our parents knew where we were; they assumed they did. We ate rice, lamb, yogurt, harriseh, and baklawa (sweet cornbread and baklava). We had the thrill of our lives. We could not wait to tell everyone about our experience. We congratulated the family and left with smiles on our faces.

It was about dusk when we left without a care in the world. The wedding adventure was a gift from heaven; we lived as if we did not live in a war zone. We walked out with our heads high, with big smiles on our faces, and with our arms intertwined.

As we turned the bend toward our homes, we noticed our neighbors and parents in the street looking frantic. We approached them with caution. Their faces signaled anger and relief at the same time. We stood still as they advanced toward us; we untangled our arms. Our bliss turned into bewilderment. What did we do wrong this time?

Everything became apparent as my mom dragged me home smacking my head and tush. My friends' parents did the same to them. We still did not comprehend the errors we committed. My dad, who rarely punished me, was just as livid. They kept saying, "You could have been killed. We thought someone kidnapped you."

Some of the neighbors came to ask what had happened. My parents sent me to the bedroom and told me not to move. Every few minutes my mom came over and either screamed at me or smacked me. By then I was crying. She yelled at me to stop crying while she spanked me some more. She ordered my sisters not to speak to me. I went to bed without any supper. In my solitary confinement, I tried to guess what I did wrong. I could not come up with an answer. I cried myself to sleep. I almost forgot the happiness I experienced at the wedding.

I woke up the next day worried about more punishment. I did not dare look at my mom or dad. My sisters stayed away from me. Before breakfast, my parents sat us down to explain to me what I did wrong. They told me that my five-hour disappearance had created a panic in the town.

My dad said they did not know where I was, and that I didn't seem to care that they didn't know. After my scolding, they gave me my punishment. I had to do extra chores at home. They ordered me to stay inside the house, even during the day, and worst of all, they banned me from playing with my friends. Later, I learned my friends received the same treatment. Afraid of my mom's wrath, my sisters did not dare to help me.

The baker immediately apologized to my parents. He thought they knew where I was. Later in life, I realized the gravity of what happened when I disappeared. I could only imagine the horror my parents felt during those five hours. For weeks after this wedding episode, my neighbors, the nuns, and other relatives reminded me of my error as they shook their heads in disbelief.

I must have told the story about the wedding a thousand times. The day is etched in my eternal memory; a day of joy that ended with severe and memorable punishment. For years, I thought about the Abu Jebreel family and the celebration at their home.

An accidental encounter in July 2012 reunited me with the groom's grandson, who was at that same wedding. As I walked the lobby of the hotel where the American Federation of Ramallah, Palestine, conference was being held, looking for Arabic CDs, my eyes fell on a vendor and his two daughters. Their name tags said "Abu Jebreel." The girls, who wore hijabs, stood dismissive behind the counter.

Nonchalantly, I mentioned to the father that I knew the baker Abu Jebreel and mentioned the wedding I attended at his home when I was a child. The man smiled, shook my hand, and exclaimed his disbelief at the coincidence of us attending the same wedding in Ramallah. He and I talked about the details of the wedding as if it happened yesterday. My husband and sisters, who have heard the story several times over the years, listened to us recounting the experience. The solemn atmosphere of the minutes before changed in a flash to a happy encounter. The girls who had frowned at us earler now smiled and started talking with us. The man identified the groom as his grandfather, who married his second wife at the wedding I attended.

I closed the circle by inviting the groom's grandson and his great-granddaughters to a reception held in my honor for being elected to the presidency of the American Federation of Ramallah, Palestine. We are forever intertwined in the memories of moments bliss, among the disproportionate memories of the grief of war.

18 / No One is Spared
(The Golda Meir Era)

In 1969, the curfews were still there, but they were less predictable. If it was a school day and the lockdown had been lifted, we woke up at 6 a.m., dressed, ate breakfast, and went to school. Since we lived across the street from the school, we left a few minutes before the first bell rang.

After Tony's beating, we stopped lingering or playing along the way. We ran to and from school, avoiding eye contact with anyone, especially if the soldiers were prowling around. The soldiers not only physically harmed some of my friends and neighbors, they also terrorized the Palestinian society, especially children.

As kids, we did not know the true reasons we became the victims of vicious and heartless rulers. We heard that King Hussien was no longer our leader, but we did not know who now reigned over our lives. All we knew was that the Israeli government hated us because we were Palestinians. We also learned that they were Jewish and not Arab. They certainly did not want us to remain in Palestine. They did everything in their power to get rid of us.

We started hearing names like Levi Eshkol, the prime minister of Israel; Moshe Dayan, a celebrated military leader with a patch on his eye; and Yitzhak Rabin. We also heard the name Golda Meir. These names spelled terror for us. According to radio reports, they oversaw the killing and maiming of our people and the dismantling of our neighborhoods. We did not know them, but we feared them. I prayed to God to punish them. We were glad that Levi Eshkol died in office because we heard he was an evil man. After all, he sent the soldiers to our homes to beat us. Of all these people, no one was more brutal than the celebrated Golda Meir. She ruled us with an iron fist.

While the world celebrated and heralded the election of Golda Meir in 1969, and called her a hero, the Palestinians, including my family, became exposed to a severe and sadistic kind of brutality that many in the world call war crimes. Under her rule, the abuses we endured were not only inhumane but were in violation of the provisions of the Fourth Geneva Convention, which stated that rulers are obligated to protect the people under their occupation. The brutality of Golda Meir's government dwarfed Eshkol's heartless rules.

The admired Golda Meir, a Russian Jew who grew up in the United States, had no connection to Palestine. She became the first woman prime minister of

Israel. This icon of courage, leadership, and kindness was a vicious brute who did everything in her power to try to cleanse Palestine of its indigent people. Meir supported the ethnic cleansing of Palestinians, who she said had 'never existed' in the first place. "There is no such thing as a Palestinian people ... It is not as if we came and threw them out and took their country. They didn't exist."[12]

This statement shows the level of hatred she harbored for the Palestinian people.

Meir had no problem forcibly removing people from their homes and kicking them out of their birthplace. As early as 1960, she lived on the upper floor of a Jerusalem Villa of Harun Ar-Rashid, which was confiscated by Israel and divided up into apartments. During her tenure as prime minister, she increased the arbitrary arrest of Palestinians without charges.

She imposed military laws for the Palestinians and civilian laws for the Israelis. The Palestinians who lived under military laws were not subject to due process like the Israelis who lived under civilian laws and were offered all aspects of justice. She confiscated land belonging to the Palestinians, demolished people's homes, and expelled many young men from their homeland.

My Father's Beating

It was during Meir's tenure as prime minister that my family endured the worst nightmare of our lives. One day, during a curfew, as my family sat for breakfast in a back room away from the window, we heard a commotion, as if someone broke the steel front door. We heard loud footsteps coming toward us. Within seconds, soldiers confronted my dad. They dragged him to the front door and began to beat him in front of us. They beat him with the butts of their guns as they screamed at him for leaving the front door open. They ordered him to put his hands above his head and took turns beating, spitting, and kicking him. They broke the lock on the front door but accused my dad of defying their order. In terror, we followed as the soldiers hauled my father toward the street. My mom begged the soldiers to leave her semi-blind husband alone.

Terrified, we tried to come between the soldiers and our dad. When my sisters pulled at my dad, a couple of soldiers kicked us out of their way. By then, they had him pinned to the wall outside the front door. My mom continued to plead. "Stop, stop; he is a harmless man." They ignored her plea and our sobs. They knocked my dad's glasses off and proceeded to strike him. My older sister and I reached out to my father and pulled his shirt trying to free him, while my mom tried to wedge herself between my dad and the blows. They yanked us away. Desperate, we screamed.

A nun, Sister Pia, peaked out her dormitory window and saw what was happening. She yelled at the soldiers to stop. "For God's sake, how can you beat a father in front of his kids!" One of the soldiers aimed his shotgun at her and fired. She moved and was not hit.

---

12 "Golda Meir statement to the (London) *Sunday Times*, June 15, 1969

Nothing was going to stop them. The soldiers, high on adrenaline, took pleasure in the beating and the fear they inflicted on us. They cursed as they kicked my dad. My father looked helpless as he tried to shield himself from the blows. I did not dare look at his face. I was scared. We wanted to save him and did not want the soldiers to take him away. My dad almost collapsed.

Just when we thought the worst was about to happen, a soldier with stripes on his shirt stopped his Jeep and ordered the soldiers to stop. Grateful for the kind soldier, we took my dad inside and tended to his wounds. Although he was badly hurt, his injuries were not life-threatening. During that period, my parents taught us a lesson of forgiveness that stays with me to this day. After anger over the beating had subsided, my parents asked us to pray for the soldiers because they were afraid and did not know what they were doing.

As soon as the curfew was lifted, my dad went to the doctor, where he learned the soldiers had bruised his kidneys, ribs, and liver. We also learned the same soldiers went from house to house, beating each male, including the elderly and the mentally ill. At age twelve, I witnessed man's inhumanity toward man, but learned about the spirit of kindness, fearlessness, and forgiveness in the worst of circumstances.

This lesson sustained me a few months later.

I had gone out to look for my mother during one of these impulsive curfews. In the distance I saw a few soldiers patrolling on foot. I also saw a truck parked near an alley. Just in the nick of time, I slid under it. I tried not to breathe or make any noise. The soldiers stopped by the truck and started to talk to each other. They munched on watermelon seeds as they spoke in a different language. Terror engulfed me. I thought I was going to die. I wanted to cry but did not dare. If I had moved at all, they would have discovered me and killed me.

I don't know how, but I overcame my fright. I remember my parents talking about the soldiers and how young they were. I also remembered that the soldiers were like us, fearful. I calmed myself and began to pray for myself and the soldiers. For twenty minutes, I did not move. I recited the rosary and the Lord's prayer.

I looked at the Israeli soldier's boots and thought of the kind Jordanian soldiers with their shiny shoes. I also thought about our neighbors. After what seemed like forever, they finally left. I waited until I heard no more noise, then bolted for home. I entered through the basement door I had left unlocked. My mom came home a few minutes after I arrived. She had also waited until the soldiers had left the area before she returned home.

Under the Israeli occupation, we all endured various punishments. Our homes stopped being safe havens. These punishments could have destroyed our bodies and our souls if it had not been for my parents, and many other parents, who decided to take extraordinary steps to bring peace and healing to our hearts by teaching us the values of love and forgiveness.

After a couple of years of fear and anger, my semi-illiterate parents decided that while the Israelis could take everything away, even kill us, they would never put hate in our hearts. The turning point came when the soldiers beat my dad. It was hard to forget the pain of seeing him beaten. The scars can last forever, but the idea of hate terrified my parents more than the wounds of the flesh. Through their example, they taught us the power of forgiveness. They understood the power of hate and rejected it for our benefit. It is amazing that this lesson still sticks with me, especially since I rarely listened to their instructions.

Throughout the Israeli occupation, Palestinians suffered physical oppression and humiliation. The Israelis had the capability to kill, maim and destroy the livelihood of my people. But we learned that although physical peace was impossible, we could survive with inner peace and dignity. Many times, I heard people say that they would rather be oppressed than be the oppressors. We were comforted by the fact that we were not the perpetrators. Our opponents conquered our homes and country, but they never captured our hearts and minds. They may have stolen our present, but they could never touch our hopes and dreams.

Time never stood still during the occupation. We always had to be prepared for the worst and even though our future was uncertain, we believed it would be brighter. As days went by, we took ownership of our lives. Out there in the darkness, we saw the light of liberty, and as with other oppressed people, a strong force gave us the power to rise above our fears. Eventually we stopped being scared. We received strength that guns and military power could not destroy.

As time passed my sisters, friends and I mocked the soldiers for their cowardice. We whispered to each other, "Look, they have guns and tanks, but they are afraid of little children." Sometimes, we mustered the courage to laugh at the soldiers, who stood close by but were not within hearing distance. We had the hearts of lions, but we believed the soldiers were timid. They had no real sense of who we were as a people and therefore they feared us.

Over the years, Israel perfected its use of fear as a weapon to create a sense of unattainable security. From its creation until today, Israel has built a brand based on using fear and propaganda as a strategy to steal Palestinians' land and keep the Palestinian people under ultimate control. Like their government, the young drafted Israeli soldiers, who grew up with insecurity and fear, were no match for people who want to live free in their homes. We grew up loving life and our neighborhood; the Israeli soldiers were duty bound to suppress us and to further a twisted colonial power. No matter how much they tried, unless they were psychopaths without conscience, the oppression hurt them more than it hurt us.

Living the Best We Could

No matter how dark life became, we still experienced moments of pure love, hope, beauty, and adventure. My beloved Uncle Zouzou asked for his cousin's hand in marriage, and her parents agreed. Pregnant with my youngest sister, my mom held an engagement party for my soon-to-be Aunt Rozette and invited everyone in Jifna, Rozette's hometown. The party was a hit.

Uncle Zouzou lived in Livonia, Michigan, and sent money and papers for his fiancé so she could be with him. My mother, Rozette, and Rozette's mom went on a shopping spree to buy new clothes and jewelry for the bride-to-be, as was the custom. For days, we waited eagerly to see what they bought for this special occasion.

We took professional pictures to send to my eager uncle. I and my older sister, Ghada, wrote letters on behalf of my mom and dad to Michigan to keep them informed about Rozette and her travel plans. My great-grandmother from Jifna and her daughter, a nun, came to visit several times. Each time they brought goodies. If it weren't for the soldiers and all their curfews and home invasions, one would think life proceeding as normal.

The plane ticket was finally purchased and Rozette left for the United States on March 16, 1969, the same day my mom gave birth to my younger sister, Marguerite (Maggie).

My mother began her labor after 4 a.m. My dad summoned our neighbor to stay with us and went to get the midwife. My sisters and I woke up after hearing the commotion but thought the soldiers were invading our house again. Our neighbor Um Salem told us not to worry, but to stay in our rooms because my mom was having the baby. By the time the midwife arrived, there were a couple of nuns already in the room with my mom.

My father sat with us waiting for the news. After an hour, we heard the baby cry. My dad left us to be with my mother. We heard a combination of joy and ... oh, another girl. Both my parents were happy the baby was healthy and that my mom's labor was not too hard. The neighbors and the midwife cleaned the room and brought us to see the baby. She was tiny with dark hair; she looked like a doll. We wanted to hold her but were told we would a little later.

The day Rozette left, and our sister was born, was crisp, almost spring-like. Since it was Sunday, we dressed and went to church. We couldn't wait to tell everyone about the new baby. My mom's cousin Laila, our seamstress, was thrilled. She came by to congratulate my mom. I was in and out of the house, helping to greet well-wishers. We served them coffee and sweets. The nuns brought gifts for the baby.

The next day, I left for school early to study with a few other kids. As I ran around practicing for gym class, I noticed a couple of dead birds. But when I turned the bend, there were more than 100 dead sparrows on the ground. The other students saw them and went to tell one of the sisters. No one knew the cause; some speculated the mysterious death of that many birds was caused by Israel, trying to poison everyone. I never learned the reason behind the dead sparrow mystery, but that was the first and last time I saw so many dead birds all at once.

Maggie's birth brought joy to everyone. My mom had not wanted any more children, but as soon as Maggie arrived, the whole neighborhood, including the nuns, adopted her. As older sisters, we pitched in to help. When my mom went to work, she took Maggie with her. The nuns set up a makeshift bed by the kitchen window where my mother worked. In a way, Maggie became the school mascot. Everyone wanted to play with the adorable child who smiled and giggled all the time. The nuns, teachers, priests, and other staff brought her toys and clothes from their travels. By nine months old, Maggie began to babble and pronounce words. We had normal, even in abnormal circumstances.

Moments of happiness existed in the midst of horror. We tried to take advantage of the happy times. We did not give in to despair.

When we lined up for a class every morning, Maggie stood by herself or the Mother Superior held her. Sometimes, Maggie giggled in the midst of prayers or instructions.

By the time Maggie was born, I had four best friends — Deanna Jamil, Najwa Kreitem, Deanna Khanou, a new student in our school, and Sana'a Kaabni. I still played with the boys in our neighborhood and occasionally hung around with Henry and Giovanni, but I was entering puberty and was aware of the changes happening in my body.

I paid a little more attention to my appearance and tried to dress more fashionably. I still liked to climb walls and catch butterflies, but I no longer played with marbles. I traded the small marbles for basketballs or dodgeballs. I loved track, and although we did not have an official registry, I know I was one of the fastest runners in my class.

I also discovered reading for pleasure. The school had a small library, and I began to check out books. I liked reading about women saints. I believe I read every book in the library. I also began to recognize the value of books and therefore stopped shredding them, as had been my custom when I was younger. But for every joyous occasion, the soldiers stationed in our town reminded us that we were not free people; we were still under Israeli dominion.

Coming of Age Under the Occupation

My friend Deanna Jamil and I spent a lot of time together. With permission from my parents, I sometimes went to her house to visit and took my sister Maggie or my brother, Micheal, with me. But even with this small freedom, I was always monitored by my parents or the neighbors, who were afraid we would be harmed. It was hard enough just to be a regular teenager in life, but it was challenging to grow up in a violent environment.

Our parents imposed restrictions on our movements. They replaced our freedom with confinement. We rarely ventured to a friend's house without adult supervision. On the rare occasions when they permitted us to go out, mostly to church or school functions, or when I was permitted to go to Deanna's house, our parents strictly enforced the rules of when, how and where we could go. Suffice it to say, we felt as if we had a noose around our necks. If my father was late returning from work, the family panicked. Alarms went off until he appeared again.

In the middle of all this turmoil, life went on. My family strived to create a healthy environment for us. They enrolled my older sister and me in activities at school. We joined the JEC (Jeunesse Etudiante Chretienne); The Young Christian Students, a Catholic organization. The group was led by the young associate priest and Sister Ida, a young nun who guided us in prayers and civic activities. It was a youth organization for people between twelve and 25 years of age. Its goal was to educate responsible, committed citizens. They gave us spiritual nourishment and guided us in developing social commitment.

The JEC appealed to me more than anything else in my life at that time. I was determined to do my very best for this organization. They gave us the freedom to explore our visions and to set goals. I rarely missed a meeting.

For the first time in my young life, I began to consider the possibility of becoming a nun. I was not alone. I vocalized my dream. I volunteered for every project. By then, the school and church started to take us on field trips to Jerusalem and Bethlehem to participate in the high holidays and to have spiritual retreats with other Catholic schools. These activities gave us a respite from the daily grind of the occupation. But, still, we were never safe. Numerous times, our buses were stopped so soldiers could inspect and question everyone. The nuns and priests, especially those with French or Vatican passports, served as buffers between the soldiers and the young boys in our group.

One day, we watched in horror as soldiers targeted one or two male students and attempted to force them off the bus. Father Boulos and Father William tried to appeal to, and negotiate with, the young soldiers about the important faith of those two students. The priests were determined; they succeeded in keeping all the students on the bus and away from the soldiers. Sometimes an appeal to a higher ranking officer worked.

The priests and nuns gave us hope when hope was hard to come by. As I observed the nuns and priests demonstrate their commitment to their pupils, I became serious about what I thought was a spiritual vocation. But my desire to defeat the Israelis was stronger than my desire to serve the Lord.

I continued to question the restrictions put on us. I no longer tolerated the ill-treatment of my teachers, friends, and neighbors. I began to speak rudely to soldiers. Once, when I saw a young man running from some soldiers, I made sure to find him a place to hide, against my parents' will.

I devoted myself to listening to patriotic music, which was illegal. I read and passed along to others illegal leaflets distributed by the underground. At school, the administration prohibited any mention of politics. They expelled anyone caught talking about the Israelis or singing patriotic songs. Nevertheless, we seized every opportunity to show our patriotism and our love for Palestine.

We sang songs off key, but from the heart. We sang about freedom, our love for Palestine, and the need for an uprising. In our own way, we dissented peacefully against the occupation.

Since that time, I've come to believe that extreme patriotism contributes to xenophobia. Blind loyalty to one's country separates and divides people and makes unnecessary enemies. But back then, I reveled at the opportunity to show my allegiance to the oppressed Palestinian people. Among my favorite songs, is the Palestinian National Anthem:

> My country, my country
> Oh my land, Oh land of forefathers
> Fedayee, fedayee (Self-sacrificers)
> Oh my people, Oh people of eternity

By my strong will and my inflaming rage, my volcanic revenge
By my yearning blood for my land and home
I have climbed the mountains and combated struggles
I have subdued in the impossible and smashed the shackles

By the storming winds and the firing arms
By my people determination, by the land of strife
Palestine is my home, Palestine is my fire
Palestine is my revenge and the land of resistance

By vowing the oath beneath the shade of the flag
By my land, by my people, by my firing pain
Fedayee I must survive, fedayee I must proceed
Fedayee I must sacrifice until I return

Another popular song I like is:

We were burned by fire, but we never faltered
But we never gave up.
You are the mother of our martyrs
You are the home of the prophets and the martyrs
Oh how beautiful is my country

We developed a high degree of political consciousness. Although I never went to a demonstration or threw stones at soldiers, I was becoming nationalistic. Like many who lived under the occupation, we began to direct our anger at not only the Israeli soldiers but also at King Hussien of Jordan. We believed he sold the Palestinians to Israel to save himself. Some people in our community considered him treasonous, like his grandfather, King Abdullah.

Rumors about him talking to the Israeli government leaked and people who supported him began to question his support of the Palestinian people. I neither resented him nor admired him. Like my family, I stayed neutral on the issue of King Hussein. Rumors of assassination attempts on his life prompted him to further suppress the Palestinians. The Jordanian army had launched a full-scale attack on Palestinian guerrillas in towns all over Jordan. This news devastated our community.

Many young people took to the streets to demonstrate against the king. Of course, the Israeli soldiers rounded people up and imprisoned them for demonstrating. I saw my grandfather's sister tear her hair at the news of a clampdown on the Palestinians in Jordan. Her only child and her grandchildren lived in Jordan. She was afraid the Jordanian king might kick them out of the country. One of the lessons the Palestinians learned from their experience was that nothing was permanent, everything can be taken away in the blink of an eye. We vowed to stay active and beat both the Israelis and the cowardly Jordanians.

Israel continued to target innocent people for punishment. They imprisoned a young woman named Esther Habash. Esther and her elderly parents were refugees from Lydda and lived a few houses away from us. She was a shy and reserved young woman of 23, the same age as my aunt. She was not the kind of woman who stood up to the authorities. I remember Esther as a slim lady who always dressed modestly, rarely ventured out of our neighborhood, and was always with her mother or sister-in-law. She graduated from high school, and I believe she studied sewing at the women's center at Al-tireh. She was the last person on earth to be involved in politics.

The Israelis detained her for a few weeks. They had hoped she could connect them to her distant cousin, Dr. George Habbash, the founder and leader of the Popular Front for the Liberation of Palestine (PFLP). Her arrest shook the community. The arbitrary detention and harsh treatment of this young woman sent shivers up our spines.

After her release, Esther refused to talk to anyone outside her family about her experience, but her mother later told my mom about the abuse she had endured. They tortured her when asking about Dr. Habbash and his family, and threatened to harm her immediate family. They interrogated her for 20 hours non-stop. They deprived her of sleep and food. They refused her the benefits of basic hygiene. They made her stand for hours at a time without moving. They sexually harassed her.

After Esther's arrest, my mother became more alarmed and obsessive about our activities, especially about mine. But that did not deter me from cautiously exploring the resistance movement. Of course, I did not have any avenues through which I could learn about the resistance. My form of resistance was challenging authority by listening to songs that were banned in the occupied territories.

Golda Meir continued her aggressive and racist attitudes toward the Palestinians. She had disdain for the Palestinian people and waged a war of attrition on the Palestinian society. To absolve herself of the crimes she and her government committed, she blamed the Palestinians for their predicament She was regularly quoted as saying, "We can forgive the Arabs for killing our children. We cannot forgive them for forcing us to kill their children," as well as "We will only have peace with the Arabs when they love their children more than they hate us."[13]

The Death of Gamal Abdul Nasser

Bleakness and darkness ascended on the Palestinian people. They felt trapped by the Israeli occupation and betrayed by close Arab allies who publicly promised their support but left us to suffer alone at the mercy of cruel rulers. Many Palestinians, including our neighbors, felt that the only real Arab leader with integrity was the Egyptian President Gamal Abdel Nasser. His nationalist policies appealed to the grassroots Arab populations, including my neighbors. They viewed him as a symbol of Arab dignity and freedom.

The charismatic leader led many to believe he would create a Pan-Arab nationalism and liberate Palestine and the Golan Heights. His long speeches,

13 "Golda Meir, Israel's 'Iron Lady', left behind a complex legacy" By Jordana Silverstein, ABC News, July 19, 2021.

heard by millions, mesmerized his followers. I always thought he just spoke for too long and accomplished little, but I was in the minority. When he died in 1970, the Palestinian people, along with many in the Arab world, felt the tragedy was too much to bear.

Students from different public schools took to the streets and chanted Nasser's name and vowed to follow in his footsteps. Women from the refugee camps and the old section of town grieved the Egyptian president. They wept and shouted his name. For a few hours, the Israelis allowed the outpouring of grief to spill into the streets. But within hours, they issued a curfew and started to round up people who took part in the street demonstration. They took the opportunity to expand their aggression against an occupied people who had just lost their beloved leader.

It appeared that Nasser died after securing a ceasefire between King Hussein and Yasser Arafat in Jordan. Many believed Nasser was murdered. Of course, there was no evidence, but in the Arab world conspiracy theories continue to be part of our DNA.

At the time of Nasser's death, the Palestinian resistance and leadership was still in its infancy — young, fractured and with limited military power. The resistance relied on many Arab states for support. Then the Palestinian Liberation Organization (PLO) was established. An extreme element in the PLO hijacked international planes. Such acts were stupid and proved disastrous for the Palestinian people.

We cautiously supported the PLO. I overheard people talk about the courage of the PLO and how they would save us. Nasser legitimized their leadership and treated them as equals to other regimes in the region, but when he died, many were worried we had lost our protector in the Middle East.

Israel continued its persistent aggression toward the Palestinian people. Every day we experienced or heard of a new form of cruelty against innocent people. They targeted public schools and dragged teachers out of their classrooms. They either dragged them to jail or hauled them to the streets and had them kneel for hours at the time.

In 1970, both the United Nations and Amnesty International issued reports charging Israeli authorities with practicing torture in the occupied territories. The International Red Cross and Israeli lawyers also reported the continuous use of torture in Israeli prisons.

Strategically, Israel began a new form of collective punishment. They started seizing land belonging to people who were either absent or who had committed small infractions. They targeted areas in Jerusalem and its surrounding areas. They then began to uproot olive trees, a valued symbol for Palestine. They shut off the electricity and water without notice. They implemented plans to restrict our movements. They issued IDs for anyone over the age of 16. Anyone caught without the ID would automatically face detention.

To improve their economy, Israel opened its doors to Palestinian laborers. Some of my neighbors who needed to work found either domestic, construction or farm employment in Israel. They attracted workers by paying them more money than they could make in the occupied territories. Some became the subject of abuse. They worked for months without getting paid. They also suffered mistreatment from some Palestinian people who accused them of being traitors.

Everyday life was made more difficult. Most times, all these humiliations were endured in silence. Sometimes, brave women confronted the soldiers and their brutality. Sometimes, brave Israeli soldiers stepped in and objected to some of the mistreatment. When this happened, people showered these soldiers with blessings for their kindness. Again, I learned that during horrific circumstances, there was always bravery and compassion. I also learned these soldiers were not evil. They were young, fearful adults implementing evil policies.

During that period, we heard news from the United States that my grandfather was sick and wanted to see my mother. My uncles planned for my mom to visit Detroit for a month. By then my father had steady work; it was going to be difficult to leave us at home without supervision, but with the help of the nuns, neighbors and our family, my mother could leave for Detroit without worries.

With her departure, of course, we felt free to misbehave and neglect our chores. My parents had recruited an army of volunteers to keep an eye on us and make certain we were fed, kept clean, and stayed out of trouble. Every morning, my nearly deaf aunt came to check on us. After a few days, we drove her crazy by pretending to say something and refusing to talk loud to her; she gave up on us and left.

Other neighbors filled the void, much to our disappointment. Mrs. Eways, the old lady who lived behind our house with her husband, came over on Fridays to help us with our laundry. Each day, a neighbor came over and helped cook our dinner. My older sister was always helping them in the kitchen.

My mom's Aunt Moudalalah, my grandfather's younger and bellicose sister, arrived around 1 p.m. every day and made our lives a living hell. She yelled at us for every infraction. She stayed until my dad came home. Mandy' grandmother (we did not know her name), the old lady who lived a few houses away from us, came daily to visit with my aunt and see if we were okay. Of course, we were not happy with all the attention. We were grateful for the help but wanted our freedom to have friends over and visit friends. We complained to my dad, but he did not budge, he was worried the soldiers would harm us if we were left by ourselves. We tried to convince him that if anything happened, one of us would reach him at work.

After several days, we found ways to get rid of my aunt. With the help of a young, unsuspecting nun, we convinced my aunts that we had projects at school and therefore we did not need them. Sister Elizabeth confirmed our arrangements. My sister Stella delivered the message to my aunts, who were happy the nuns were supervising us. Everyone, including my oldest sister, Ghada, was in on the lie. Since my older sister was involved, my aunts had no reason to doubt us.

Just in case they were watching, we left the house and waited for fifteen minutes until the coast was clear. We searched to see if our aunt was in the vicinity. With no sighting of her, we returned home.

We had a burning desire to be free, even if only for one day. We circumvented all supervision. Our neighbors' kids gathered at our house. We sat around and talked. Hilda, our new next-door neighbor who came to live with her grandfather, was among the kids who joined us. We wanted to do something fun where everyone could participate. Of course, I wanted to show off my running skills. I still played soccer and climbed walls, but my new passion was running. It was hot; therefore, running was out of the question. Fretting about what to do, someone suggested a water fight. Everything was calm in town. The soldiers were patrolling the main roads and did not come into the neighborhoods during the day. Most of our neighbors were taking advantage of the hot weather and taking their afternoon naps.

The water fight started with a cup of water and then escalated to pots and pans filled with water. We desperately wanted to cool down and have fun. We unleashed all our energy and began to use water from the well my parents and neighbors had as a reservoir from the rainy season.

Kids joined us from a different neighborhood; It seemed everyone under the age of 17 was participating in our water fight. We were soaked. We screamed, laughed, ran and jumped. It was the perfect escape on a dull day. We did not consider for a moment all the precious water we wasted. We did not ruminate about the consequences of our actions. We were kids who wanted to breathe; to play and enjoy the summer, without any restrictions. Most of the adults were taking a nap, but with the noise we made, one would have thought someone would have been alarmed.

In the summer of 1971, we experienced freedom, thrills, and pure bliss before one of the nuns peered from her window and was horrified at all the soaking wet children playing in the street. She shouted at us to stop. At first, we pretended not to hear her, but one by one the adult neighbors came over and ordered us to stop. We did not need to wait for my dad for our punishment; our neighbors took care of that. They took us to the woodshed. They screamed at us and spanked us. They all had shocked looks on their faces. They kept asking us what we were going to do without water?

It turns out we had depleted the much-needed water my parents and our neighbor next door had preserved during the rainy season for the summer. The water supply in Palestine was scarce and was made more so by the limits of the Israeli policies. The adults were sickened by the amount of water we had wasted that day. Wet and now miserable, we went home and waited for my dad. He already knew what we had done, so es sat in silence and went to bed without any supper.

A harmless water fight was an example of something our parents had to worry about under the Israeli rules. Every little infraction had consequences that children never thought about. As the occupation progressed, our parents became more and more anxious and we, in turn, developed anxiety disorders. This invisible psychological damage manifested itself in our misbehavior in school. We stopped trusting each other and our schoolwork lagged, but most of all, we had non-stop nightmares. Even when the soldiers were not around, we woke in the middle of the night screaming and had regular flashbacks of soldiers beating us up.

When my mother came back from Detroit, my parents talked about leaving Palestine to be with the rest of the family in the United States. We were not the only ones; a few of our neighbors who had relatives there also began to think about their safety and the future of their children and developed plans to leave. I did not want to go anywhere. I was in eighth grade and loved my friends and school. I had developed a tight circle of friends and was popular among my peers. I participated in after-school activities and was a running star in my school. I found a way to live a happy life, despite the occupation. Still, I slowly began to explore the possibility of joining resistance groups but did not know how.

By September 1971, I entered ninth grade, a pivotal year where students not only had to succeed in their studies, but had to pass a national test. The pressure was very high; students who did not pass would have to find alternative ways to continue school. I had to set my ambition to resist the Israelis aside, so I could concentrate on school. My parents did not decide whether we would leave for the United States until 1972.

Everything around me was changing. I was still a tomboy, but as I mentioned earlier, as a teenager, I began to care a little more about my appearance. I did not protest when my mother took us shopping and bought me mini dresses and miniskirts and high heels. When I left the house, I made sure that my clothes were pressed and neat. I took care of my hair. Unlike some of my friends, my body developed early and therefore, I had to wear bras. Some boys stopped viewing me as a pal, and those who did not know me attempted to tease me; they learned their lessons very fast. I still hung around the boys who had been my buddies since childhood.

Our teachers gave us insight into a life far away from the Occupation and the pain of war. Sister Claire thrilled us by reading *The Scarlet Pimpernel* and *The Count of Monte Cristo*. We read *Les Miserables* and *The Merchant of Venice*. They had us participate in school plays and compete in art shows. To the naked eye, all seemed normal until you saw the ever-present soldiers and heard the war stories.

Ninth grade was stressful, but with only sixteen students in the class, we all became fast friends. I was an average student who applied myself to the classes that I liked and ignored the others. Two years after the occupation, tenth, eleventh and twelve grades transferred to the Latin Patriarchate School. We had a couple of new students join us that year, and two others left for the United States. One student got married and left before she finished the school year.

Except for the Occupation and some school stress, everything was going my way. In 1972, I passed the National Exam and was happy, until my mother told me I would not be enrolling in school for the next academic year because my older sister and I were leaving for Detroit. She then shipped us off to live and work with her aunt, Sister Marie Stella, a nun at the St. Joseph Hospital in Jerusalem.

Everything came crashing down on me; I was devastated. My pleas to her and my dad did not work. I cried almost every day. I was 14. I may not have applied myself to my schoolwork, but I always loved school. I enjoyed the teachers, my friends, and my studies. While my friends prepared to go to tenth grade, I was cleaning cancer patients' rooms in Jerusalem.

My sister and I joined six or seven other women, all older than us, in a dormitory. We stayed in Jerusalem for five days a week. They assigned me kitchen and cleaning duties. I was tormented by the sight of young and old people dying of cancer. I became depressed. Most people I worked with were kind, but they were old. They were not my friends. I went from being a popular teenager in an exclusive school to being a maid in a hospice awaiting exile to the United States of America.

My aunt did not want to give us preferential treatment. In fact, she demanded more of us. While I hated my life and missed my friends, I was introduced to gentle nuns and friendly Jewish people who did not carry guns. Since we could not go home, I was able to explore the city. I walked through the old streets of Jerusalem. As I walked for hours in the narrow alleys and explored all the shops, I felt at peace. After several visits with some of the nuns and the other women, the shopkeepers began to recognize me. They were friendly and often invited me to have tea with them. In the Christian Quarter, I stopped at St. Savior around 4 p.m. and joined some older women in reciting their rosary.

There were tourists from all over the world. I watched as they inspected the merchandise and attempted to bargain with the shopkeepers. I still saw soldiers in every corner of Jerusalem, so I stayed away from troubled areas like the Aqsa Mosque or the Western Wall. I sulked at my misfortune and thought of my friends, but after a few weeks, I refused to go back home. I was embarrassed by the fact that I was not enrolled in school; I did not want to face my friends. I sent my pay back home with my sister and found excuses to stay in Jerusalem.

If it weren't for Sister Claudette, who oversaw the kitchen at the hospital, I don't know what I would have done. Without telling her or anyone else of my embarrassment, she recognized my misery. She took me under her wings and made excuses for me when I did not want to go home. Although she was obese, she was light on her feet. She had a great sense of humor and made me laugh. When she went to the market, she took me with her and indulged me. She treated me as her equal.

During the week, and after a long day at work, the women and I sat on the second-floor balcony overlooking the Yaffa Gate and watched the tourists walking in and out of the old city. We became a regular audience to the sins of the city, such as young men and women making love in the field by the Ottoman-built wall. We saw hippies with long, dirty, braided hair smoke hashish and play guitars. We laughed at young, awkward Arab boys as they tried and failed to pick up women. Part of me felt emancipated from my mother. I no longer had to worry about her rules, yet I still yearned for and missed my old life, but I resigned myself to my fate.

Despite my calamity, I again began to think seriously about becoming a nun. I started to read the Bible every night before I went to bed. A few times, I encountered soldiers in the hospital visiting members of their families. They were different; they were friendly and polite. While at the hospital, I met and interacted with a Muslim woman from a refugee camp for the first time in my life. She told my sister and me about the hardship in the Dehashe Refugee camp near Bethlehem, and about her two brothers who were in jail for political reasons.

Everyone treated me as a younger sister, including the Jewish physicians, the nurses, the security guard, and his family, who lived in a house adjacent to the hospital, and the nuns. Before I went to bed, Sister Claudette and Sister Christiana came to check on me to see if I needed anything. Because the hospital was located inside the green line, the internationally recognized border of Israel, the soldiers did not invade our rooms. I still had nightmares of soldiers running after me, but while in the hospital in Jerusalem, I felt safe.

My mom visited us a few times in Jerusalem. I still did not understand her motive for taking me out of school. Unlike my sister, I was not satisfied with her answer that "school will be a waste of money since I would be leaving to the United States." During one of her visits, she took my sister and me to a professional photographer, so we could apply for residency in the United States. My uncles sent the necessary sponsorship papers required by the State Department. A week later we went to the American Consulate in Jerusalem and applied for a green card. Within months, our residencies were approved. I protested every step of the way. My mother convinced me that if I stayed, I would end up in jail, like so many other young people my age. Although I never believed in violence, I became increasingly vocal about the abuses under the Israeli occupation.

After a few weeks at the hospital, I adjusted to the routine and got to know some of the Jewish patients and their families. I openly criticized the brutal Israeli occupation. Some, like young Doctor Jack, agreed with my criticism. Others complained about me to my aunt, who told my mom and once again, I was reprimanded.

It became clear that I would be leaving for the United States within months. We went with my parents to a travel agent who agreed to loan us money for airline tickets if we paid half the cost upfront. To raise funds, my mom postponed our travel until December, so my sister and I could continue to work and use our wages to help pay for the tickets for the three of us. My mom was determined to escort us to Detroit.

I worked at the hospital for more than eight months. Initially, I visited home frequently. At first, I was anxious to visit, but after the third or fourth visit, I felt like a failure, especially around school registration time. My friends were excited about entering high school, but they knew I had to quit school. They did not know how to act around me.

I later found out that my religion teacher and mentor was leaving for South Sudan. I met with him and bid him well. We promised to write to each other. True to his word, he kept in touch, and we wrote to each other about our lives in the diaspora. He was my salvation during my first two years in the United States. He urged me to stay strong and continue the pursuit of my goals in life.

I went home only to shop for the trip to the United States; otherwise, I stayed in Jerusalem. People my age were in school. Therefore, the only friends I now had were the nuns and the older workers who adopted me and took care of me. I had a strained relationship with my family back home, but my older sister visited them almost every week.

I was grateful for the guidance of some of the nuns, who encouraged me to weather the storm and work on a better future. I was ashamed of who I was and the fact that I was not in school. I avoided my friends and family. I no longer went to the church in Ramallah; I joined the church in Jerusalem and became an introvert. When not working, I watched television in the hospital lobby.

Despite everything, I was looking forward to watching the summer Olympics in the coming weeks.

The Munich Olympics

With few television broadcasts back then, the Olympics always brought joy and excitement to the Palestinian people. As a child, I dreamed of running in the Olympics. In September 1972, several friends had gathered to watch the already recorded segments of the Olympics before the curfews. I was home for the weekend when news of the terrorist massacre of Israeli athletes and their coach blared from our neighbor's television. When the broadcast was suddenly interrupted, we turned to the BBC and listened in horror to the announcer report live on the happenings in Munich. The broadcaster interviewed officials who claimed the perpetrators were Palestinians.

Upon hearing the news, everyone went into shock. A debate developed among some of the neighbors who supported the massacre as a form of defense against the Israeli occupation. The two people who seemed to defend the Munich violence were rebuked by everyone else.

My family and neighbors immediately understood that Israel would avenge the deaths by collectively punishing the Palestinian people. We were right; retaliation was swift and immediate. Israel assembled a team that targeted those in Palestinian leadership around the world and began a covert assassination campaign. Operation Wrath of God was authorized by Prime Minister Golda Meir. The movie Munich, directed by Steven Spielberg in 2005, depicted part of the campaign.

Cruel punishment and pure terror were unleashed on every Palestinian. Israel shut down our towns. They shut off our water, our electricity, our transportation and instituted more severe curfews. The Israeli Army and the Mossad did not hide their contempt for, and abuse of, the Palestinian people. They did not only want revenge, but they also wanted to strike sheer terror in every Palestinian, young and old.

They killed, injured, and maimed. They indiscriminately demolished the homes of anyone they thought might be connected to the resistance. They took to the streets and began imprisoning people. I went back to Jerusalem in a car with an Israeli license plate, which signifies that the driver has access to all roads. I saw rows and rows of blindfolded men and boys kneeling in the hot sun on hot asphalt without food or water.

Of course, the militant, terrorist leaders and their gangs were wrong; they did not have the support of most Palestinians. The terrorist of the Munich Olympics, Luttif Afif, whose mother was Jewish, and whose father was Christian, was looked upon as an extremist. The terrorist attack was devastating, on so many levels. As much as we did not like the Israelis, we never wanted to hurt civilians. We viewed the Olympics as a sacred venue — where the world came together in the spirit of brotherhood to compete in a peaceful way. All I heard the adults say after that was "Allah Youstrana (God protect us)."

We always understood that our safety depended on the benevolence of the Israeli troops. No doubt our lives were in jeopardy. The world witnessed the horror of the Munich massacre, but no one batted an eye at the revenge Israel exacted on the Palestinians.

The Israel Mossad and the IDF went from home to home and smashed heads of people whose only crime was to be born in Palestine. The thousands of Palestinians victimized after the Munich killings suffered alone while the world poured out sympathy for the eleven Israelis killed at the Olympics.

Since 1948, my parents had seen a trend of abuse that would eventually kill us and, so after years of resisting, they decided enough was enough; it was time to leave our homeland.

My parents believed it was only a matter of time before I would be hauled off to jail for standing up to the Israeli soldiers. Therefore, they sought to change our airline tickets to the United States to an earlier departure. That would have cost more money, so they set a departure date for December.

I had gotten used to working with Sister Claudette and did not want to leave her. She became a kind, surrogate mother. She showed me unconditional love, gave me hope, and helped me reconnect with my friends. She encouraged me to stay in touch with them. A week before we were scheduled to leave for the United States, I left Jerusalem and went back home. One by one, my friends came to see me and bid me goodbye. My former teachers came to see us.

My last day in Palestine was bittersweet — my relatives, friends, classmates, and neighbors all came to say farewell. I sat with my friends and reminisced about my school days. I promised I would stay in touch. Henry came with his classmate, my cousin Zahi. We laughed, we cried and then it was time for them to leave. I hugged all of them thinking this would be the last time I would see them. I did not want to leave my home. I cried and sulked all day until my friends surprised me and came to spend the night with me. Although it was December, I remember it was not terribly cold.

My mom's uncle gave me whiskey to drink; it tasted awful, but it gave me a buzz. My head was still spinning from the alcohol when my parents woke us up to leave. We hugged everyone; I hugged my father and the nuns, who reminded me to listen to my grandmother and my aunts in America.

During the flight, I refused to talk to my mother. I was mad at her for her decision to ship me to a foreign country. I was also afraid; it was my first time on a plane. The combination of a hangover, anger, and fear made my journey to a new world a flight from hell.

Part III
Going to America

19 / A Palestinian in America

The pain of leaving the only home I'd ever known was excruciating. I replayed in my head the last hours with my friends. On the plane, I refused to speak to my mom or my sister. I was miserable. I left behind not only my friends, but also my dad, and my siblings and I knew that my mother would be returning without us.

We arrived at Detroit Metropolitan Airport via Boston on December 18, 1972. My aunts, uncles, and cousins were waiting at the arrival gate. I recognized Uncle Zouzou and my aunts Samira and Salma and my grandmother. My grandfather had died a month after my mom visited him earlier. Everything was strange. We arrived at the international terminal and went through immigration and customs without any problem. More than 30 people came to the airport to greet us. After getting our luggage, we left the airport in my Uncle Zouzou's (Joe's) car. Most of the people who came to meet us went to my uncle's home, while two cars followed us to downtown Detroit, which my uncle wanted to show us. I was tired, upset, and disoriented. Everything was different.

The streets were covered with snow. Christmas lights adorned most buildings. Instead of going to Livonia, where I would be living with my uncle, we took I-94 to see the lights at Hudson's building in downtown Detroit. My Statue of Liberty was the large Uniroyal tire near the airport. My mom and uncle chatted while my sister and I stared at the vast highway, buildings, and cars. Before we approached Detroit, I was spellbound by the Parklane towers of the Southfield Freeway and the Ford Glass House, the Ford Motor Company headquarters.

As we approached downtown Detroit, I saw the skyline. We exited the highway and went toward the Hudson's department store building. We took Larned Street and passed by the Pontchartrain Hotel. We saw the Buhl, Guardian buildings, and other Detroit landmarks. We turned on Woodward Avenue and saw the Spirit of Detroit for the first time. Although tired, I was awe-struck by the massive gold statue. I stayed quiet while looking outside trying to grasp the views. Nothing made sense to me. I was numb and upset about coming to a new country. Nevertheless, I could not help but be fascinated with the hustle and bustle of the streets and the absence of soldiers.

The streets were full of people shopping at Hudson's. Most had beautifully wrapped packages with them. The Christmas decorations ornamenting the store were fairy tale like. We did not have anything like it in Palestine. After a short tour, my uncle took us back to his house in Livonia. He drove on Interstate 94 and exited on Ford Road. I fell asleep before we arrived at the small bungalow on Hugh Avenue, a block away from Joy Road and Middlebelt Road.

Unlike downtown Detroit, the homes on my uncle's block all looked alike. Except for the Christmas decorations, the houses on Hugh Avenue had similar structures.

More than 50 people were waiting for us. After all the hugs and introductions, I went to sleep. I woke up to the sound of a new aunt, who came to welcome us; I recognized her from pictures.

The first few days, we met many people from the old country. They were strangers to me. They spoke in foreign tongues, neither English nor Arabic. They mixed the languages together making it hard for me to understand them. My cousins were as curious about me as I was about them. Few were my age. I had a hard time connecting with them. We simply had little in common, other than being a blood relative. We had completely different life experiences. My oldest cousin was married with two children, her brother and sisters were in school and had their own circle of friends. The rest of my first cousins were in diapers. Yet, everyone was kind and tried to reach out to my sister and me.

They took us shopping at the massive Federal's department store. I could not believe all the merchandise under one roof. All the stores in Ramallah could fit in that store. I had a new experience of rummaging through the racks. In Ramallah, a clerk helped fetch the items we needed from the shelves. It was an eye-opening experience. The styles on the shelves at Federal's were passe. I was amazed that the fashions in America were a bit behind. We followed the fashion trends from France and Lebanon.

I laughed every time my cousins spoke their falhi (peasant) Arabic. In some ways, my sister and I grew up in a less culturally restricted environment. We had no problem having boys as friends. We also participated in all after-school activities. My cousins were limited to school and people from the Ramallah community, specifically their cousins. They lived under the confines of their parents' understanding of an old-fashioned culture from the 1950s. I felt like an alien visiting earth for the first time. Nothing made sense. I was bewildered by the differences. I enjoyed seeing my uncles and aunts but longed to go back to my life in Ramallah.

Before she returned to Ramallah, my mother informed me that I would not be going to school as planned. She explained that I would have to work to help bring the family over and pay for my living expenses. It was another blow to my heart and doused my hopes and long-term vision. She shut down my dreams of finishing school and college without my permission. Her decision devastated me. I felt pain deep in my heart.

I walked around with a sobering melancholy; I thought it would kill me one day. I cried for hours upon hearing the news. I did not want to live. But my aunts and uncles helped me get over the shock by promising to help me find ways to go back to school in the evenings after work. The promise of going back to school did not materialize until three years later.

Before my mother left, my uncle took me to a couple of restaurants and introduced me to the Arabic owners. I was hired as a dishwasher at Cordoba

Restaurant in Livonia Mall. The owner, a friendly Jordanian man, gave me my first job. Later in my career, I became a good friend of his son. I worked more than forty hours a week, cleaning dishes and bussing tables. In the meantime, my sister found a job at another restaurant doing the same thing. They paid me minimum wages of $1.65 an hour. Most of the money went to my living expenses and my family back home. I was able to save some money by babysitting.

After a month my mother left, and my sister and I began our new lives in America. It was a lonely time for me. I could not count the tears. I cried more at that period than any other time in my life. I missed everything about Palestine. I had many firsts during that period. First time without my friends; first time without my church; first time without friends my age. Many nights, I stifled my cries as I went to a bed I shared with my sister, who did the same.

My host family — Uncle Joe, his wife, and grandmother — was very kind. They strived to help me and compensate for my loss. They included me in all their activities. They had many friends. They loved everyone, and people loved them back. They constantly entertained people. My uncle worked as a car salesman in Dearborn. He had a gigantic two-tone Impala. My aunts and uncle kept up with the latest styles. Uncle Joe sported an afro hairdo. My grandmother and aunt kept an immaculate home. They spent most of the day preparing dinner. In the afternoon, my aunts sat and watched soap operas. My grandmother occupied herself by knitting clothes for everyone.

They also entertained many people. Except for one or two individuals, the people I met at my uncle's home were of Palestinian or Jordanian background. I had a hard time understanding them. At first, I chastised myself for not practicing my English enough. I should have been more diligent. But after a couple of months, I realized that they spoke neither English nor Arabic. They had invented their own language. They intertwined Arabic and English together and made-up words, for example, they said, "vacaimna el house," (We vacuumed the house)" They used the English words and conjugated them in Arabic.

As time passed, I started to adjust. However, I still longed for my previous life. It was hard to communicate. It cost half my wages to call home. I went to the post office next to my work and bought airmail letters. I tried to write at least once a week. In the early days, some of my friends wrote back immediately, but as the time passed, the letters were less frequent. I wrote to Father Boulos Marcuzzo in South Sudan. He wrote back with encouragement.

In the evening, I entertained myself by watching television. News agencies such as ABC, CBS, and NBC kept up their coverage on the Munich attack but neglected to mention the plight of the Palestinians. They referred to the Palestinians as terrorists. They rarely cited the Israeli occupation and the killing of Palestinian people. The omission of positive Palestinian stories blurred each time a story about the Middle East was brought up.

My other uncles, who either worked in the factories or owned their own businesses, told me to say that "I am Greek or Syrian." I did not understand why. So, I refused to do it since I did not speak Greek, and I was not Syrian.

Everyone we met tried to help and include us in their daily activities. My cousin Jezelle and Jacqueline Judeh made individual efforts to be attentive to our needs. Jezelle, who worked two jobs to help her family, came over at least once a week to check on us and take us places. She continued to support us even after she was engaged to be married to Boulus, her husband. Jezelle, Jacqueline, Judith, and Jumana took me to my first drive-in movie, *Live and Let Die*, in Dearborn. Although I had just turned 15, they tried to convince the cashier I was ten. He was not satisfied but relented and allowed the car in. It was another new experience for me. Sitting in the car and watching the movie while drinking Coke and eating popcorn introduced me to a unique aspect of America.

After a while, my sister and I adjusted to the routine of living with my uncle, his wife, his 2-year-old daughter, and my grandmother. They lived a happy life. On weekends, my aunts and uncles went to nightclubs or weddings, and my sister and I babysat my younger cousins. My Uncle Issa, who worked at Detroit Diesel, sang at a nightclub on the weekends and many in the family went to be entertained. If they did not go to the nightclub, they attended weddings at Roma Hall, where my uncle also sang.

I had no interest in the nightclubs or in weddings, so I occupied myself by watching my favorite police shows like *Adam-12* or *Hawaii Five-O*. I also got hooked on *Marcus Welby, M.D.* I fell in love with James Brolin. But no matter how I adjusted to my life, I still dreamed of my school and life back home. I wondered what my friends were doing, I paid attention to the calendar and kept tabs on what I would be doing if I was back in school. The TV and my family tried to divert my attention, but the ache and pain of being uprooted were too deep.

I was still angry at my parents, especially my mother, who did not consider my feelings when they decided to relocate me. I could not understand why she would just take us from our environment to a strange new world. Later in life, I learned she and my dad were trying to protect us.

Making the best of it, I began to adjust to working as a busgirl and a dishwasher. Most of the customers were very friendly. The other employees were older than me but helped me adapt. I befriended people from work. A few kids from high school worked during the afternoon shift. At first, I was afraid to speak English, but within months, I started to carry on limited conversations with my co-workers. When I did not understand something, I looked up the words in the dictionary. When someone laughed at me, I laughed with them. I learned phrases such as "son of a bitch" and "go fuck yourself" — words we did not learn at my Catholic school. Uncle Joe could not believe the language coming out of my mouth. He explained to me the meaning of these words, so I stopped using them. I also developed a habit of reading the newspapers left by customers. I still love reading newspapers today.

At first, my uncles and aunts took turns driving us to work. But within months we were taking the bus to work and back. In my free hours, I went shopping at the Livonia Mall.

I did not last long at the Cordoba restaurant. My uncle made me quit after I burned my fingers and was not sent to the emergency room. After my fingers healed, I went to work at a Big Boy restaurant with my sister Ghada. I enjoyed the atmosphere at Big Boy. My Lebanese American manager was funny and cussed a lot. He worked hard and demanded that we work just as hard. When the business slowed down, he had us clean the restaurant and help prepare the food.

My sister was promoted to fast food cook. I still worked in the dish room with a drunk named Ray. We made a good team. His southern accent coupled with his slurred speech made it hard for me to understand him. He entertained me. I became efficient at my work. I liked the waitresses and cashiers, and we became friends. We developed a beautiful camaraderie. Every other week I got paid and was thrilled that I was responsible for my own money. I did not object to my workplace, although it was smelly and reeked of grease and stale hamburgers. I did my job with pride ... that is until my manager demanded that I sweep and mop the kitchen floor. I was indignant. I considered sweeping the kitchen beneath my dignity. I refused. He became angry and threatened to fire me. I took my apron off and told him I was quitting.

With my head held high and my dignity intact, I left the restaurant and walked out onto Seven Mile Road, with only a nickel in my dirty uniform. While waiting for the bus, I walked to Dunkin' Donuts and asked the cashier for an application. I knew that I needed a job, so I did not want to waste any time. I was not a high school graduate. I had limited English proficiency. And my uniform smelled like stale eggs and hamburger. I walked out without thinking of the consequences. I had just had it with being treated like a pauper; mopping the floor was beneath me, or so I thought. The young lady who handed me the application gave me a look that said: "not a chance." When I asked her for a pen, she rolled her eyes and continued to talk to a customer seated at the counter.

I disregarded the look and proceeded to fill out the application. I had no problem with the first three questions. I inserted my name, Social Security number, my telephone and so on. Then, I stopped. I read the question "Sex" with two small boxes; one had an "M" next to it and the other an "F." The word "sex" stupefied me. I never read the word before. I did not know what to do, I completed the rest of the application. I kept going back and forth to the sex box and still did not know what to put down. I did not know anything about dough-nuts, and being a counter girl was a long shot, but I had nothing to lose. After I finished the application, I went back to the sex question. Next to the "M," I put "medium" and next to the "F," I wrote "fair." I handed the application to the counter girl, who gave it to a man in the back office. Despite the counter girl's attitude, I felt good about my chances. I felt a sense of ease when I boarded the bus to go home.

By then, the driver knew me and greeted me with a smile. My grandmother and aunt knew I had quit my job; my sister had called them from the restaurant. They were kind enough not to berate me for my hasty decision. The call from Dunkin' Donuts never came. I stayed home for a couple of days, while my uncles put feelers out for potential restaurant jobs. When none came in, my uncle took me back to Big Boy and had me apologize for my attitude. Kass, the Lebanese general manager, gave me my job back.

Except for my caring family and work, I was lost and had no social life. Jezelle's mother and dad were my grandmother's best friend and frequent visitors. When not working or babysitting, I visited my aunts and uncles. Winter was brutal. I loved the snow but did not like the temperature. I brought with me a few small books and pictures. I read and reread the prayer books until I memorized them. I read newspapers and magazines left by the customers.

My English began to improve. TV became my English teacher. I occupied myself by listening to Arabic music. I befriended people at work, but my uncle did not allow me to go out with them. My social life consisted of my family. Sometimes, when I left the job early, I walked to Livonia Mall and looked in the shops. I loved to browse the bookstores. With my babysitting money, I began to buy cheap novels to read. I cherished Danielle Steel's novels. In the summer, I went with my family to Kensington Beach. I ached to socialize with people my own age. My older sister and I had our differences, we did not coalesce as friends. We hung together at work but stayed out of each other's way at home.

I still liked going to church. However, I did not like the church my family belonged to, The Sacred Heart Byzantine Church on Six Mile in Livonia. After a couple of months, I walked to St. Demian Church in Westland. The service was exactly like the service in Ramallah. Unlike my home church, I did not feel I belonged, I did not know the people. They were strangers. During the sermon, I tried to recall the last sermons I heard in Ramallah. I felt isolated.

Sunday was the hardest because I had special memories. I missed the melody of the church bells. I missed the smell of hot kaak (hot bread and sesame). My mind kept going back to the times when my dad shared his bottle of beer with us during Sunday dinner. When I became overwhelmed with the memories, I went to my room, closed the door, and rummaged through my pictures and the autograph book my friends and teachers signed. I read and cherished every word. I closed my eyes often to remember the great time I had in Ramallah.

When I turned 16, people my grandmother's age asked if I was ready for marriage. I insisted I was going to be a nun. Although I was a teenager, some old ladies who hung around my grandmother always lurked around to find a suitable mate for their sons and grandsons. Since my sister and I were not in school, they thought we were in the market for a groom. My grandmother took the pressure off us by saying that I was going to be a nun and my sister needed to help my family. I continued to resent that I was not in school. I dreamed of the day I would return.

When I was depressed, I did not know it. I kept on moving. Instead of school, I read magazines; my favorite was *Reader's Digest*. I read books and was active with my family. Rozette, who was a few years older than us, treated us like younger sisters. She took us shopping and entertained us with her friends and my other aunts. Every now and then my grandmother and uncles warned me about talking to non-Arab people my age. I did not have to pretend. No one my age had anything to do with us.

I did not know anything about the United States when I came to this country, but it was not what I imagined. Sure, I had studied some American geography and history, but I did not know anything about its culture other than the stuff I watched on American sitcoms that made their way to Palestine. I knew many of the stereotypes but nothing about real life. What was supposed to be the best time of my life as a teenager was spent cleaning dishes for people who did not see me. My only reprieve was the thought that one day, I would go back and reunite with all the people I left behind.

In Palestine, the Israeli occupation curbed my freedom, but my life was full of friends, activities, and things I loved. My first year in the US, I lost my liberty to rules I did not understand and people I feared and didn't know. Since my extended family was kind, I worried about disappointing them, so I did not hang out with non-Arabs.

The flow of information from Palestine was limited. My mother was always critical and asking about money. Like many people who took a journey like mine, one learns to adjust. I became addicted to TV shows like *Adam-12, Mannix* and *The Rookies*. I still had nightmares of soldiers going after my family, but they paled next to what I experienced in real life under the Israeli occupation.

Within a few months of my arrival, I developed a healthy habit of daydreaming of a better future. This allowed me to go beyond my circumstances and look forward. It kept me away from depression.

Regardless of what I was doing, I kept an eye on the news. I came to the United States at a very tumultuous time. People were divided over the Vietnam War. I learned about it and heard talk at work about the catastrophic effect of war on young people. I also heard about the young people who protested the war.

Early in 1973, it was apparent that the bombing of Vietnam was a failure and thousands of soldiers had lost their lives. On the news, I saw people take to the streets to protest the war. I heard about members of the Democratic Party of the U. S. House of Representatives who voted to cut off funds for the war. President Nixon, whom I liked because he did not kowtow to Israel at that period, and his party continued to support the war. I did not know why. Although I fully understood the war I left behind in Palestine, I knew little about the Vietnam war. On the news, I just heard that people hated the soldiers, or so I thought.

My family did not participate in the debate. They were too busy making a living. My uncle's home was a happy home. Occasionally my grandmother and aunt had some disagreements but nothing major. Everyone worried about my family in Palestine. My grandma knew about my difficulty with my mom and made sure to tell me that she loved me. When I had a difficult phone call with my mom, my grandmother made something special for me so that I did not feel bad. If my sister felt isolated, I did not take notice. I was trying to survive the best way I knew. I knew that she enjoyed her job and made friends with the people we worked with. I never bothered to ask her. I knew that she was as lonely as I was because I heard her muffled cries at night.

My aunts lived at the London Townhouses, an apartment complex in Westland, Michigan, stepped in to support us as well. They, along with our uncles, made sure we were not excluded. On Saturdays, my Aunt Samira and her husband often took us for long drives where we stopped at garage sales in different neighborhoods. My Aunt Salma and her husband took us to visit their friends, and when appropriate, took my sister to weddings. I did not want to go.

At their apartments, my aunts became acquainted with families whose sons went to Vietnam. One day while I was visiting my Aunt Samira, one of the soldiers who lived in their apartment complex surprised his parents and came home. The whole neighborhood erupted in cheers and tears. A week later, the family invited everyone in their court to a party celebrating the safe return of the soldier. I sat outside of my aunt's home and watched the event until about midnight. I had mixed feelings, I was happy for the family, but did not know how I felt about the soldiers. The more I heard about Vietnam, the more I sided with the protesters. I also wished they would protest on behalf of the Palestinians. That was only a dream.

On TV and the radio, the news highlighted the protestors and sometimes, like in Palestine, the protest music appealed to my soul. *Where Are You, My Son?* by Joan Baez spoke to my heart. The sirens at the beginning of the songs reminded me of the jet noises I heard during the first few days of the 1967 war. And the lyrics reminded me of Musa's funeral.

In 1973, I became attached to popular music. The first time I heard, *Tie a Yellow Ribbon* while riding in the car with my cousin, Jezelle, I cried as if the song spoke to me. I was not into the Beatles, but *Imagine* by John Lennon touched all my senses. I learned the lyrics and tortured my young cousins by listening to the song again and again and again. American, French and Arabic music gave me an escape from my lonely, friendless life.

I continued to pay attention to the news about Palestine. The coverage was cemented with negative images of the Palestinians while the Israelis were portrayed as victims. Egypt, with help from other countries, launched a surprise attack against Israel on Yum Kippur. They were gaining ground until the United States came to Israel's rescue.

During that period, getting news from Ramallah was sporadic. After the Yom Kippur War, communication with my family stopped completely. The lack of news was excruciating. Everyone was anxious. My grandmother worried about my family, her mother, brother, and sisters. We listened intently to any shred of news from back home. Someone came back from a trip home and told us that my family was in the process of obtaining residency in the United States and as soon as they received their papers, they planned to buy their tickets to join us. My sister and I started working extra hours to help my parents with the tickets. I sought any opportunity I could find to make more money, such as babysitting kids from the neighborhood.

Around Christmas, my mother called my Uncle Joe and told him of their plans. They were packing and getting rid of all their belongings. With their clothes and some photos packed in their suitcase, they arrived at Detroit Airport on June 27, 1974. They came without my sister Stella, who stayed behind to finish the ninth-grade national exam. I was happy and anxious at the same time. I wanted to see the family, but I had become accustomed to living with my grandmother and uncle. Also, I was worried about supporting a large family on Ghada's and my salary. We did not have enough money to buy or rent a home for nine people. Of course, we counted on everybody to pitch in, but in 1974, Detroit was in the middle of a recession. My dad was 50 years old with limited eyesight and some disabilities from the beating, but our hopes were high that he would find a job as a carpenter.

With my parents in the United States, we became whole again. My mother found a job as a maid in a motel right away. My younger sisters pitched in by babysitting. My father tried to find a job but could not. We stayed with my uncle and his wife for over a month. We found an empty home at the corner of Joy Road and Inkster. With the help of my uncles and my father, we fixed the place up and made it livable. The house had four bedrooms and one bathroom and was adjacent to a locksmith shop. Frank and Gloria were our landlords and owners of the store, were kind people. The rent was very cheap. We pooled our money and began our lives as a family again.

My uncles taught Ghada and me how to drive. Once we got our driver's licenses, they helped us to purchase a car, which had rust and many dents. We took turns shuttling people around, and after a few months, my mother received her driver's license. My father did not pass the eye test. It hurt him tremendously, but as always, he never complained. While we worked, my father took care of the house. He did everything but the cooking. Everyone in my extended family pitched in to help us settle. My aunts took my sisters and brother and enrolled them in school. I put my dream to go back to school on hold. I needed to help my family.

Before the end of 1974, we settled as a family in Livonia. We began to venture out with friends from work. My sisters and brother excelled at school. During the summer, my father built an organic vegetable garden in our backyard. He planted tomatoes, moulkye (a plant resembling spinach but tastier) cucumbers, and zucchinis. Aside from putting fresh food on our table, he made a small profit by selling the crop to family and friends.

In 1975, at age 18, I went to the administration office of Franklin High School in Livonia and enrolled as a freshman. I met with the assistant principal and told him my situation and my desire to go to school full time. Since I looked young for my age, he did not object. On Tuesday, September 2, 1975, I started high school anew. I still had to work full time to help my family. I worked the afternoon shift and went to school in the morning. High school was the first step toward a bright future. I did not have time to participate in after-school activities. I made a few friends at work and school. I loved the social science classes and enjoyed my first computer programming class. I settled into a routine of work and school. Despite my mediocre grades, (since I worked and did not always have time to do my daily homework) I thrived. I aimed to go to college. Since I knew my parents could not pay for my school, I began saving for tuition. I worked extra hours and babysat my cousins and some neighbors.

My family kept an eye on what was going on in Palestine. We were worried about my uncles, aunts, and cousins left behind. Although the news was skewed, we knew the situation had deteriorated. I became interested in politics but did not know how to get involved. Every now and then, my family attended activities at the local Ramallah Club, but we did not participate much in their local activism. My cousin Jezelle and her husband involved us in a local Palestinian organization, but again, we were busy trying to survive in our new country. We nevertheless kept attuned to the situation in the Middle East. When Jimmy Carter became president, we had no confidence in his ability to fix the problems in the Middle East. We thought he was like the rest of the politicians of his time; we believed all they cared about was oil and Israel.

I followed closely his attempt to broker peace between Egypt and Israel. I grew angry when the administration excluded Palestinian leaders from their negotiations. We did not know his overall strategy of changing the Middle East, one country a time. I thought he sided with Israel.

This took place around my graduation from high school in 1978. As Carter brought together Egyptian President Anwar Sadat and Israeli Prime Minister Menachem Begin to negotiate for peace, I became enraged that once again, an Arab country sold Palestinian lives for few million dollars. I did not understand the complexity, or the intention, of the peace negotiations Carter had put forward. Later in life, I came to appreciate his work and his dedication to genuine peace in the region.

Although I was moving forward with my life in the United States and began to make friends and live a comfortable life, I still had to live with the stereotype of Palestinians as terrorists. Behind my back, students called us terrorists. My close friends jokingly called me "rag head," "terrorist," or "camel jockey."

At that time, Carter faced many humiliations, especially from Begin, who was defying the terms of the agreements. He left the negotiations several times and threatened to quit. Sadat dramatically went to Jerusalem, and the United States promised military and financial support; only then did Begin sign the agreement. It was the first step in stopping the violence between Egypt and Israel. Carter intended to pursue a just solution for both people.

During that time, the Arab American community was weak and fractured. To his credit, Carter forged ahead with the peace initiative despite opposition from every camp. As everyone was ready to throw the towel in on the Camp David Agreement, the White House hosted a triumphant signing ceremony before 1,600 assembled guests in March 1978.

Again, at the time of the Camp David Agreement, peace in the Middle East was not relevant to most Americans. The issue of Palestine was secondary. At that time people in the United States were more concerned about the energy crisis. This specific peace treaty did not provide the Palestinians with a concrete resolution to their conflict with Israeli, but it was the beginning of a new era of recognizing that the region would not be stabilized unless the conflict was resolved peacefully without armaments.

Although vilified for keeping the Palestinians out of the peace process, President Carter started an era of direct American involvement in brokering peace in the Middle East. I knew very little about Jimmy Carter, but I liked his politics, I liked his commitment to human rights, justice, and genuine peace. He was sincere and folksy. Unlike many in our community, I was willing to wait and see. My philosophy then and now is negotiation is better than war. Any peaceful initiative is better than none. The exclusion of the Palestinians hurt; however, I understood that negotiating peace is far harder than waging war. Peace is more complicated and involves baby steps which, when once achieved, will be irreversible.

History has proven that Jimmy Carter did not abandon the Palestinian people. However, when people are held hostage by war and conflict, time is of the essence. With other distractions in the Middle East, the Iranian hostage crisis and Carter's re-election defeat, the Camp David Agreement fell short. The agreement gave Egypt $1.3 billion and Israel $3 billion annually. The accord neutralized Egypt, which made Israel more secure but did not address the plight of the Palestinians. The agreement entirely ignored Palestinian grievances. In fact, it furthered Israel's brutality against the Palestinians. But a seed was sown at the White House that made it harder for subsequent presidents to avoid the conflict in the region.

I was not able to enroll in college right away. So, as not to waste time, I enrolled in the Livonia Career Center Program. I loved it. I discovered and was intrigued by computer programming. It was fun, innovative, and new. For the first time since I came to the United States, I found my bearings. I saw my future. At the end of the year, I applied and was accepted at Schoolcraft Community College. Maneuvering college was not as easy as I thought it would be. I did not know the rules regarding dropping classes. I thought one could drop courses without affecting one's grade point average. I was wrong. It took a couple of semesters before I wised up. The computer professors were not as good as the instructors at the Livonia Career Center, so I switched my major and continued to take a class here and a class there until I graduated.

Ghada and Stella, both now married, and I were the ones my parents counted on for support. My younger sisters worked, but they were still in school. They could not work overtime or have an extra job as I could. We all pitched in to help. During the summer, my father's small farm worked wonders. He was able to bring money into our home.

While in college, I continued to work part-time at Big Boy while working the midnight shift at Rosa-A-Lee Donut shop. During the summer, when school was out, I worked two full-time jobs. I worked the midnight shift at the doughnut shop and worked at Big Boy during the day. Two of my younger sisters worked at the same place in the afternoon.

I did not consider working at the doughnut shop a hardship. I met many people, especially police officers from various departments including Livonia, Farmington Hills, Redford, and Southfield. The cops came in daily for free coffee and donuts.

I befriended many police officers; I even dated a couple of them. They introduced me to the ins and outs of local government. Aside from my work, I volunteered with the City of Livonia. I became intrigued with domestic politics. By the time I graduated from Schoolcraft College, I had obtained some skills that helped me throughout my life. I realized the value and power of volunteerism. Through the Livonia City Hall, I became involved with local youth programs. At age 24, I gained my independence.

My initiatives to help did not go in vain. My cousin Jezelle and her husband, Boulus, recruited me to help with the Palestine Aid Society, a leftist secular organization that helped Palestinians in the refugee camps in Palestine, Jordan, and Lebanon. I liked their mission; however, I was not mature enough to understand the politics of the organization. She and her husband introduced me to many wonderful people who dedicated their lives to helping the Palestinian people. Although grateful for their help, I leaned toward volunteering in my local community. Jezelle also helped me find my first professional job as an intern at the Consulate of the Yemen Arab Republic.

I served four different counsel generals in Detroit. The community was different than the population in Livonia. Most of the people who frequented the consulate office were men who worked in either the service industry or factories. They lived in the United States but were isolated from the greater community, including other Arabs in southeast Michigan. Most who frequented the Yemeni Consulate either resided in southeast Dearborn or Hamtramck. I helped process passports and became liaison to the non-Arabic community. Although they paid well, I still had to work another job so that I could continue my education and help my family.

After graduating from Schoolcraft College, I registered at the University of Michigan-Dearborn and joined the Livonia Police Department's police reserve program. I also pursued volunteer work, both in the Arabic-American community and with the City of Livonia.

I began to blossom on my own terms. I became integrated into American society. Livonia Mayor Edward McNamara, a man I hardly knew at the time but who later became my boss, appointed me to the Livonia Youth Commission. Every step of the way, I was aware of my obligation to help the Palestinian people who were left behind. Some of my younger sisters who attended the universities introduced me to the Palestinian activists in their colleges.

I went to a few events but did not like how they went about promoting the Palestinian cause. Instead of working with churches and local social justice organizations, the students and their leaders aligned themselves with fringe groups that were viewed as communist sympathizers. I did not want to waste my time. Unlike my sisters, who joined for social purposes, I opted to stay away from these organizations.

During that period, many saw Saddam Hussein and Hafez Assad, the heads of the Baath Parties in Iraq and Syria, as their saviors. So many students aligned themselves with the Baath Party. They advocated Arab Nationalism. Rumors of funding from Saddam Hussein were rampant throughout the Arab-American community and the Arab world.

During that time, I was trying to get involved in local Arab-American organizations. Although I attended a couple of parties with two of my sisters, none of the activities appealed to me. People were more interested in factions and alliances than the cause of justice. Most meetings were shouting matches about the right and wrong leaders. Those aligned with Saddam Hussien did not tolerate any criticism from anyone who opposed his views. While the Jewish community was organized and active, the Arab community was fractured and ineffective. To the broader community, we appeared to be unruly and foreign. If the people were inclined to support us, we lost their support with our antics. Therefore, we had no influence whatsoever in the political arena.

As for my family, we were geographically away from the conflict but still embroiled in its consequences. We still had family in Ramallah and news about the occupation was still disturbing us. As Palestinians, we were incensed about the United States' alliance with Israel. Coming from the occupied territories, we were wary and fearful about joining any political activities. But armed with new citizenship (the United States was the only country to bestow me with citizenship; since I left the occupied territories before I reached age 16, I was not a considered a citizen in my birth country), I explored more avenues to get involved.

While volunteering, I found out that most Americans, including those involved in politics, knew very little about Palestine and the cause of the conflict there. Most had negative views but were willing to listen. Most viewed Israel as a victim of Arab aggression and saw the Palestinians as armed and always dangerous.

While working with the Livonia Police reserve during this period, I, like the rest of the reserves in my unit, had been trained to shoot weapons as a requirement for the job. I was a terrible shooter. I barely qualified to join the force for this reason. On one particularly lousy training day, my trainer stopped the exercise and began to shout on the loudspeaker "I just can't believe my fucking luck; I inherited the only Palestinian who can't shoot a gun." We all laughed at his comments.

Even with all the negatives surrounding the Palestinians' issues, most people were open-minded and willing to change their beliefs if given the opportunity. Because most Arab Americans were not participating in local politics, the stereotypes were being upheld. While maintaining my volunteer activities, including an eight-year stint with the Livonia Police reserves and serving on several mayoral campaigns, I got involved with the Arab-American community.

20 / Turning the Tide with the ADC

By the early 1980s, I was volunteering with local Palestinian organizations but soon became disillusioned with their goals. There was no collaboration among the agencies. They worked from the heart, but some of the work was counterproductive. They did not reach out to the non-Arab communities. Some in the organized Jewish community built a case to criminalize all Palestinians through their outreach programs. As for the Palestinian people, we had limited resources and few leaders like Dr. Edward Said, who inspired us into action. The few Palestinian organizations that worked spent countless hours spinning their wheels without effecting change.

A significant number of activists were not ideologically aligned with each other. All agreed that Palestine is for the Palestinians and should be returned to the Palestinians. Some wanted to make a concession for the sake of peace, others wanted to fight and regain every inch of stolen land. The internal politics of these organizations derailed and disheartened many of us who ended up seeking volunteer work somewhere else.

Even with this dispirited outlook, many kind-hearted Palestinians and Arab Americans worked hard to help the Palestinians in refugee camps in Jordan and Palestine. Members of the Palestine Aid Society and the Holy Land Relief Fund tried to raise money for the unfortunate people in these camps. But the amount raised paled in comparison to what was needed, especially after the massacre at Sabra and Shatila in 1982, when the Lebanese Christian Militia, with the help of Arial Sharon, slaughtered hundreds of innocent, unarmed men, women, and children who could not escape because Israeli soldiers blocked their routes to safety.

The Israeli invasion of Lebanon and the slaughter of innocent people woke the community from its dormant sleep and brought the expulsion of Palestinian leadership from South Lebanon. This major catastrophe alarmed Arab and Palestinian leaders in Michigan and brought them to their senses. They began to work together as a unit despite their differences. The situation in Palestine and Lebanon, coupled with the mounting discrimination and the targeting of Arab Americans by law enforcement, specifically the FBI, prompted them into action. Local leaders such as Abdeen Jabara, Harold Samhat, Jessica Daher, and Nabeel Abraheem came together with Senator James Abourezk and Dr. James Zogby to push for a national organization that would defend the rights of Arab Americans. Another goal of the group was to dispel the years of propaganda promoted by Israel and its allies and present an accurate picture of what was happening in Palestine and Lebanon.

The American Arab Anti-Discrimination Committee (ADC) was established in 1980 to protect the rights of people of Arab descent and promote their rich cultural heritage and dispel stereotypes of Arabs as bombers, belly dancers, and billionaires. During the Lebanon invasion, the ADC became the counterbalance to the one-sided coverage of events in the Middle East, particularly the Palestinian/Israeli conflict.

The credibility of former Senator James Abourezk of South Dakota and Dr. James Zogby helped establish the organization and gave the media alternative sources to quote besides Israeli spokespeople. In addition to countering media biases, the agency began a grassroots effort to recruit people into its ranks. As a college student, I was thrilled at the prospect of working with a team with a great mission. I volunteered to help at the office and to recruit people into the fold.

Within a few years, the ADC became the most significant Arab/American organization in the United States. Neither the success nor the activities of the ADC escaped the scrutiny of the FBI, hate groups and Jewish organizations, both moderate and extreme. The Anti-Defamation League (ADL) started a campaign of distortion against individuals active in the ADC, accusing those who spoke out against Israel of being anti-Semitic. In Detroit, Richard Lobenthal, executive director of the ADL, went after our leaders in the media. The FBI began to be more visible in the local Arab and Palestinian communities. The local FBI office visited individuals as well as organizations and collected membership information without due process. They collected literature and, in conjunction with US Immigration Office, monitored individuals daily, deterring them from participating in activities focused on Palestine.

Although the FBI and the ADL spread fear in the community, they were not as successful as the Jewish Defense League (JDL), a Jewish hate organization headed by founder Rabbi Meir David Kahane, who used violence to paralyze the progress of the ADC. The JDL's terrorist attacks at national and local ADC offices resulted in injuries to civilians in California and police officers in Boston. They were implicated in the murder of Alex Odeh, the California regional director of the ADC.

The attempt to silence activists in the ADC was unsuccessful and only intensified its efforts and growth. When the ADC executive director from Detroit, Kathy Eadeh, moved to Washington, D.C., I was asked to fill in until they recruited a new executive director. After a couple of months in the position, I was asked to become the ADC regional director.

Although my mandate was to work on dispelling Arab stereotypes, I felt compelled to put attention on the erroneous coverage of the Palestinian/Israeli conflict. With the help of a great board of directors, we worked with the local media to dispel the long-standing bias that was popular when covering Palestinian issues. We began by meeting with media executives and reporters to provide them with alternative sources for their coverage.

The increased attention was not limited to the media; hate groups like the KKK and neo-Nazi groups began to target our office. My hate mail during that period was as much as my regular mail. The hate mail was so frequent I started to call them my "love letters." As I received the letters, I read them and filed them in one of my desk drawers. On my day off, Joe Borrojo, a dedicated volunteer, discovered the letters and called the FBI. Alarmed, the FBI opened an investigation into the frequency of the mail. Through profiling, they targeted several groups and one individual from Flint, Michigan. In many ways, the FBI inquiry would open a positive relationship between several agents and me.

During one interview, the agents were concerned that some of the mail indicated that the writer was monitoring my moves. They wanted to know if I noticed anyone following me. I said no. The next question was: "Do you have any enemies or anyone who wants to harm you?" I replied, "Look, I am an Arab, take a number." The question that followed was: "Do you know the person in the letter who called you a 'fucking whore that should be killed'?" I responded with a smile and said anyone who knew me knew I wasn't dating and had not had sex in a while.

Despite their professional demeanor, they laughed at my responses and lectured me about the danger I was in. They then instructed me not to open the mail, but if I did, I must use latex gloves and forward the letters to the FBI. Within six months, they arrested a man from Flint responsible for some of the hate mail.

The FBI told me I was not his only target. He hated anyone who was different. Although it was not up to me, I opposed his prosecution. When he was sentenced, I told his probation officer that instead of jail he should be enrolled in a class for cultural diversity. I was overruled. They sentenced him to six months in prison.

Working with the national ADC Office in 1986, we encouraged reporters and politicians to visit Israel and the occupied territories with a program called *Eyewitness Israel* to report on the situation. The media like the *Detroit Free Press* and the *Detroit News* independently sent stellar reporters like Tom Hundley, Steve Franklin, and David Turnley to Israel, Palestine, and Lebanon. They wrote terrific exposés on the reality on the ground. The stories they wrote reflected the reality of the situation.

Through this program, the tide began to change as reporters now questioned Israel's tactics. Also, politicians, like Paul Findley, a former Congressman from Illinois, spoke out against this country's blind allegiance to Israel. As a Palestinian American, I took comfort that our blind loyalty to Israel's policies was being questioned for the first time. The success in the media sparked young Arab Americans to volunteer for the ADC, which in turn resulted in the Arab-American community building alliances with other minority communities, including some in the Jewish community.

The occupation was "always a brutal and mortifying experience for the occupied" and was "founded on brute force, repression and fear, collaboration and treachery, beatings and torture chambers, and daily intimidation, humiliation, and manipulation."[14]

This led to the Palestinian children in the West Bank and Gaza starting a mass uprising in December 1987 against the Israeli occupation. This unarmed

14 'Righteous Victims: A History of the Zionist-Arab Conflict, 1881-2001," Vintage (2001) by Benny Morris.

revolution, or Intifada (which means "shaking off" in Arabic), was developed under occupation and involved hundreds of thousands of people, many with no previous resistance experience, including children, teenagers, and women. For the first few years, it included many forms of civil disobedience, including massive demonstrations, general strikes, refusal to pay taxes, boycotts of Israeli products, political graffiti, and the establishment of underground schools (since regular schools were closed by the military as reprisals for the uprising). It also included stone-throwing, Molotov cocktails and the erection of barricades to impede the movement of Israeli military forces.

From 1987 to 1991, Israeli forces killed over 1,000 Palestinians, including more than 200 under the age of sixteen.

For the first time since the start of the conflict, the horror that afflicted the Palestinian people was making the front pages of the local newspapers including *The Free Press* and the *Detroit News*. Reporters could not ignore the stories that Israel was trying to suppress, and, for the first time, coverage did not portray Palestinians as hoodlums bent on killing Israelis. With programs such as *Nightline*, which featured articulate Palestinians who described the occupation to the American public, the Palestinian children started to be viewed as David going after Goliath ... and for the first time since immigrating to this country, I wanted to witness the events for myself.

21 / Revisiting Horror

Through *Eye Witness Israel*, a program run by the American-Arab Anti-Discrimination Committee, I was afforded the opportunity to travel to my homeland. I returned to Jordan with twenty non-Palestinian people in July 1988. At the Israeli border, it was immediately clear I was an unwelcome visitor. As the only Palestinian in the delegation, the border patrol put me through intensive scrutiny. Unlike with my fellow travelers, the border patrol opened every item in my luggage, spread my underwear and other personal things on a table in public view. They checked and rechecked my stuff. They took my toothpaste and directed me to go to a private room for further inspection.

The rest of the delegation waited as an unfriendly female guard ordered me to take off all my clothes and proceeded to pat me. I decided not to show her my discomfort. Secretly, I wished I had my period to gross her out. After all the checks, I still had to wait for further interrogation. I felt terrible for the rest of the delegation, who were patiently waiting for me. After four hours, they let me go without an apology.

My discomfort could not compare to what most Palestinians went through. The border at that time was divided into two sections, Palestinians, and non-Palestinians. Movement for Palestinians was prolonged and rough while non-Palestinians were treated with kindness and dignity unless the reviewer focused on one's Arab surname or birthplace.

As a member of the Livonia Police reserves at the time, I knew the difference between proper and improper security procedures. It was, and continues to be, evidence that Israel profiles people based on their Arab or Palestinian ethnicity. The questions they asked me were meant to trick me. It was a good cop-bad cop routine until they gathered the necessary information they wanted. Why was I visiting? Who was I visiting? How long would I be visiting? Who was my grandfather? Where was he born? How come I don't have a Jordanian passport?

When I left Detroit, I was somehow secure in the notion my American passport would protect me. I discovered then, and continue to believe now, that Israel decides who is an acceptable US citizen and who is not. Judging by their practices and demeanor, I am like a second-class citizen in the Jim Crow days of the South. The Israelis continue to view the Palestinians as a threat and therefore have sanctioned policies to dissuade Palestinian Americans from visiting their homeland.

The fact that Israel tried to deny me my full-fledged American citizenship annoyed me. At the time of my visit, I totally believed in the American ideals and values of constitutional rights granted to me when I took my citizenship oath. Their profiling and dismissal of my American citizenship meant more to me than many who were born in this country and took their citizenship for granted.

After that unfortunate delay, I left on a bus with a very sympathetic delegation. I pretended I was not bothered by the violation of my fundamental rights. I began to joke about my body search. We rode through Jericho in the heart of the Israeli occupation. This was my first visit back, so I was filled with conflicted emotions. I did not want to miss a sight. I remembered the picnics in Jericho my parents and school had taken us to before the occupation. I recalled the banana and palm trees. As the bus zigzagged from one dusty road to another, everyone began to clap as we saw a Palestinian flag pulled by a string and balanced by a black shoe high up on an electric wire. Although I am not overly crazy about flags (I believe that flags divide us), I wiped an uncontrolled tear from my eyes. I could not believe that I choked up at the sight.

I have always kept up with what was going on in Palestine; however, after a sixteen-year absence from my homeland, I was unsure of what had become of the occupation. Once there, I saw firsthand that what I had heard on the news was just a fraction of the reality; everyone under the occupation was touched by the brutality.

Area hospitals in Ramallah, Jerusalem, Gaza, and Nablus were filled with young men and children fighting for their lives from injuries from bullets, rubber bullets (hard metals wrapped in thin rubber), and tear gas. I saw newborn babies in incubators who had a hard time breathing because Israeli soldiers had shot tear gas inside their homes. I saw broken elbows, knees, and other joints of young men, women, and children who were beaten by soldiers' clubs. I also saw dead children lying in hospital hallways waiting for the curfew to lift so they could be claimed by their families for proper burial.

As horrible as the injuries and deaths were, nothing prepared me for the body-snatching game that Israel and the Palestinians perfected during the Intifada (rebellion). While Israel tried in vain to prevent any news coverage of the occupation, reporters, including brave Israeli journalists, were leaking stories of the suffering Palestinians. Israel, in turn, tried to block access to any scene that might shed light on the reality of the situation.

Israel Defense Minister Yitzhak Rabin established the "Iron-Fist" and broken arms policies and abolished all Palestinian funerals as a punishment for the Palestinian Intifada. It was a cloak and dagger game of hide and seek. The mostly unarmed civilian Palestinians protested the Israeli occupation. The Israeli defense forces, including sharpshooters, targeted individuals and shot at them with live or metal-coated rubber bullets. Once a Palestinian was killed, a curfew was declared in the immediate area and IDF would try to snatch the body to quell further demonstrations at the funeral. During this period, the Israelis permitted no more than five people to attend the funeral. Israel was not worried about the protest. They knew the Palestinians were weak. They were concerned about their image in the West. They did not want the press to capture the truth.

The Palestinians, at their wit's end and were not afraid of Israel's bullets, made every effort to snatch the body before Israel did. I was at a hospital in Nablus when young Palestinian men came running in with a dead body hoisted on their shoulders and requested sanctuary in the hospital. Hospital workers, including doctors and administrators familiar with the body snatching game, sprang into action. They directed the men who held the body to a safe route. The women went out to the front doors to delay the patrol cars fast approaching. They stood at the front gate and attempted to block the soldiers from entering the hospital. The soldiers began hitting the women with their billy clubs while the administrators, doctors, and other staff frantically tried to hide the body and its guardians. Like a well-practiced drill, they provided civilians with hospital uniforms or ushered others to empty hospital beds and gave them hospital gowns. It was very surreal and unnatural to see such barbaric human behavior and courage intertwined during a moment of danger. The whole episode lasted less than fifteen minutes, with soldiers entering an operating room while surgery was in progress, disregarding international protocols. It was evident this was a daily occurrence of occupiers exerting their might and occupied people wielding their defiance.

During my fifteen-day visit, I witnessed the beatings of children, shooting of tear gas inside homes (I brought home some of these canisters), detention of people in the hot sun for hours, curfews, and other human miseries that can only be described as barbaric. I also spoke with many men, women, and children of all ages who were beaten or shot by Israelis without any provocation.

Before I immigrated to the United States, I viewed the people under the Occupation as meek and fearful, submitting to their oppressors without a whimper. Upon my return, I encountered a new generation of courageous younger Palestinians. Without weapons or any defense, they stood tall against brutal Israelis. I met a generation of Palestinians who were fearless. They took pride in their defiance of Israeli authority.

I heard so many stories, but the one that stood out is a story of Hanna Shatara, a friend of my cousin. As we sat on my aunt's balcony drinking lemonade, he described the beating he received months earlier at the hands of Israeli soldiers. He spoke with animation and joy. He told about the blows to his arms and legs and the kicks to his stomach. With a smile on his face, he said, "I refused to cry. Blow after blow. I held my tears." He said, "Boy, I was so hurt, I wanted to cry so bad, but I kept thinking that I will not cry in front of these bastards, but when I got home, I wailed like a baby." With a smirk on his face, he said, "I would rather have died than let them see me cry."

In 1987 and 1988 the Palestinian people, under the Israeli occupation, saw hope through the courage of their children. Born and raised under the occupation, this new generation of Palestinians disobeyed their elders, took fearlessly to the streets and began hurling stones at the soldiers who were shooting at them. As criticism against Israel mounted, the Israeli public relations machine began to dehumanize the Palestinians with quotes from major politicians in Israel to spread around the world. The most popular quotes were: "They send their children into the streets to be killed," and "They hate us more than they love their children."

Everyone I spoke with said the occupation left them without authority, and they felt helpless about their children. The children, witnessing the atrocities befalling them, felt they had nothing to lose. They wanted to live free. They ached for a moment of independence. They merely wanted to roam the roads as I did when I was a child without being stopped, harassed, injured, or killed. They just wanted to be children, but Israel suffocated them with their brutal occupation.

The 1987-88 Intifada began and continued because every aspect of Palestinians' lives was touched by violence, humiliation, and deprivation. Normal life ceased to exist under the Israeli occupation. Israel shut down all the main institutions like schools, universities, and municipal buildings. They criminalized education and proclaimed schools a risk to Israel's security. In the name of security, Israelis killed, maimed, imprisoned, and robbed people of their human rights.

Violence against the Israelis was minimal. According to the Middle East Monitor, by the end of the Intifada in 1993, almost 1,500 Palestinians and 185 Israelis had been killed; more than 120,000 Palestinians had been arrested. The Swedish branch of Save the Children estimated that "23,600 to 29,000 children required medical treatment for their beating injuries in the first two years of the Intifada;" one third under the age of ten.

The killing, checkpoints, beatings, and imprisonment of Palestinians were part of an overall collective punishment meant to drive the Palestinians out of their homeland. Israel did not foresee the outcome — the Palestinians refused to leave. When their schools and universities were shut down, the Palestinian people, and without proper leadership, erected underground schools and universities to ensure their education system was not disrupted. Teachers started to work without pay in their homes.

One day I sat with my ten-year-old cousin Wael, getting to know each other. I heard some gunfire and jumped. He looked at me with amusement and tried to calm me with a laugh. "Don't worry, you are safe, the sound of the guns is not near." As the gunfire intensified, he began to describe what kind of bullets we heard. Without seeing the weapons, he explained in detail the type of guns used.

"Ah," he said, "this bullet is from an Uzi. This bullet is shot from an army tank." He also described the kind of vehicles roaming the streets from afar. "This noise is the sound of a Jeep," or "this racket is the noise of an army tank." I felt like a little child schooled in the art of occupation. When I asked how he knew the sounds without seeing them, he replied: "I have lived with them since birth."

In 1988, I began to experience the power of the women living under the Israeli occupation. I walked from my hotel to the old city in Jerusalem. The town was bustling with people near the Damascus Gate. Peddlers were selling their goods. For centuries, the Damascus Gate or "Bab Al-amoud" has stood at the entrance to the Old City of Jerusalem, sometimes called East Jerusalem. The Palestinians call it "Al-Quds." Its doorway is an impressive gate built in 1537 under the rule of Suleiman the Magnificent, sultan of the Ottoman Empire. It opens to a packed makeshift market, village peddlers, and tea houses and is the main gate to the Muslim quarter in Jerusalem. Usually, tourists can be seen for miles taking pictures and trying to buy cheap souvenirs from the peddlers who compete for customers.

Since the Intifada was underway, I saw few tourists. The place was calm, with only local Palestinians shopping and running their daily errands. The air was tense. Few people smiled. I noticed more women than men running around. The Israeli mounted police rode back and forth looking for troublemakers. They pushed some of the peddlers aside. Some taxi drivers yelled, "Taxi, taxi ready to go." People were trying to go on with their lives, but everyone was on alert. I recognized one of the nuns coming toward me, and just when I was about to approach her, all hell broke loose.

I saw a mounted policemen grab a young boy and drag him behind his horse. The boy started to scream and cry. Everyone turned as other officers began to drag other kids. Women from all walks of lives, some wearing peasant thoubs (traditional Palestinian clothing), others in fashionable attire, Christian and Muslim women, and a couple of nuns, jumped in and tried to snatch the crying boys away from the officers. Anger erupted everywhere. The rage of the police officers intensified as they gripped and dragged the kids while hitting the women with their nightsticks. They hit them indiscriminately; no one was spared. Within seconds, an army patrol converged on the area. The cops continued the beatings; this did not deter the women. They were determined to save the children. Some women shouted, "Leave my son alone!" Fear engulfed me. I did not join the women, and I did not turn away.

I was a trained police officer, serving in the Livonia Police reserve department. The beating was against all police training. It was not justified. Plus, the kids were minors. I tried to take a photo as evidence of this brutality, but my hand shook so much, the image did not turn out right. A policeman saw my camera and came toward me. I turned away pretending to leave. He went back to the task of helping the other officers. I stood twenty feet away and watched the extraordinary cruelty; I was amazed at the courage displayed by women who, clearly, did not fear for their lives. I noticed that my hand shook as I tried to take another picture; I managed to botch that photo too. The women snatched a couple of the boys and ran in my direction. The police officers did not follow them. They moved away from the crowd. No one was arrested.

When I caught up with the nun, I asked her the reason for the scuffle. She shrugged her shoulders and said with disdain, "This is the norm, this is the Israeli occupation." She continued with sadness, "It is our collective punishment, they want us to know who is in charge."

It turned out that the women who saved the boys were not related to them. As part of the Palestinian resistance to the Israeli occupation, Palestinian women took it upon themselves to protect the children at all costs. They became the shield that protected any child they saw in harm's way. The Israeli government targeted children and men. Over a thousand unarmed civilians were killed, including 273 children. Also, as many as 29,900 children suffered injuries that required medical attention because of beatings inflicted by Israeli soldiers during the 1987-1988 Intifada. In this first uprising, the women played a pivotal role in hiding and protecting any Palestinian who faced danger from the Israeli forces.

I returned to my hotel that night, skipped dinner, and stayed in my room until Terry Balata, our local host and organizer, came to take us to the hospital, where some of the children injured the days before languished between life and death, separated from their villages and their families. In one room, I saw a young boy with bruised eyes, a swollen head, and covered with bandages from head to toe dying with only his brother with him. His mother and father could not come to see him because of an imposed curfew on his village.

His brother was inconsolable. The staff tried to help them. I felt the loneliness of this young man. I sensed his pain. He could not reach his parents to tell them about their child. As we left his room, I took a picture of the dying young boy. The doctor said that the kid was not going to make it. I wanted to hug him and his brother, but I did not dare approach them, nor was I capable of uttering a word of encouragement. I was numb, holding back tears.

Most patients in the hospital were young pre-teens with injuries to their heads, knees, elbows, and other vital body parts. The Israeli armies aimed to kill or disable children for life. That night, I cried myself to sleep in my helplessness. What haunted me was not the injuries or the death of the young boy. I cried and continued to tear up when I thought of the loneliness the injured boy and his brother must have felt not being able to have their mom and dad with them to comfort them. The cruelty of the occupation denied parents the chance to say the last goodbye to their dying son. It was such an inhumane act that I still cannot come up with words to describe it.

I thought for sure the world would not stand idly by as the Israelis killed unarmed civilians. I came back from Palestine thinking that if I told my friends in the local media what I witnessed, they would act and help stop the killing field. The Palestinians gained some sympathy, but not enough to hear the outcry from civic and political and religious leaders. Civil rights and human rights leaders stay away from criticizing Israel for fear of being accused of being anti-Semitic.

I came back from Palestine determined not to stay silent. I brought with me my first-hand account of what I saw, including an empty tear gas canister with a warning of danger if people breathe the fumes of the gas, and bullet shells I collected during my visit. I developed my pictures of injured children and civilians. My voice, and the cries of others like me who believed that the indigenous Palestinians were in grave danger, were no match for the alternative narrative Israel and its supporters provided. They poured money into their propaganda and used fear to stop our advocacy. They drowned out our voices by proclaiming that Israel's values are the same as American values. They labeled the injured Palestinian children as terrorists. Israel claimed, and continues to claim, that it is the only democracy in the Middle East, though *The Economist*'s Global Democracy Index for 2019, which ranks countries by five democratic criteria, lists Israel as a "flawed democracy." The country is marked down for such criteria as "government functioning, political culture, and, in particular, civil liberties, where Israel scores just 5.88 out of a possible 10." [15]

Israel is an apartheid state that grants more rights to Jewish people, even though 20 percent of its population are indigenous non-Jews.

---

15 "Israel's democracy: a systemic problem," by Ian Parmeter, *The Interpreter*, February 17, 2020

Accroding to Human Rights Watch, throughout most of the area between the Mediterranean Sea and the Jordan River, "Israel is the sole governing power; in the remainder, it exercises primary authority alongside limited Palestinian self-rule. Across these areas and in most aspects of life, Israeli authorities methodically privilege Jewish Israelis and discriminate against Palestinians. Laws, policies, and statements by leading Israeli officials make plain that the objective of maintaining Jewish Israeli control over demographics, political power, and land has long guided government policy. In pursuit of this goal, authorities have dispossessed, confined, forcibly separated, and subjugated Palestinians by virtue of their identity to varying degrees of intensity. In certain areas, as described in this report, these deprivations are so severe that they amount to the crimes against humanity of apartheid and persecution." [16]

I spoke to the media and showed them my evidence of the bullets and tear gas canisters I brought with me. The press took interest for a few weeks. I gained the attention of some Israeli supporters, including some who labeled me anti-Semitic. I organized people in our community to try to persuade the politicians to withdraw support for this oppressive occupation. But my work and funds paled in comparison to the money that poured in from AIPAC (America's pro-Israel lobby), aimed at influencing people to support Israel. They painted the Palestinians as the aggressors who wanted to "throw Israel into the sea," despite the facts on the ground that prove otherwise.

The occupation did not stop at the border of the West Bank and the Gaza Strip; it followed us to America. Some activists became the target of the FBI and local law enforcement, and many in our community began to receive visits from law enforcement agencies.

Before leaving for Palestine for the first time since I came to the United States, I knew the amount of funding Israel and its supporters poured into the campaign to defend Israel and discredit the Palestinian people. Any criticism of Israel was labeled anti-Semitic. As regional director of the American-Arab Anti-Discrimination Committee, I saw how Israel tried to stifle our voices. They accused some in our community of potential terrorism and incitement of hate. I refused to be silent. Likewise, many in the Jewish community began to question Israel's tactics. For the first time since I came to the United States, I had fleeting glimpses of hope.

With the Intifada raging, the Reagan administration carefully condemned the violence. They tried to be balanced in their condemnation. Or so they said. They feared offending prominent people in the Republican Party who support Israel. They equated the victims of a well-armed forces with the little boys who threw stones at them. They blamed the Palestinians for their own victimhood. Nevertheless, they sent a message to Israel that the violence against children should stop. With Secretary of State James Baker, a man viewed as pro-Arab, Israel began to look for a resolution to the Intifada. They started to explore the possibility of a peace conference among the Arab countries surrounding Israel and Israel. They wanted to create peace in the Middle East as part of their strat-

---

16 "A Threshold Crossed: Israeli Authorities and the Crimes of Apartheid and Persecution," Human Rights Watch, April 27, 2021

egy and global vision, after the end of the Cold War. Although the Soviet Union supported the establishment of the State of Israel, it shifted its alliances in the 1960s and aligned itself with some Arab States.

Baker and Dennis Ross, Director of Policy Planning in the State Department under President George H. W. Bush, the special Middle East coordinator under President Bill Clinton, dealt directly with the parties in negotiations. When Ross retired, he joined the Washington Institute for Near East Policy, a spin-off of the American Israel Public Affairs Committee. They began the process of bringing all the parties to the conflict together, except for the Palestinians and their leadership.

The first Palestinian Intifada, which I witnessed, lasted from 1987 until the Madrid Conference in 1991. Israel's leadership does not bother me as much as the citizens of good will who continue to stay silent. They knew the facts on the ground in Israel and the occupied territories yet remained supportive of Israel and its illegal actions. Many of my good friends in the Jewish community who stand for the rights of everyone, looked the other way when the abuse was committed by Israel.

22 / An Invitation
to the Oslo Accords Signing

Children of wars tend to find ways to hope, usually overcoming bleak circumstances and seeking brighter futures. As a student of ancient history, I know that empires come and go. I also know that the will of people who want to be free will never be extinguished.

From an early age, Palestinian children learned about freedom. They learned about their heritage and learned to value the commitment of society to the ideals of liberty. Despite what I witnessed and lived through as a child, I believe it is only a matter of time until justice will be served, and the people will be free.

My grandfather and grandmother felt this belief in the depth of their hearts. They died clinging to the dream of a peaceful, just life for all people. Despite all the horror my grandparents lived through, they always understood that there are good people on all sides of a conflict. They believed that if people only talk to each other, hate will disappear. In their storytelling, they spoke of the friendly Jewish neighbors who lived among them. My mom and dad did the same.

So, I grew up knowing that peace is just a matter of time. Regardless of what I witnessed, I knew that good will overcome evil, and that as human beings who belong to the one tribe of humanity, we must live together regardless of the hurt.

So, in 1991, I became hopeful. I did not fully understand the military industrial complex and the role it played in the Middle East, and how one group's interest changed the dynamics of the situation. I did not understand that there were military and political technicians devising strategies that did not consider people who lived in a target area. I thought colonialism was a thing of the past. With all the advances in the world, I believed people could serve their interests without victimizing others. I was wrong; I dared to dream. So when, in the aftermath of the 1991 Gulf War, President George H.W. Bush and his secretary of state, James Baker, formulated a framework for peace between Israel and its neighbors, I felt cautious but optimistic.

My hope, and the hopes of many of my brothers and sisters, faded when the letter of invitation to the Madrid conference from the United States and Russia excluded the Palestinian Liberation Organization (PLO), the formal representative of the Palestinian people. Leaders of the Madrid Conference invited Israel, Syria, Lebanon, and Jordan. Israel insisted the PLO be excluded, or they would not participate. To save face, leaders of the conference invited prominent members of the Palestinian people who lived under the Israeli occupation to be part of the Jordanian delegation, signaling that the Palestinian people are part of Jordan. The Palestinian members of the Jordanian delegation included Saeb Erekat, Faisal Husseini, Hanan Ashrawi and Haidar Abdel-Shafi. Despite Israel's objection, members of the delegation stayed in constant communication with PLO leadership in Tunis.

The Madrid Conference was to serve as an opening forum for the participants. It had no power to impose solutions or veto agreements. It inaugurated negotiations on both bilateral and multilateral tracks that also involved the international community. The Syrian and Lebanese negotiators agreed on a common strategy.

For those of us who lived through years of broken dreams and broken promises, we rejoiced at the prospect of eventual peace. We were concerned with Israel's objection to including the Palestinians, especially the PLO, in this process. However, we decided to wait and see rather than prematurely reject the outcome.

Among the people invited to the conference was Dr. Haidar Abdul Shafi, head of the Palestinian delegation, whom I met in 1988 when he spoke about the occupation and its toll on the people of Gaza. Despite his upper-class status, he was viewed as a visionary with whom people in refugee camps could identify and trust. Unlike other leaders in the community, his emotions did not guide him. He believed in compromises and did not view all Israelis as evil. While he admired the Palestinian's leadership in Tunis, he was critical of some of their tactics. I was pleased with his selection as one of the negotiators. His opening speech indeed summed up the feeling of the Palestinian people both inside and outside Palestine. His speech was poetic and reached my soul.

> We, the people of Palestine, stand before you in the fullness of our pain, our pride, and our anticipation, for we have long harbored a yearning for peace and a dream of justice and freedom. For too long the Palestinian people have gone unheeded, silenced, and denied our identity negated by political expediency, our legal struggle against injustice maligned, and our present existence subsumed by the past tragedy of another people. For the greater part of this century, we have been victimized by the myth of "a land without a people," and described with impunity as "the invisible Palestinians." Before such willful blindness, we refused to disappear or to accept a distorted identity. Our Intifada is a testimony to our perseverance and resilience, waged in a just struggle to regain our rights.

The Palestinian participants echoed our sentiments regarding our status in life and our aspiration for a better life. We were euphoric with the anticipation of peace based on justice. A lasting solution to the conflict seemed to be just a matter of time. During this period, I authored an opinion article published in the local paper expressing hope for the negotiations' success. I had such high hopes that peace was imminent that I began to imagine Palestinian and Israeli children living side by side in peace and prosperity.

But as time passed and Israel, helped by the blind support the United States, curtailed every Palestinian proposal, my wishful thinking began to wane. Israel continued to expand its settlements and occupation without interruption. This celebrated initiative took three years and only resulted in defining a process forward.

The delay of negotiation emboldened the extremists and gave them power. Some resorted to violence, including suicide bombing. On a spring day in 1993, Tamam Nabulsi drove a van into a parked bus and detonated a bomb. Two passengers were killed and five were injured.

Until 1987, the use of violence by Palestinians under the occupation was sporadic and rare. Palestinians submitted to their status with little or no resistance. The few who dared to speak out against the occupation or were rumored to be active, including local public officials, were arrested without due process and put in jail without charges for months, if not years, or injured by the army and Israeli settlers. Israel continued its annexations of Palestinian land to build settlements. The mostly unarmed and non-violent Palestinian populations had no rights.

Although the uprising (Intifada) was non-violent, more than 1,000 Palestinians were killed by Israeli forces, including 237 children under the age of eighteen. Tens of thousands more were injured. According to the Swedish branch of Save the Children, as many as 29,900 children required medical treatment for injuries caused by beatings from Israeli soldiers in the first two years of the Intifada. Nearly a third of them were ten or under. In comparison, between 1987 and 1993, approximately 150 Israelis were killed by Palestinians, including about 100 civilians.

Notwithstanding the brutality of Israel, the Palestinians were eager to reach a peaceful settlement. My family was tired of worrying and hearing about the violence. My dad's brother and his family still lived in Palestine, and every time someone mentioned Ramallah on the news our alarm went up. After my visit to Palestine in 1988, I wanted to expedite the peace process, but the Madrid Conference was doomed to failure. How can a peace process proceed without including the leaders of one of the parties? How can peace succeed when the facts show that Israel continued its aggression and collective punishments of the Palestinian people who live under their occupation?

The Palestinians in the West Bank and Gaza Strip were not safe. Israel used every method of punishment to suppress the Palestinian people. They confiscated their properties, closed schools, imprisoned people without due process or charges. Israel seized their identification (similar to ID used by Germany and South Africa for Jews and Blacks), which rendered them prisoners in their own homes, and physically and mentally abused them.

No one was safe, not even my elderly Uncle Oudeh, who had a massive stroke, but the Israeli Defense Forces forced him to go outside to remove debris, rocks, and logs from in front of his house. When my aunt appealed to their sense of mercy, the soldiers threatened to throw her in jail and confiscate her home. Limping and dragging his left foot, he slowly removed the rubble as soldiers watched and mocked him. My uncle was not alone. His neighbors were forced to paint political graffiti and forced to remove burned tires while the soldiers had their guns pointed at their heads with their fingers on the triggers. No one dared to protest. They just followed orders for fear of further punishment, including death.

During that period, and in complete secrecy, in 1993 Israeli and Palestinian negotiators working without intermediaries, hammered out the Oslo Accords, which forced both sides to come to terms with each other's existence (although Yasser Arafat recognized Israel in 1977). Israel agreed to accept Arafat as its partner in peace talks and decided to recognize Palestinian autonomy in the West Bank and Gaza Strip by beginning to withdraw from the cities of Gaza and Jericho — essentially exchanging land for peace. The Palestinians, in turn, recognized Israel's right to exist on 78 percent of Palestinian land, while also renouncing the use of terrorism and its long-held call for Israel's destruction.

I did not want the world to equate the suffering of the Palestinian people with that of the Israelis. It was not the same and never was. The Israelis were the invaders and were, and still are, the oppressors. But for the sake of the children who continued to suffer, I believed we must compromise. Therefore, I was delighted at the prospect that the Palestinians would live side by side with the Israelis in peace. When I received an invitation to the signing of the Oslo Accords at the White House, I floated on air. I felt in my heart that our tragedy would finally come to an end and children on both sides would find freedom and flourish. I only wished that my grandparents, father, and uncle had lived to see this historic moment.

23 / The Beginning of the Peace Process

I lost my beloved father on April 6, 1992. I came back from a women's protest in Washington to find my mother waiting to tell me that he was in critical condition at the hospital. Within hours, we lost the quiet patriarch of our family, a kind and gentle man who supported and unconditionally loved his family. The marker on his grave says, "simple and kind man." These words summed up my father. He was born into poverty; his life was full of struggles and hard work. A man of few words, he was considered by all who knew him to be kind, gentle and giving. Although we were poor, my father once borrowed money to assist a neighbor who was in more need than we were.

Once he came to the United States, my father's goal was to obtain citizenship. He viewed citizenship as a right of passage to becoming a whole human being, protected by a government that cared for him and his family. Living under Jordanian and Israeli rule, he was a nobody and just a resident of his own birthplace. For a year before he obtained his US citizenship, he and my mother studied daily for the citizenship test, amazing us all with their knowledge of American government. Unlike us, my parents took their citizenship seriously. At his funeral, we talked about the importance of his US citizenship and his courage in leaving his chaotic birthplace to provide a better life for his children. We also boasted of his kindness and lack of bitterness toward those who beat him just because he was Palestinian.

Before my father died, I had established a good life in Michigan, working as an executive director for the American-Arab Anti-Discrimination Committee, and then being appointed by Wayne County Executive Edward McNamara to work on his executive staff. I was also active in Democratic Party politics, both on the local and national level, and was honored to be selected to the credentials committee for the Democratic National Convention in 1992.

My parents, especially my dad, thought that with my connections and influence, I could become instrumental in finding peace in the Middle East. I only wish I had had that power. Equally important as his citizenship was my father's dream of peace in the Middle East. He truly believed that peace is always achievable if people want it. So, when the peace process was revived, he was hopeful and optimistic. Yearning for peace was part of both my parents' make-up. Since birth, their lives had been laced with unwanted violence, colonialism, and wars. They did not want wealth and privileges; they just wanted justice and peace. The death of my father represented yet another generation dying with an unfulfilled desire for peace.

When rumors of a new peace process were circulating, I wanted this initiative to succeed in memory of the father who departed this world without seeing peace in his country. I also wanted the peace process to work for the sake of all the innocent children who deserve better.

I believed that the Oslo Accords would resolve the conflict once and for all. Being politically active in Detroit, I worked on President Bill Clinton's bid for election in 1992 and was invited with 3,000 other people to attend the signing of the Oslo Accords in a ceremony at the White House on September 13, 1993.

The agreement provided a framework for a solution, rather than an actual solution, but I believed in the goodwill and the rhetoric of those who worked and supported the deal.

So, on September 13, 1993, the world was treated to the unlikely spectacle of Yasser Arafat and Yitzhak Rabin shaking hands, and of Palestinians and Israelis talking of peace for the first time since 1948. I sat on the White House lawn and cried tears of joy as President Clinton pushed Rabin to shake hands with Arafat. This first agreement stated that Israeli forces would withdraw from unspecified areas in the Gaza Strip and a small area around Jericho in preparation for a Palestinian government election. Letters accompanied the declaration from Arafat, who promised to change the PLO Charter that called for the destruction of Israel. Rabin then proclaimed Israel's intent to allow normalization of life in the occupied territories.

I was naïve.

Although it was not explicit in the agreement, Israel recognized the Palestinians as people for the first time since the beginning of the conflict, erasing the notion that "Palestine was a land without people for people without a land," a widely cited phrase associated with the movement to establish a Jewish homeland in Palestine during the 19th and 20th centuries.[17] Before leaving for Washington, I co-wrote an editorial with David Gad-Harf, executive director of Detroit's Jewish Community Center, about our hope for genuine peace between our two peoples.

The prospect of peace thrilled me, and I was willing to overlook all the atrocities committed against my people, specifically my family, and trust in Israel's willingness to give peace a chance. Like many Palestinians, I dared to imagine. I also knew that to achieve peace, we must all compromise. For several years the Palestinians talked implicitly and explicitly about abiding by the United Nations Resolutions 242 and 338 — land for a peace initiative that asked for Israel to return to its pre-1967 border. As a descendant of a refugee, I did not want the refugees to be forgotten, and I did not think that the right of return was a possibility, but I wanted a resolution for the people who were still lingering in refugee camps. They should have the right to be citizens in their own country and have their issues addressed. In the meantime, I did not want Israeli families who occupied the land to face the same fate as my family.

For more than 45 years, some Israelis were born and raised on the land they confiscated from the Palestinians. But, right or wrong, I did not think they

---

17 "On the Origin, Meaning, Use and Abuse of a Phrase" by Adam M. Garfinkle, *Middle Eastern Studies*, London, Oct. 1991, vol. 27

should be removed from their homes. To remove them would only cause another unnecessary tragedy. On the other hand, I believed that immigration to Israel should be curbed and Palestinian-Israelis should have the same rights as those of Jewish background. The preferences given to Jews were counterproductive and a deal breaker. It was a matter of basic human rights.

The week of the signing, I had a migraine, but I did not want to miss being a witness to history. I arrived early in Washington and waited with the others by the White House gate for entrance to this historic event. There was a swarm of media who interviewed as many people as possible regarding their reaction to this signing. Everyone was euphoric about witnessing Arabs and Jews walking side-by-side, clapping hands, hugging, laughing, and talking about the prospect for peace.

After being checked in, I was asked if I was a government official. I said yes since I was working for the Wayne County executive. I was ushered in and directed to sit in the rows that were designated for elected public officials, like governors and senators. I sat in the second row on the right-hand side of the stage, next to Gov. Evan Bayh of Indiana. While waiting for the ceremony to start, everyone around me talked about this historic moment and their hope for the peace process to succeed. As the only Palestinian in my row, people asked me questions about my history and background. None of the officials I was with had met a Palestinian who had lived under the occupation.

They had traveled to Israel, but never went to Ramallah, so their questions were laced with ignorance. Most were shocked to learn that I was a Christian and asked if I converted when I came to the United States. I was saddened by their ignorance but not surprised; Israel's public relations machine was superb. Let's face it, the Palestinians failed to grasp the importance of their public image in the West. They simply thought that their cause was enough to change people's minds about the conflict. They were wrong. Television was an essential medium to shape people's opinions. Judging from the comments I've heard through the years, most people view the Israelis as victims and the Palestinians as the terrorist oppressors, a contradiction of the reality on the ground and objective statistics.

As President Clinton ushered Chairman Arafat and Prime Minister Rabin to the stage to begin the ceremony, I had tears in my eyes. I listened intently and when Rabin said, "Enough is enough," I whistled and clapped as if I were at a sporting event. When Arafat spoke in Arabic, I was mesmerized with the elegance of his Arabic speech. He summed up the feelings of three generations of Palestinians who were denied a voice for 45 years. The climax of the ceremony came when Clinton had the two parties shake hands, and the place erupted with claps that were echoed throughout the world. When the formal event ended, everyone around me extended his or her congratulations. Between tears and laughter, I hugged and shook hands with almost everyone in my section.

Before we traveled back, President Clinton invited about 200 people from the Arab/Palestinian American and Jewish-American communities to a meeting to discuss "The Builder for the Peace" initiative. We were ushered into the White House press room and sat, reminiscing about the ceremony and the optimism. Both Arabs and Jews were in an unusual mood of trust, hope, and exuberance about the future. I felt that for the first time, we were talking to each other rather than at each other. In that room I did not see enemies, I saw people who loved their own people and wanted to ensure that they didn't suffer. After an hour of casual conversation, President Clinton, flanked by Vice President Gore, Gen. Colin Powell, and other senior White House staff, entered the room to talk about the day's events and about our role in this new initiative.

For almost an hour, Clinton talked about the historic moment and the importance of our role in it as both Arab and Jewish Americans. He then asked us to join Vice President Gore in "The Builder for the Peace" program which would improve economic conditions in the West Bank and Gaza. It was hoped that American private sector investments would boost support for the peace process and lead to a reduction in cultural barriers, ending longstanding animosities.

Everyone in the room, including me, received this program with enthusiasm. We promised to work together to achieve this specific goal. President Clinton designated Mel Levine and Jim Zogby as co-chairs of this action. [18] Within months, this small initiative fizzled.

I had high hopes but was fully aware the Oslo Accords were only a roadmap to a solution. I thought the recognition of the Palestinian representatives was the first step to a solution. Plus, I felt there were concrete steps for a withdrawal. Despite that fact, I was excited because for the first time our representatives were legitimized by the United States. In addition, the proposal dictated immediate incremental withdrawal by the Israeli armed forces from the occupied territories. I called my cousins in Ramallah to ask about their feelings and was told they had a hopeful but wait and see attitude. After years of bloodshed, the Oslo process represented a non-violent way to resolve the conflict. Like many Palestinians, I believed that people on both sides could achieve a negotiated outcome.

According to the US State Department archive, the agreement was summed up as follows:

> The Declaration of Principles gives the general guidelines for the negotiations to come and lays the foundations for a regime of Palestinian autonomy in the West Bank and Gaza for a transitional period of five years. After this period, a permanent settlement based on Security Council Resolutions 242 and 338 should enter into force. This settlement shall deal not only with the permanent juridical form of the Palestinian entity but also with Jerusalem, refugees, Israeli settlements, global security arrangements, borders and other matters of common interests.[19]

Anxious for a new era of non-violence, we trusted that the negotiations would be carried out in good faith. President Clinton portrayed himself as a

---

18 "How Opposites Attract : Politics: An advocate for Israel and a supporter of Arab causes are working for economic development in the Middle East. Mel Levine and James Zogby have their differences, but they're doing business." By Mathis Chazanov, *Los Angeles Times*, March 27, 1994
19 "The Oslo Accords, 1993," US State Department Archive

truly honest broker and convinced us that the United States was entering a new era of a balanced approach in the negotiation process. Oslo was a historic breakthrough for all of us; it was an agreement full of hope and cooperation. Israel permitted the exiled leadership to return to Jericho to assume responsibilities. The talks between the two parties continued, and milestones were set. But as time passed, the Palestinians realized that the negotiations were nothing but the reconstruction of the occupation. After some reflection, it was apparent that the failure of the agreement was evident and the ceremony at the White House was just, unfortunately, a perfect "Kodak moment."

The Oslo Accords did not achieve its outlined goals for peace. Instead, it became a massive failure. The most significant source of this failure was a lack of balance among the respective powers involved and within the agreements themselves. While there were many reasons for the eventual failure of the Oslo Accords, the main three were: A) The wording and meaning of the actual agreement were out of balance and emphasized the wishes of Israel over those of the Palestinians, B) There was a significant imbalance of power between Israel and the Palestinians, and C) there was a lack of stability in the political leadership on both sides. In the years following, the Accords failed because Israel refused to handle future concessions contained in the agreement. From the start, the peace agreement was out of balance, which doomed it to failure.

To the Palestinians, Oslo was a straitjacket that further confined them and created a new form of occupation riddled with checkpoints and a stranglehold on the people. The Oslo Accords, which were to be implemented in phases, made no mention of occupation and postponed negotiations over the most contentious issues of borders, refugees, Jerusalem, and settlements until the final stage.

Oslo failed to address the fundamental power imbalance between Israel, regional hegemony, and Palestinians, a stateless, occupied population. Palestinians hoped the Oslo process would lead to the end of occupation and the creation of an independent state in the West Bank and Gaza Strip. Instead, Oslo's phased process and the absence of an effective enforcement mechanism or a clear end goal allowed Israel, as the more powerful party, to continue a policy of territorial expansion and brutal occupation leaving Palestinians with little recourse.

While Israeli and Palestinian negotiators were haggling over areas in which Israeli troops would redeploy, Israel continued to build settlements in the occupied territories. Between 1994 and 2000, the Israeli settler population doubled. Concurrently, Israel constructed a network of "bypass roads" to connect the settlements to each other and to Israel. Palestinians from the West Bank were to be shot dead if they used the bypass roads without a permit.

By early 2000, nearly 250 miles of bypass roads had been built on confiscated Palestinian land. Israeli settlement building went primarily unchecked by the US, supposedly an "honest broker" between the two sides.

What the world perceived as a "peace process" resulted in a marked decrease in an already weak standard of living for Palestinians. Israel continued to maintain its control of the land and resources of the West Bank and Gaza Strip through a series of increasingly restrictive checkpoints. These checkpoints controlled the movement of individuals as well as goods coming in or out, so Israel only altered its form of occupation, but not the content. The Palestinians continued to be under siege.

24 / A Country of Checkpoints

As naïve as it sounds, life for the Palestinians was easier before the "Peace Process." That is not to say the occupation was not brutal, but before Oslo and Prime Minister Rabin's death, Palestinians living in Gaza and the West Bank were able to travel freely from town to town under the watchful eyes of the Israeli occupiers. But after Oslo, Israel changed its form of occupation. Instead of posting their soldiers in the centers of a town, they placed them at checkpoints between cities and villages. In essence, the Palestinians were put in prisons.

Only 10 percent of the population was, and still is, free to go from town to town. Besides the checkpoints, every Palestinian must carry an ID that indicates what town they live in. If a Palestinian is caught in the wrong city at a certain hour, Israel will imprison him or her. Aside from the ID, Israel has created an apartheid system of license plates. Cars with green or white plates were denied crossing at the checkpoints in Gaza and the West Bank. Therefore, if someone has permission to travel through the checkpoints, he or she must abandon the car at the checkpoints and take a taxi or a bus to the destination. Israel claimed that these checkpoints were set in place to deter terrorists from harming Israel. However, the placement of these checkpoints between Arab towns on Palestinians' land clearly shows that their primary goal was humiliation and discomfort.

Still euphoric about the prospect of peace, and despite all the obstacles and the reports of abuse, I met with the executive committee of the Federation of Ramallah, Palestine, and proposed that they sponsor a project in the city of Ramallah where young men and women from Palestinian background could volunteer their time on a community service project.

The Federation was enthusiastic about the proposal and authorized me to organize a project with people in Ramallah. With the help of old friends in the city, we put together a program called Project Hope. I recruited young first- and second-generation immigrants from across the United States, and we traveled to Ramallah in August 1997 to fulfill our mission. Many participants were younger than twenty-five. I met the group in New York and we hit it off. Most were college graduates or college students who believed in serving their community both in the United States and abroad.

Most were going to Ramallah for the first time and their awareness of the situation was limited. We talked about the expectations of each volunteer. It was breathtaking to witness their enthusiasm. So, with that, we left for Amman for two days of retreat and relaxation at the Dead Sea, Petra, and the Red Sea, and we packed to go to Ramallah. Upon crossing the Allenby Bridge, our enthusiasm evaporated quickly as we saw a sea of Palestinian people lingering in the hot August sun waiting to go to their homeland. We were ushered to go with non-Arab tourists to a separate building.

Having heard of the situation before leaving with a group of 50 young people to participate in Project Hope, I was still hopeful that the cruelty was exaggerated. I was wrong. Israel's brutality defied my imagination.

Since we had our American passports and all participants except for me were born in the United States, we thought the crossing would be easy. We were wrong. Upon looking at our surnames, Israeli agents gathered our passports and told us to wait. One by one, they searched us, searched our luggage, interrogated us, and ordered us to wait. After five hours, they let us go without any explanation.

Our hosts waited for us outside of the bridge. When we attempted to apologize for the delay, they laughed and told us how lucky we were that the Israelis had not delayed us any longer or turned us away. They explained that what we encountered at the border was a standard procedure that Israel instituted to deter Arab-Americans, especially Palestinians, from visiting their homeland.

As we drove on the highway to Jericho, we suddenly saw a Palestinian flag waving from afar. We all started clapping and whistling and hugging each other for this beautiful sight. We also had tears of joy in our eyes. We asked the bus driver to stop so we could take a picture of the flag. We saw people milling around in Jericho. It was late in the afternoon. After we ate. Our hosts explained to us that we would be leaving soon for Ramallah.

They told us we would be going through several checkpoints. They advised us on how to behave during the inspections. When we asked how long the trip should take, they responded that it should be an hour, but with the checkpoints, it could be four.

We traveled in growing dismay. The first checkpoint was one mile outside of Jericho. Two soldiers entered the bus, took our passports, and asked us to wait. We waited, and after a few minutes they returned with our passports and sent us on our way. We thought that wasn't so bad. But before we started to relax, our hosts told us that this was only one of many checkpoints. They asked us to stay tuned. Sure enough, after about three miles, we had to stop at another checkpoint. The same routine, but this time, our host was interrogated further. As we sat watching the situation unfold, we saw lines and lines of people waiting their turn to go to their home. This time, after half an hour, we were on our way. After several stops at checkpoints, we finally made it to Ramallah at about 10 p.m. The trip that should have taken us an hour and a half took us five hours. Again, with claps and whistles, we arrived home.

Anticipating the obstacles, our hosts gave us a day of rest. They wanted us to explore Ramallah. So, we walked in the main streets, going to the center of the city. Everything seemed normal. But Ramallah had changed since my departure in 1972. It had become an urban city and an economic hub. Shops were busy, and crowds, especially young people, walked the main street aimlessly. At first, we thought nothing of the situation, but after a few days, we realized these idle young men had no place to go. The middle of town looked like a parking lot. There were cars everywhere with no place to go. Drivers were honking their horns, inching their way to their destination. Again, their destinations were limited. With their white and green license plates, they could not go far.

We stopped at the famous ice cream place "Rukab," and had our first taste of ice cream. True to reputation, it was delicious. The streets of Ramallah were filthy, with garbage everywhere. But it seemed only we noticed the trash. Since part of our project was to clean one of the main streets, we were wondering if we were going to accomplish our goal. It seemed overwhelming.

In the evening, the mayor of Ramallah hosted the group. A dynamic middle-aged man, educated at Wayne State University, he welcomed us and thanked us in advance for our services. As if he read our minds, he talked about the filth we encountered and told us about the breakdown in civil society because of the occupation. He explained that cities like Ramallah were more lenient on people regarding city ordinances because of the hardship people faced under the occupation. Also, he said, resources to fix the problem were scarce.

As both a mayor and an engineer, his priority was to keep the city moving. He had to accomplish this with few resources and severe restrictions on movement. He also explained that the young men we saw walking around in the main streets were unemployed with nowhere to go. At the time, 35 percent of the population was unemployed. After a wonderful dinner in the central garden of the municipality, we left for our hotel to rest for work the next day.

We got up early and went to the municipality to get our gear, so we could go to our assigned project. Crossing the street from our hotel, we saw Israeli cars speeding on the same road and were astonished that they were in the city. Our liaison told us that soldiers were free to come and go as they pleased in Ramallah. As for the tanks and Jeeps speeding in the town, they said to us, "The Israeli soldiers were going after someone." And sure enough, within minutes, we heard gunshots. Scared, we ran away from the street. With sarcasm, our liaison told us Israel's retreat from Ramallah was an illusion to show the rest of the world that Israel was sincere about peace.

After this disturbing episode, we left for our work site. I had collected garbage as a volunteer before, so I was accustomed to junk. I just could not believe the primitive method they used for us to collect the trash. Before leaving the United States, we brought with us latex gloves, garbage bags and other small tools we were able to carry with us. We ran out of supplies within an hour. The city had no garbage bags. Frustrated, we devised a plan to sweep the streets and put the garbage by the nearest bin. The most adjacent container overflowed with waste. With one garbage truck in the municipality, we waited until they came and hauled the garbage away. Our efforts to clean the streets were met with speculation and admiration. As we cleaned, people honked, clapped, and showered us with compliments. But none volunteered to work with us.

In Ramallah, like the rest of the Arab world, society consists of various social classes. Garbage men come from the lowest caste in society. We worked hand-in-hand with the garbage men who worked for the municipality. As we worked together, we got to know each other. They could not believe we came all the way from the United States to help them with their jobs. They were astounded when I told them I was a government appointee in Wayne County, the largest county in the State of Michigan. They just did not think it was possible for a person of my status to work with them. These comments saddened me. Public officials in the Arab world, especially those with a high rank or position in government, are treated like nobility, they rarely associate with their workers, especially those who do menial work.

At lunch, we broke bread with our co-workers, learning about their families and the situation in the occupation. One of the gentlemen teared up because we treated him with respect. It turned out it was the first time people from a perceived higher social status treated them as equals. I was ashamed.

The next day, our job was to plant trees in the city. The job was easier and more sanitary. Again, the people gave us accolades for our work. At one point, a woman stopped in the middle of the street and shouted to the people around her. She said in Arabic, "Look, look how wonderful the people from America are: We should all be learning lessons from them. We should all be ashamed of ourselves for having people come from across the ocean to clean our filthy city."

As we planted trees on one main street, it became apparent that water resources were limited. There were no sprinklers in the streets. With no water faucets, the water hauled in on the trucks was recycled so the people would not waste water. Our handlers told us access to water was another form of punishment Israel used against the Palestinian people. They controlled the water resources.

As I visited my family during the trip, my cousin informed me that the water was shut off, and therefore, they had to adjust their day. It was just a matter of fact; they were not angry. The shutoff of electricity occurred at least three times a day. Families in the West Bank prepare themselves to work with these inconveniences.

This specific problem of water and electricity control bothered me until we attended a party at the Catholic Church in the city of Birzeit. It was late evening and we had just finished eating in the backyard. Our team was getting acquainted with the local team. The music began from about a mile away. We could see a village extremely well lit. Our host said the well-lit community was an Israeli settlement. Once again, with no warning, our hosts lost electricity. The place was pitch black. The only ray of light came from the Israeli settlement a mile away.

Our group was a little confused. Our host and the young people brought candles and continued with the celebration as if nothing happened. They urged us to pay no attention to these minor inconveniences. A young man screamed, "Let's show them that they can't break our spirits." Sure enough, we spent the evening partying by candlelight. Their defiant mood amazed us. After the party, the priest helped us with taxi cabs. He arranged for us to go to our destination without going through the checkpoints. It took us an extra hour to get there.

Because we were Americans traveling in Palestine, our host arranged for us to travel by a bus with an Israeli license plate. This permitted us to move through checkpoints with minimal inconvenience. The priest from Birzeit urged me to take my group through the barriers used by the few Palestinians who had permits. Only 10 percent of the people were allowed through these horrific barriers; the rest could not leave their towns. He wanted my group to experience the miserable life of the few lucky Palestinians.

Since I did not want to jeopardize the safety of my group, I went by myself to live a "day in the life of Palestinians." So, the next day, set aside for relaxation, I followed the priest's instructions and went to the checkpoints. They were bottlenecked barriers scattered through the West Bank by Israel so they could build a wall and network of roads to be used by Israeli settlers. People at these barricades were subjected to daily humiliation, indignity and human rights abuses by teenaged military personnel who were trained to hate Palestinians.

I took a taxi to the Qalandia checkpoint, the nearest checkpoint to Ramallah between the city of El-Bireh and Beit Hanina. I went through the lines with the rest of the Palestinians. I watched as soldiers milled around and harassed people, especially young men. They randomly took young men or women with a hijab out of line and interrogated and searched them. I watched as women with traditional Muslim garb waited in line holding young babies and grocery bags. I gazed at old men who waited a few hours for a chance to enter the checkpoints, only to be told they could not cross and had to go back. People stood for hours without a whimper to pass so that they could visit their families or go to a hospital or go to work. I left my hotel very early in the morning, and I was in line for at least three hours. It was a nightmare in which people were mistreated, and I could not do anything about it. After about three and a half hours, I was able to pass with no problem because I had an American passport.

I left the checkpoint and proceeded to catch a regular taxi to Jerusalem. I was sharing the taxi with several other Palestinians. A mile from the inspection, an army patrol stopped our cab. We were still in the heart of the West Bank, and not in Israeli territories. The soldiers demanded our papers. They took them and came back and returned all the documents but two. They ordered the two passengers who had all the right papers and just passed inspection earlier to go back. The other passengers looked with despair at the two people and told them not to cause any trouble. Trying to be helpful, the driver said to them that they could try again. They might get lucky. I just sat and observed the absurdity of the situation.

Once the patrol was out sight, everyone started talking all at once. I asked if this was normal.

They all said, "This is nothing. Sometimes everyone is told to go back." Then one by one, they told me tales of horror they all experienced at one point or another. I mentioned that I would like to visit Bethlehem (about a ten-minute journey.) The driver recommended I travel the way that 90 percent of the Palestinians travel, "You must take a cab that goes to alternate routes to an Arab town." The rest had to weave through back roads that resemble white water rafting. I agreed to go the route he recommended. He found me a taxi and instructed the driver where to take me. I rode with four women, two young men, and an older gentleman. It was a journey from hell. The route was dangerous and treacherous.

The other passengers were nice and curious. When they found out I had an American passport, they asked me why I chose to travel in this taxi, when clearly I had other choices. I told them I wanted to learn first-hand what they were going through. The other passengers wanted to honor me by paying my way. I thanked them but declined the offer. The driver refused to let me pay. Their kindness overwhelmed me. We rode and talked for about four miles.

The driver received a message from his station that the road was blocked by the Israeli border patrol. He apologized and ordered us to disembark with regrets in his voice. He said, "Allah Yeounkoum, May God help you." I was nervous, but not scared. I left on foot, following the other passengers. We walked about a quarter of a mile on the road riddled with potholes and rocks. Other Palestinians were walking in the same direction. Everyone seemed to know where they were going, I followed blindly, trusting the people I met in the cab.

As I walked, I saw an elderly lady struggling with the items she was carrying. She had a bag of flour which she balanced on her head, three large bottles of pop, and other grocery items. I offered to help her. She accepted graciously and showered me with blessing. Two women maneuvered along the road wearing high heels. They stumbled and held each other's arms as they walked. The men walked in a hurry with their bags. With the woman's groceries in my hand, I struggled for balance as I walked in the heat on the uneven road. Suddenly we all stopped by a short wall. One by one we climbed the three- to four-foot partition. Some of the young men stood by the wall and helped those who needed assistance. Others were on the lookout for Israeli soldiers.

It turned out that the road was closed to Palestinians even though it was in the heart of the West Bank. I did not know how to process this horrific inconvenience and how the people put up with it. The lady I was helping went first, and I followed her. Teenage boys assisted us on the other side. We jumped. I followed everyone again. We walked about a half mile to catch the taxis that on were standby to help people. Although I was in excellent physical shape, going down the hill with the groceries in my hands was very tiring. Everyone was occupied with their own thoughts and misery. Someone helped me to catch the right taxi.

Two people who rode with me earlier jumped in the same cab. I sat next to a woman who was agitated. I inquired about her problem. She told me about her journey from hell. She was a principal of a school in Hebron. Five days before I met her, she left there for a two-day conference in Ramallah. She had all the proper permits from the Israeli authorities. After the meeting ended, she attempted to go home to her children. I met her three days after her third bid to return home. She still was not sure that she was going to make it. She was worried about her young children and family. Everyone in the taxi had a story.

By the time I left the taxi in Jerusalem, I was disgusted with the world, especially the US, which allowed such abuse to continue. As I exited the taxi, I wished everyone the best of luck. I was not sure if that was appropriate. They asked me not to forget them.

The twenty-minute trip to Bethlehem took me about five hours. I met with a friend of mine and ate a late lunch and recounted my excursion. He told me,

"This is normal; it is normal." There was nothing normal about this abuse. I did not want to be out in the dark, so I opted for a shorter ride in a taxi with an Israeli-approved license plate; at least that was my intention. I thought my troubles for the day were over. I was wrong.

I arrived at Qalandia checkpoint near Ramallah. The line was long, but moving. While I waited in line, three young men, who appeared to be in distress, asked to cut through the line. Everyone they asked allowed them to proceed. When they got to me, they politely asked to jump in front of me. They said they were on their way to their brother's funeral in El Bireh, less than half a mile from the checkpoint. Of course, I gave them my condolences and allowed them to proceed. One by one, the people gave them their sympathy and permission to move forward. As I approached the table where the soldiers stood to inspect all the documents, the three young men were standing in disbelief as the young soldier refused to let them through. He rudely told them to go back. And in rude Arabic, he said, "Rouh, rouh, rouh." (Go, go, go)

The men did not know what to do. They were in shock. They stood frozen, living in a non-ending nightmare. The crowd averted their eyes, afraid to see the pain and afraid to anger the soldier. The young soldier yelled "next." I was next. Since I had an American passport, I felt compelled to say something to the soldier. I told him politely that his treatment of the people and his conduct toward the three men were despicable. I was incensed by his behavior, and I wanted him to know. He looked at me and in perfect English he said: "I don't make the rules." He then approved my paper and ushered me to his superior to talk with me.

His superior and I had a lengthy conversation about what transpired. He explained to me that their goal was to ensure security for everyone. I replied that their actions were not about security. They were about power and humiliation. I then told him he has no business in setting a security check between Arab cities. We went back and forth for at least 20 minutes. People looked at me and tried to distance themselves from me, clearly a crazy woman who dared to question the soldiers. They kept to themselves. They worried that if they were caught looking at the soldiers or me, they would be punished.

The conversation was cordial. The commander told me he was doing his job. "I don't make the decisions about where the checkpoints are erected, I just follow orders." I told him, "Wrong is wrong. Complying with this racist policy makes you just as guilty as the people who follow the system without questions." After the lengthy discussion, we shook hands and wished each other a genuine peace. He was a nice person. He was not evil. He was just doing his job.

My plea for mercy did not change the decision they made about the men. They did not allow them to attend their brother's funeral. After I left the checkpoint, I walked toward a taxi a little away from the soldiers' view. Several people greeted me as if I was a hero. Everyone wanted to shake my hand for standing up to the soldiers. I recognized one of the people from a shop in Ramallah. They thanked me profusely for being their advocate. As I mounted the cab to go to my hotel, several offered to pay my fare. Again, the driver told the other riders that he would take care of the ride. I truly was humbled. When I sat and thought about what I did, I wondered if my advocacy would backfire, and the soldiers would avenge themselves by being hostile to the rest of the people still waiting in line. From my experience, oppressive people do not like to be challenged and embarrassed.

Upon reaching the taxi station, I bid everyone goodbye and left to ponder what I saw. I was overwhelmed with a sense of hopelessness. How can a friendly and decent soldier follow criminal policies and not question the abuse? The soldier I spoke with could have been someone I might work with or go out to dinner with, but his disregard for the cruelty he applied against innocent people baffled me.

The hotel provided me shelter from the ugliness all around me. I stayed in the courtyard and chilled with the young participants who wanted a reprieve from the occupation. We chatted about the upcoming trip schedule for the next few days.

Our group was scheduled to go to Yaffa, Haifa, and Nazareth. These Palestinian towns are now part of Israel, which occupied them in 1948. I looked forward to visiting Yaffa, my mother's birthplace. We left Ramallah with more than 50 people. The glaring difference between the Palestinian side and the Israeli side hit all of us the face. In the occupied territories, the roads were dusty, dirty, and not well maintained. The streets in Israel were first class, with flower beds by the sidewalks and intersections. There was a very small number of tanks or army present.

We arrived at the beach in Yaffa, which was jammed with people escaping the heat. If there were Palestinians present, they were blended with the population. As I walked the beach, I sensed that the Israelis had little or no knowledge of what was going on just few miles away. It is hard to empathize with or understand something that you don't see or experience. It dawned on me that most Israelis are ignorant of, or choose to ignore, what is going on in the West Bank and Gaza. They live as if the Palestinian people are not their concern. They had no reason to pursue peace.

The lack of interaction between the two sides terrified me. After a couple of hours on the beach, where my grandfather swam and fished and where my mother played as a child, I felt refreshed from the water and sun and sad for the injustice that took place in 1948. The inequity altered my family's life and continued to cast its ugly spell on the people whose land was stolen from them. As an American, I felt depressed because my tax dollars subsidize this inequality.

From Yaffa, the bus took us to Haifa and Nazareth. Haifa, a city with a mixed population, was thriving. Aside from being a university town, it is the primary waterway to the rest of the world. Its infrastructure was robust and well maintained. We visited the Bahai temple and garden. The grounds just took our breath away. It was a striking contrast from the checkpoints riddling the West Bank. The Temple sits at the top of nineteen terraced gardens. The Temple was planned in 1891 and finished in 1921. The place was magic. It was a place where one can experience the life of peace and serenity. It was a contrast to the reality of how people live in the area.

After a few hours' tour, we left for Nazareth, the historical city where Jesus spent his youth. Upon entering, we noticed the difference between an Arab town and a Jewish town in Israel. In the Arab towns, the streets were narrow and untidy. Although we felt more welcome in Nazareth, we noticed that the streets were not well maintained and congested. They have limited sidewalks. The business area was not zoned well. This sacred city where Jesus was raised did not have the funds to upgrade its electric grid or maintain its infrastructure. But it was a great urban city struggling to maintain itself with limited funding from the Israeli government.

We met with community leaders, including the mayor. He told us Arab towns receive one-third the resources of Jewish cities. The deputy mayor said that its popular mayor was always under investigation by the Israelis. Everyone we met explained that although the Arab population are Israeli citizens, they are still considered second-class, not unlike African Americans in Jim Crow America. From job discrimination to fund allocation, the Arab citizens of Israel fare worse than their Jewish counterparts.

Even if the funding was available, Israel prevented Arab towns from making progress by denying permits to proceed with projects. Although we set aside our day for fun and relaxation, we could not help but be exhausted with the inequality we witnessed and experienced first-hand. I wondered how people could cope daily with these situations. As I struggled to comprehend the ugliness of such inhumanity, the people I met reminded me of the spirit of all people who want to be free and that would never diminish.

We returned happy, haggard, and exhausted to Ramallah after midnight. We worked the next day and spent the evening in Ramallah shopping for gold and silver. We ate at Abou Iskandar Shawarma, a local famous hole in the wall eatery. And the next day, we went to Hebron (Al-Khalil). Just when I thought that life after Oslo could not be worse, I stumbled into the lion's den by going to Al-Kalil. Our host took us on routes designated for Israelis and settlers only. Our bus driver had an Israeli license plate. The summer heat overwhelmed us. The stench of urine and garbage gagged us. In the distance, we saw the terraced hillsides stacked in the landscape to catch rainfall as they had for centuries. You can see pine trees planted in nature reserves to deter Palestinian encroachment on the land. Although the property was owned by Palestinians, we saw the Israeli settlement expansion. New trailers traced the hilltops all along the route to Hebron.

As we passed the Israeli military bases, we saw the showcase of physical infrastructure required to maintain the Occupation: We saw the military Jeeps, Kalashnikovs, barbed wire, checkpoints, tanks, and the various units of young soldiers assembled around Kahlil.

Hebron, or AL Khalil, is one of the oldest Palestinian cities and considered the second holiest Jewish city after Jerusalem. The Bible mentions Hebron in connection with Abraham. It is the site of the Cave of the Machpelah, also known as the Tomb of the Patriarchs/Matriarchs, which is enclosed by the Mosque of Ibrahim, also known as the Avraham Avinu Synagogue. It is the traditional burial ground of the ancestors of Abraham and Sarah, Itzhak and Rebecca, and Jacob and Leah. According to Jewish tradition, the cave was built by Herod, King of Judea during the Second Temple Period some 2,000 years ago.

Although for hundreds of years, Palestinians, Muslims, Christians, and Jews had lived peacefully in Al-Khalil, tension between Muslims and Jews began to rise when on November 2, 1917, British Foreign Secretary Arthur Balfour promised Lord Rothschild, a leader of the British Jewish community, a national homeland in Palestine. Although this unlawful declaration promised to safeguard the local Palestinian population, it meant tension and upheaval to residents of the region. Before this declaration, the Jews at that time were a tiny minority who lived as Palestinians with limited problems. By 1929, anxieties ran deep and people began to distrust their Jewish neighbors.

That year riots occurred. Muslim Palestinians massacred 67 Jewish Palestinians in Al-Kahlil. This massacre became a symbol for Jewish extremists seeking revenge. So, after the 1967 occupation, Al-Kalil became a hotbed of resistance against the occupation. Messianic Jews took it upon themselves, with the cooperation of the Israeli government, to confiscate Palestinian land and live in settlements in the middle of the city. Then 250 settlers held the city hostage. They wanted to avenge those who died in 1929. These Jewish colonists had no relationship with the Palestinian Jews killed in the massacre. In fact, some of the native Jews who trace their ancestry to Al-Khalil rebuked the settlers, who came mostly from the United States and Europe.

After the occupation, violence against the mostly unarmed Palestinian civilians became the norm. They live at the mercy of both the fanatic settlers and the Israeli Army that protect them. The most recent violence in Al-Khalil centered around dividing up the Cave in 1994 for Jews and Muslims. The brutal circumstances enabled settlers to provoke and harm the people who live under the protection of the Israeli government. So, in 1994, Baruch Goldstein (an American Jewish physician who immigrated to Israel) opened fire and killed 29 Palestinians who were praying at the mosque. He then was lynched by an angry Arab mob.

As we rode into town, we stopped near the center of the city, where peddlers sell and buy their goods daily. The dusty streets smelled of sewage and rotten vegetables. A few feet away milled clusters of Israeli soldiers. As we moved into the city, we saw soldiers on every road working as security for the settlers. Hebron is the frontline in the Israeli/Palestinian conflict. Unlike other cities, Israeli settlements are in and around the city. The settlers who live in the town are some of the most militant in Israel. In 1994, the town was home to 150,000 indigent Palestinians and 500 militant Jewish extremists.

Our bus stopped near the market not far from the tomb of the Patriarchs and Ibrahim Mosque. The streets to the Mosques were clear except for IDF soldiers, and about a dozen settlers strolled the streets as if they owned the town. As we walked through the market, we looked up and saw metal netting over our heads with garbage, bricks, bottles, and other garbage on top. Our tour host told us the trash was thrown at people by the settlers. The netting was installed for protection. But the settlers became more creative; they threw urine and dirty or hot water at people indiscriminately. Although the area is 100 percent Palestinian, soldiers and settlers arbitrarily enforce a curfew and erect blockage checkpoints so settlers can walk through the old market. We watched in horror as the settlers strolled to their destination hurling curses at the shopkeepers. The soldiers walked by them trying to prevent a fight.

After a brief tour of the mosque and the market, we tried to return to our bus across the street. A soldier informed us that we couldn't cross the street; we had to go around several blocks to catch the bus. When we pointed out the obvious to the soldiers — that our coach was parked right in front of us — he shrugged, said something in Hebrew, and again told us we must go around to reach our bus. Another soldier with an American accent told us the street we crossed on earlier was now designated a military zone. "Only Jews can cross the street." We were forced to take a taxi and drive for two miles just to cross the street.

What we saw in the old city of Al-Khalil is only a small glimpse of Palestinian life under the Israeli occupation. The 500 fanatic settlers forced 150,000 people to live in terror daily. It is madness. It was the same as African Americans living in the South in the 1930s to 1950s. Israel had forced many families to abandon their homes, business, and livelihoods to appease the settlers. Many, however, refused to go, and endured daily humiliation and abuse. Entering Hebron is like walking into a lion's den: you don't know when you are going to be attacked, but eventually, you will be hurt.

As we waited for others to come back to the bus, I struck up a conversation with an Israeli soldier standing by with his hand on his rifle. He was an American Israeli soldier. I asked how he could justify such ugliness. He looked at me and said that if I did not like it, I should not have visited this area. I was nearly speechless, but before I left, another soldier who heard the conversation approached me and told me to disregard his friend's comment. He said that the group was operating under stress, and therefore they acted mean. I thanked him and asked him the same question. He said he would rather not be in this situation and would prefer to serve somewhere else; however, it was not his choice. At least, this soldier could distinguish between right or wrong.

We returned to Ramallah. Our host arranged for us to meet Yasser Arafat in his compound, nestled between residential and office buildings on the outskirts of the city. The building was surrounded by high walls and was guarded by young Palestinian soldiers.

We arrived early. Security was mediocre at best. Arafat's staff ushered us into a conference room. We had our cameras ready to snap pictures of the symbol of Palestine. I was never a fan of Arafat, but I went to school with his wife's sister. We waited for a few minutes before President Arafat entered. The room erupted in cheers as he shook hands with everyone. I was amazed at the softness of his hands. I almost asked what kind of hand lotion he used. I thought the better of it.

President Arafat, or Chairman Arafat, as the Palestinians call him, welcomed us to his office. The president of the American Federation of Ramallah, Palestine, thanked him and his staff. He talked about our programs in the United States, invited Arafat to visit the United States to speak at our annual convention. We had a chance to exchange various ideas with Arafat, who encouraged us to work with the Palestinian people in Palestine.

Since we met him not long after the assassination of Yitzhak Rabin, Arafat talked about the lost opportunity with Rabin's death. He genuinely believed Rabin had been a real partner for peace with the Palestinians. Arafat did not trust Benjamin Netanyahu, the then new prime minister. Arafat felt that peace was within reach with the help of President Clinton. He urged us to lobby Congress to support the peace process and Clinton. He insisted Palestinians and Israelis could live side by side with economic prosperity. Before we left, we posed for a photo as we wished Arafat and his administration success.

When my official duties ended, I visited friends, former teachers, and relatives. I told them what I witnessed and experienced during my visit. People were becoming more cynical about the Palestinian government and rumors of corruption. It occurred to me that people in the West Bank just wanted a functioning government. I heard stories of corruption all around, but could not attest to their validity. Israel used the report of corruption to stop funding from going to the Palestinians. As I heard these accusations, I questioned the proof. No one could tell me they had hard evidence, other than "look how the people in government live." The only thing they were sure about was that exiled Palestinians who came from Tunisia were less trustworthy.

I ached to go home to Detroit. The suffering of the Palestinian people distressed me. I did not think I could live under such circumstances. Families were exposed to bleak conditions that impeded their daily happiness. Yet, they continued to move forward with their lives. I, on the other hand, had choices. And with these opportunities comes guilt. Hence, after every trip to Palestine, I vowed to keep their voices alive.

25 / Visiting Palestine with Senator Levin

I was not the first choice to go on 2006 trip to Palestine with US Senator Carl Levin to examine economic development between the Palestinian and Jewish communities. Although Senator Levin and I have worked together for years, I heard about the trip from my friend Samir Mashni. When a member of the party backed out of the trip, I inserted myself without shame.

I first met Senator Levin in the early 1980s when I took a delegation to meet with him about the Palestinian issue. I was fully aware of his stand on Israel, but that did not deter me from arranging a meeting with him and members of the Ramallah community in Detroit. During the 90-minute meeting he listened, was gracious, and he did not deceive us. He told us what he could do to help, including setting up meetings with the US State Department and following up with more sessions. As I became involved with the Democratic Party and Wayne County, I found Senator Levin and his staff to be helpful, accessible and the epitome of faithful public servants.

After several meetings in Detroit with members of the Jewish and Palestinian communities regarding preparation for economic development for the two-state solution proposed in the Oslo Accords, Senator Levin asked me to join the small private delegation going to Israel and Palestine. With the senator as a lead, the group developed "The Michigan Fund for Peace and Economic Development Inc." The group and the trip were not part of Levin's official duty as a Senator. He emphasized the mission as personal.

The idea was to create investment funds to improve the lives of the people in Gaza and the West Bank. If successful, this would be a demonstration project of cooperation between the Jewish and Palestinian American communities in Michigan. I thought the idea was naïve and would not work if Israel continued to confiscate land and suppress Palestinians. However, I did not want to reject a noble idea without exploring the possibilities. I believed in the idealism of good people.

As I committed to going, I made my view known that economic development will not be a substitute for justice for the Palestinian people. Also, I made sure that in his capacity as a United States senator, he needed to witness the occupation for himself. This was a huge issue since he was a member of Congress who supported Israel's military and its economy. I had no doubt that Senator Levin was genuine in his pursuit of a peaceful and just solution for all parties. He and I have the same philosophy on every issue except Israel. Like many American Jews of his era, he was brought up to believe in a utopian Israel. I will continue to disagree with him on this notion until Israel stops its colonial policies toward the Palestinian people. I like to believe that if the table was turned, I would stand with all oppressed peoples.

After several weeks of preparation, I began my journey a few days ahead of the delegation, visiting my family and friends in Palestine and attending Holy Week events in Jerusalem. My flight from Newark to Tel Aviv was uneventful; my seatmate was an Israeli. I believed I was most likely the only Arab on the plane. All around me people were chattering with joyous anticipation of their trip to Israel, some for the first time. While they were celebrating, I anticipated the delay and harassment I was usually subjected to during trips to my homeland. To my relief, Shlomo and his son Daniel were great seat partners. During the first five minutes of our conversation, Shlomo told me he had more in common with me as a Palestinian than his Jewish wife from New York. Like my family, Shlomo was from the Yaffa region and had only moved to New York when he fell in love and married his wife, an attorney.

Between meals and naps, we talked about the government, the situation in Palestine, and our families and friends. We talked about the purpose of our trips: mine was an economic mission mixed with Easter celebration with family, and his was to attend a Bar Mitzvah in his hometown. Shlomo was not oblivious to the suffering of the Palestinian people. Since he was a Sephardic Jew (from the Middle East), he did not lump all Arabs in one category but rather based his likes or dislikes on experience rather than biased ignorance. Being of Yemeni background, Shlomo was very comfortable with Arab culture and even gave me the compliment that we could've been brother and sister.

Despite this unbiased connection, Shlomo could not believe that the Israelis would harass me at the airport. He assured me it would not happen, but I told him based on my experience, harassment at the airport was a regular procedure. Before we parted ways, he warned me about the closure of the West Bank. He attributed the closure to an Israeli holiday and festival. Even as lovely as Shlomo was, he did not see anything wrong with the imprisonment of a whole population to appease the ruling class. We departed as friends, with hope for each other.

Deprived of sleep, I was anxious about the potential harassment I thought for sure was awaiting me and hoped it would not last over an hour. I desperately wanted to get some sleep and participate in the Good Friday festivities. Luck was on my side that day, and the officer granted me a visa within 5 minutes, and I was on my way. I kept looking around for someone to stop me, but no one did. Hallelujah! I was free to go to Jerusalem and quickly headed toward the curb to catch a taxi. Once outside, I asked the man in charge of taxis if he could take me to Notre Dame in East Jerusalem and he said sure, then turned around to his friend and said: "What do I care, the fare is a fare even if she is Arab."

When I travel abroad, I want to experience what others experience in their travels, so I usually take a shared cab and sit in the back and listen. Everyone in the cab was Jewish and from the United States. From the conversation, I concluded they were all frequent travelers to Israel. To them, Israel was a resort for rich people to visit during the summer. One man was telling his wife that the best place to invest in Israel was the settlements. The sad part about this conversation was that no one talked about the stolen land or its original owners. My Jewish seatmates spoke about the deal and the profit they were going to make. The pain of this conversation haunted me. I wanted to scream, but stayed silent, maybe because I was tired, or just because I was mentally drained. To this day, I feel I missed an opportunity to tell someone the truth, but I remained mum. It breaks my heart every time I think of this conversation.

I was the last person the cab dropped off from the airport. A couple was dropped at a hotel, the rest stopped at Arab-looking homes built in the '50s or '60s around Jerusalem. One of the houses had a familiar Arab emblem above the door. Through confiscation, these Palestinian homes somehow became Israeli homes. After an hour I checked into the splendid Notre Dame of Jerusalem.

Father Shawki, a friend, arranged for me to stay in Jerusalem. He made sure I had a room available at the Pontifical Institute Notre Dame of Jerusalem Center. This allowed me to walk to the old city and enjoy the evening festivities without obstacles. The hotel, situated on one of the hills of Jerusalem, is an imposing historical structure. It has an air of castle or fortress. Neither the driver nor the other passengers knew the place. The Notre Dame Center has a statue of the Virgin Mary — a replica of Our Lady of the Salvation in Paris. The Center is surrounded by two towers with medieval battlements that complement its unmistakable beauty. The site has stood as a witness to history for almost 125 years. It is owned by the Vatican and hosts thousands of pilgrims from all over the world. Catholics who travel to Jerusalem view the Notre Dame as the heartbeat of the city.

As soon as I walked into the lobby, I felt at home. Everyone was welcoming and kind. Upon learning I was a Palestinian Christian, the staff rolled out the red carpet. They went out of their way to help find information about the Good Friday celebration. I took a quick shower and headed to the Holy Sepulcher.

Some of the most memorable events in my life before emigrating to the United States were the festivities of the Holy Week in Jerusalem, specifically Good Friday and Palm Sunday. Since I left my homeland, I had dreamt of going back to Jerusalem around Easter to recapture the feelings it evoked. By the time I arrived in Jerusalem, the via Dolorosa procession was over, but the service was about to begin. Oh, what glory; nothing surpasses the experience. People from all over the world come together to commemorate Christ's death and resurrection. Everyone has an open invitation to Jerusalem, except Palestinians from the West Bank and Gaza. They are banned from entering the city.

Although I am not religious, I love the traditions and the spirituality of these events. The festivities provided me with inner peace and serenity. I found my way inside the Holy Sepulcher and lit candles for family and friends who asked me to do so. The experience was amazing, even better than I anticipated. I met my sister's nephew, a Franciscan monk who served in St. Savior in the heart of the Old City. I did not return to my hotel until 2 a.m.

Despite my late night, I woke up early and headed to Ramallah to visit my old school, my aunts, and cousins. There were more tourists in Jerusalem than usual. The merchants I talked to were happy that the situation was stable, and the economy was better than in previous years. I walked to the Damascus gate (Bab Al-Amoud), the most significant gate to the old city, and took a bus from the old bus station to the checkpoint in Qalandia, just outside Ramallah.

I sat next to an elderly man. After a few awkward moments, we struck up a conversation. As we chatted, he told me he had dual citizenship, Palestinian and American. After the signing of the Oslo Accords, he moved his family back to his native land. I told him about our economic mission; he was excited about the prospect of joint economic development between Palestinians and Jewish Americans.

On my past visits, the barricade, or "wall," Israel erected on Palestinian land was in its infancy. This time around, a large segment of the wall was built. I could not believe the ugliness nor the size of this apartheid wall. The massive wall snaked throughout the West Bank on Palestinian land, separating Palestinians from their property, extended families, and way of life. The wall was 26.2-feet-high — twice the height of the Berlin Wall — with watchtowers in various areas. Also, they confiscated area surrounding the wall as a buffer zone, which further cut the Palestinian land use.

In some areas, they used electric fences, trenches, cameras, sensors, and military patrols. In other places, the wall consisted of layers of fencing and razor wire, military patrol roads, sand paths to trace footprints, ditches, and surveillance cameras. I later learned that, according to the Israeli Ministry of Defense and B'Tselem (an Israeli human rights organization), the wall runs between 422-440 miles, more than twice the length of the Green Line (Internationally agreed upon border), and is 85 percent of it is actually inside Palestinian land. The wall passes through many Palestinian villages, destroying communities and separating families. The wall also prevents most people from traveling for work. When completed, Israel will annex 46 percent of the occupied West Bank (area the size of Chicago) and cut off 90 percent of freshwater wells." [20]

My seatmate calmly explained to me that the wall had already separated his family and many of his friends. He considered himself lucky because he had an American passport which gave him more freedom. Even with an American passport, he could stay in Palestine for only three months. Although he did not live in the Israeli territories, he still had to have permission from Israel to live in the West Bank. Therefore, every three months he had to travel to another country and reapply for an Israeli permit so he could stay in the Palestinian territories. I could not help but be outraged at the barbaric treatment of such people.

With the radio blasting the recital of the Holy Qur'an, I surveyed the faces of the people on the bus. They all looked tired and resigned to their ill fate; no one smiled or talked. They were all pensive as if in a trance. My seatmate told me these daily trips (although a privilege for people with Jerusalem ID or special passes) were oppressive. A person must set aside half a day to make a twenty-mile journey. I came to appreciate the patience and perseverance of the Palestinian People.

The bus stopped just before the wall ended and the checkpoint began. Unlike the old checkpoints, the new and more confining checkpoint looks like a

---

funnel-wide at the entrance, where about fifty people begin to assemble side by side, at the end of an open-air shed with a ribbed tin roof. Within a few meters, everyone pushes their way around two high barriers. It reminded me of visiting my husband's family in Nebraska and the treatment of cattle in a stockyard.

Within seconds, I found myself forced and squashed so I could not move my hands to wipe my face. Everyone was packed like sardines. I was glad I'm not claustrophobic. It took about an hour to clear the checkpoint. People around me kept saying they were lucky the checkpoint was not congested that day.

Although inhumane, the checkpoint line created a bond among everyone waiting to be cleared. People talked to each other. When I voiced my concern about the checkpoint, the man to my right said: "Don't worry, this is normal." People warned me to be careful, saying things like, "Don't drop anything, because you can't bend down to get it." "Hold your passport close to your body. If you drop it, there is no way you could retrieve it." I don't know how many people surrounded me, I estimated about 300. It was worse than being in prison.

Just when I thought the line could get no worse, I looked to the front. I had to figure out when to approach the turnstile bars at the end. If not careful, I could be crushed by the bars. I watched the precision movements of the people in line with me and proceeded forward. There was no room to screw up. If a person misstepped, he could be pinned between two bars less than one foot in diameter. I moved forward with two other people, a man and woman. The woman was stressed. Her husband and son were behind her, but could not move forward until we were cleared. We were in the cell for a few minutes, but it felt like an eternity. The woman assured her husband and son she would wait for them. And just like that, a buzzer came on and we had to move fast, or we would have been pinned again by the electronic gate.

I thought clearing the gate was a relief. I was wrong. Soldiers with assault rifles were roaming around. I handed my passport to a young soldier. She studied it, looked at my visa, and asked me where I was going. She then asked me if I had a Palestinian ID. I said no and she let me go. She yelled in Hebrew "Next." I embedded my latest experience in my memory so I could tell Senator Levin and the delegation of the newest indignity Israel had imposed on the Palestinians.

After surprising my aunt, cousins, and teachers with my visit, I left to go back to Jerusalem. This time, even with my US passport, I was forced to wait for two hours before I crossed the border to catch a cab.

While detained, I watched and listened to the people waiting to pass and was astonished by the fear and calm demeanor they exhibited. From my vantage point, I was struck by the cruelty of the guards, especially toward the women, treated as if they were nothing. One female guard pushed, screamed, and laughed with mockery at the people waiting. She and the other guards must have been abused or bullied as teenagers. Again and again people told me, 'This is normal." To me, it was pure evil and madness. There is nothing ordinary about preventing people from doing simple human tasks; there is nothing normal about an eighteen-year-old with a gun holding hundreds of people hostage for hours at a time.

After a wait of two hours, it was my turn to show my passport to the young soldier, to whom I was just another number. As he looked at my passport, I muttered the word "disgusting." He ordered me to repeat what I said, I just gave him a dirty look and told him it was "None of his damn business." He gave me a dirty look and said I didn't have the right to be there. I told him I had every right to be in Ramallah; he, on the other hand, should not be stationed where he was. He handed my passport back, and I left to look for a bus. It was now dark, and the place was still busy with people scrambling to get home. I finally boarded a minivan and made it back to my hotel in Jerusalem, but not before being stopped three times, twice by the army and once by Israeli police officers.

Once again, I was told by the other passengers that this was normal, and I wondered how many Americans would put up with this type of harassment. I also wondered how many Israelis would allow this humiliation to take place if they were the ones being harassed. In the back of my mind, I kept thinking, I cannot be silent. It is my duty to expose injustice.

Holy Week in Jerusalem

In our lives, we all have taken steps that we look back on as significant. Walking into Jerusalem is one of these rare and noteworthy steps. Jerusalem during Holy Week is a world-class experience. It does not matter if a person is a believer. The Holy Week experience is forever etched in the mind of those who walked the path and always referred to with reverence. The week usually begins with Palm Sunday and ends at Easter. On Palm Sunday, pilgrims from all over the world gather to participate in the beginning of Holy Week. The harmony of the procession echoes throughout the city until dusk, as the sounds from the drums and bagpipes of the scout troops intermingle with voices raised in many different languages from the throngs of international pilgrim groups.

I was not there on Palm Sunday on this trip. But I remembered from my childhood the anticipation of going to Jerusalem on Palm Sunday. Those of us who were too young to participate in the procession used to picnic alongside the routes the pilgrims take to the city. When you walk down the path that Jesus walked, you walk down the Mount of Olives, overlooking the panorama of the city and the traditional site where Jesus wept over Jerusalem, lamenting the lack of ability to see the ways that led to peace. Today, one can't help but hear those words echoing truth 2000 years later.

From various places through the route, one could see the separation wall ripping through the middle of Palestinians' land and lives and the valley of Silwan. This was one of the earliest places where Israelis began demolishing the homes of those whose children had thrown stones in the first Intifada. As one walks the route, one can hear Christ. *O Jerusalem, Jerusalem, when will you learn the ways of peace?*

Jerusalem, the place of the Cross, is a city where one can feel close to God, but also where one can see the abyss caused by violence and man's pretensions. It is the city touched by love but also stained by walls and divisions, fear between Israelis and Palestinians, among Jews, Muslims, and Christians. The

Holy City is a place where the signs of death live side by side with the signs of the resurrection. My husband, who has traveled extensively and visited Jerusalem four times, thinks it is one of the great cities of the world. Jerusalem for me is a place of fond memories. It is where my friends and I walked the streets holding hands with our Catholic school uniforms, pretending to pray while looking at the candy stores that lined the medieval streets. Being in Jerusalem during Holy Week gave me the opportunity to relive some of the joy I left behind. I hoped I would re-live some of these beautiful moments and I was not disappointed.

I arrived in Jerusalem just in time to take a quick shower and head to the Holy Sepulcher. I entered old Jerusalem via the New Gate and headed to the Christian quarter to witness the passing of the Holy Fire. It was a world apart from the checkpoint I had just come from. Here the radio was blasting the famous singer Fayrouz' song about the streets of Jerusalem along with Easter Music. Fayrouz is an icon in the Arab World. Her songs about Jerusalem have become anthems for the Arab world for the city that was lost in 1967. Her angelic voice and lyrics bring a chill to those of us who cherish the city and know its torments:

> For you, the city of prayer … I pray
> For you, with your gorgeous houses...oh rose of cities
> Oh Jerusalem … oh Jerusalem
> Oh, Jerusalem … city of prayer … I pray
> Our eyes travel to you every day
> Walk and wander through the temples
> Hug old churches
> Wipe off sadness from mosques
> Oh, nocturnal journey … oh road of who passed through you to the sky
> Our eyes travel to you every day … and I'm praying
> The child (Jesus) in the cave with his mother Mariam, both are crying
> Both are crying … for people who are forced to be homeless … for children without houses
> For all people, who defended his land and were martyred in the entries were martyred … at home of peace
> And so justice was lost on the entries
> When Jerusalem city fell ... love retreated and in the heart of those who war lived in them
> The child (Jesus) in the cave with his mother Mariam, both are crying …

For a couple of hours, it was as though there was no occupation, even though the Israeli police and army were all around the festivities. The people ignored them and celebrated with gusto. For a brief time, they forgot the pain and problems; they laughed, danced, and sang with their neighbors and kids with candles in their hands, awaiting the Easter Light on its way from the Holy Sepulcher. It is believed that the "Light" emanates from Christ's tomb the day before

Easter. The voice of happiness intermingled with the sounds of vendors selling pastries and colored eggs.

I stood alone and watched with pleasure and tears as I tried to capture the moment with my camera. Someone gave me a candle and alerted me to what I should look for. Suddenly jubilant chaos erupted as young men hoisted on their friends' shoulders emerged with lit candles. People clapped, pushed, and reached out to light their candles. Someone lit my candle. Someone shouted, "make room, make room," The Franciscan boys and girls bands started marching, followed by the hoisted boys who led the chant "Sabet Alnour wa benaid; benaid maa Al-Massih eli bedamou eshtarana (We celebrate this Saturday of light, we celebrate with Christ who saved us with his blood)." They sang about their presence in Jerusalem. They sang about St. George who slew the dragon. They marched in the streets of Jerusalem like many generations before them. They paraded through the alleys of old Jerusalem; they wanted the world to know that they are natives of Jerusalem. They wanted everyone to know that they are an intricate part of Jerusalem's fabric. I followed them; there were few tourists. Israel warned foreign tourists not to be in the Arab section of Jerusalem. After several hours, I walked to my hotel about 1 a.m., tired but in great spirits. I did not go to bed until 3, as I participated in another celebration at the hotel. About 200 tourists and priests built a bonfire outside the hotel court and celebrated a mass welcoming Easter.

For Palestinian Christians, Easter is a greater holiday than Christmas. It is the holiday that reaffirms our lives as Christians. As a child, I always celebrated Easter with my family. We went to church and to my grandparents' home for dinner, which lasted all day. Friends and neighbors came to wish us well. We made special pastries with nuts and dates which symbolize the resurrection of Christ. So, I was not sure if I should have skipped my get-together with my family on Easter. Of course, my doubt dissipated as soon as I landed at the airport. I decided that despite the fact the rest of my family lived in Ramallah and could not go to Jerusalem, I made a great choice staying in Jerusalem so I could partake in all the activities.

After a couple of hours of sleep, I woke up early in the morning at the urging of a local man who had told me about the Easter procession in the streets of Jerusalem. The Christian sector of the city was clean and ready for the Easter celebration. Instead of going to the start of the procession, I walked to the Holy Sepulcher. I stood and watched people coming and going. Since I was early, few people were waiting. I struck up a conversation with a tour guide. Upon learning I was Palestinian, he directed me to where I should stand to get the best view. It was not long before I heard the pounding of the guards' canes announcing the procession was near.

The guards dressed in old Turkish attire, with long silver and wooden canes they pounded in unison. They were followed by Franciscan monks wearing brown robes, and Archdiocese priests. The Catholic Patriarch of Jerusalem appeared, as did my sister's nephew, followed by diocese priests, including my dear friend Father Iyad, who was surprised to see me.

As they entered the church, I followed and stood on the right side of the altar by Christ's tomb as instructed by my sister's nephew Oussama, a Franciscan friar. I was giddy with excitement. A few minutes after the mass started, a Franciscan friar motioned for me to follow him. I was worried about losing my place but went after him. He took me to the vestibule and had me wait with twelve strangers. I did not know why I was there. However, I pretended I belonged. The friar asked our names and nationalities and gave us our instructions. It turned out I was selected to give the mass gifts used during the celebration to the patriarch. At that moment, I wanted to shout from the top of my lungs, "Oh my God, I can't wait until I brag about this."

A young friar gave me a gold chalice and instructed me on how to hold it. On cue, we moved from the sacristy to the tomb where the mass was taking place. I remembered thinking, "Don't drop the chalice. Don't drop the chalice." As I came forward, Father Iyad watched me with bemusement. He knows me well enough to know I am an infrequent churchgoer. I would have paid money to capture the look on his face. After the mass, I waited for him and accompanied him and his friends to the Archdiocese of Jerusalem where I was introduced to all kinds of people.

My hours of bliss ended when I returned to Ramallah on a local bus to have dinner with my cousins. As the ride began, I was sitting next to a woman who appeared to be my age. At first, she was quiet and tired, but after I introduced myself, she began to talk. She spoke with a smile about her six-year-old son who would be waiting for her and the treats she was bringing him. She told me about her daughter, who had just graduated from nursing school and was married to a nice man. She talked about her son, who was a sweet boy, but less successful than her daughter. I found out her husband had been a political prisoner who served more than twelve years in jail.

As the bus rolled toward Ramallah, my seatmate pointed out her village (Hizmah). It was two miles away from her work near Jerusalem. With a sense of resignation, she mentioned that it takes her two hours each way to go to work. She must take two taxis and a bus. With the wall, roadblocks, and checkpoints, she goes fifteen miles out of her way to reach her village. She wanted me to know she was grateful to have a job at a school since her husband and son could not find employment because they were prisoners.

We sat silently as I contemplated the injustice of the situation. Worried she had offended me, she explained her silence. "I am just tired today; I only slept three hours." She went on to say, the Israeli soldiers had come to her and her neighbor's houses and forced everyone out, including her sleeping six-year-old son. She told me that thinking back, she had to laugh — "the soldiers were afraid of my child." It turned out soldiers came and took her fourteen-year-old neighbor. She was worried about him and his mother. She whimpered to herself, "Life cannot continue to go on like this — Inshallah — God's willing," she said, "things will change; they have to." We departed as she went to her village with a small bag of chips for her son and I went back to Ramallah and my cousins. At the checkpoint, the vendors were hawking their products, but I noticed boys as young as eight selling gum. I bought a couple of packs to help them and went on my way. I did not even look at the boy selling the gum; he was a faceless, nameless vendor, trying to make it in this cruel world.

When I arrived at my cousin's home, dinner was waiting. When I finished, my cousin suggested an elegant restaurant owned by a member of my tribe for dessert. I protested but lost. I later was told my young cousins loved the place and would have been disappointed if we hadn't gone. The owner was proud of his place, especially that the building was constructed from old Ramallah stones.

After dessert, I stayed in Ramallah. I awoke to the sound of gunshots. No one flinched except me. "It is normal," my cousin said.

After a great time with my cousins, I went back to Jerusalem. I arrived early since I was going to join the official delegation and had to change hotels. The seven miles that should have taken a twenty-minute ride took me two hours.

The Official Program Begins

I checked into the famed King David hotel a day early by mistake. Since no one from the delegation had arrived yet, I went to visit the Aqsa Mosque, the third holiest place for Muslims. I always like to visit the place. The ornate golden dome can be seen from every part of the city. It is featured in every panoramic photo of Jerusalem. As I arrived at the gate, two Israeli police officers stopped me and asked if I was Muslim. It was an odd question; I replied "no." They denied me entry. "Only Muslims allowed."

Deciding not to pursue the matter any further, I went shopping instead. I've been told that shopping in Jerusalem is an art; one must know how to shop and bargain. I am a failure at the art of bargaining for several reasons: I hate to see the shop owners sell their souls for my sale, everything was comparatively sold cheaper in the U.S, and I knew the hardship of the store owners and I was not willing to save a dime at the cost of their misfortune. I ignored my husband's advice and shopped until I dropped.

By the time I returned to the hotel, it was dark. A young police officer in civilian clothes asked the purpose of my visit to the hotel. I told him I was a guest. He asked to see my ID before I entered. I was profiled since no one else was asked to show their ID. Unlike the young man at the door, the workers, both Arab and Jews, were helpful and courteous. By then I was drained, so I went to my room, and after speaking with my husband on the phone, I took a hot bath and fell asleep in a luxurious bed until 9 a.m. the next day.

I made some calls to confirm meetings for our delegation in Ramallah. I was not due to meet the rest of the group until 5 p.m. It was the Jerusalem I knew, full of activity and vivaciousness. I saw a sea of students in various uniforms leaving schools to go home. Women rushed home with their groceries. I felt at home. Around 3 p.m., I headed back to the hotel to prepare for Senator Levin's arrival. I wanted to be ready for the meeting with the delegation at 5.

I went down to the lobby to wait for the senator's arrival. Most of the guests in the lobby were either American or Westerners. An hour into my wait, Senator Levin and two of his staff arrived.

Unbeknownst to me, Israeli security, American Embassy personnel, and an Israeli government liaison were escorting our delegation. When the senator entered, security personnel converged around him. He excused himself and approached me with a hug. The Israeli government liaison introduced himself to the delegation and informed us about our first meeting.

Tired from his trip, Senator Levin begged off to check into his room to refresh. The rest of the delegation had not arrived. I was left alone with the Israeli official. He told me he was a career government official and head of the Bureau of International Affairs for the Center for Political Research. His name was Baruch Binah and he was currently assigned to be Israel's next council general in Chicago. The first few moments alone were awkward. We made small talk about our backgrounds, and then we dived into what I had witnessed the last few days.

I told him about the hardships I encountered going to Ramallah, and the wall. He was a master of vagueness; he listened, did not correct me, and proceeded to talk about peace and hope. Like many Israelis and their supporters, he said that although things were complicated, Prime Minister Sharon had authorized a disengagement plan from Gaza. He viewed it as a benefit to the Palestinian people. The reality of the plan, however, was to reorganize the occupation of Gaza at a minimal cost to the Israelis, while imprisoning and walling off 1.5 million Palestinians and dividing them from the rest of Palestine. We moved on to several new subjects. He if he could stay in contact with me, and if I could organize meetings with him and the Palestinian community in Michigan. Before I responded, Senator Levin interrupted and we left for our first official meeting.

Senator Levin explained to Binah and others that this mission was a private one, and he was not visiting on behalf of the American government. He said that during this visit would hold some official meetings with Israeli officials regarding the war in Iraq. Binah was positive and encouraged us to pursue the project.

As I listened, I noticed that Binah interlaced the United States and Israel as if they are one and the same. He kept saying that Israeli and American values are the same.

Binah told the delegation that the Iraq war was misguided and executed wrong, but necessary. When asked about Syria and Iran, he indicated, like many of the neo-conservatives in the US, that the two countries represented an imminent threat to the United States and Israel. It was at that moment I realized there was a strategic plan to change the face of the Middle East, one country at a time. My heart ached since I knew millions would die because of colonialist thinking.

Several times during the meeting, Senator Levin challenged Binah regarding his beliefs. As a consummate diplomat, Binah listened politely.

We then met with Robert J. Tansey, first secretary of environment, science, technology, and health, and had dinner with US ambassador to Israel, Daniel C. Kurtzer, and his wife. We had a briefing from several State Department field staff stationed in Israel.

During dinner, Senator Levin explained in detail our mission to the region and asked the staff for some guidance on the best approach in working on our project. The most informative member was the head of the US Agency for International Development (USAID), who talked in detail about the extreme needs of the communities, detailing their economic needs, obstacles to achievement as well as the drive for success. He also stressed the importance of meeting with the US Consulate General, who works directly with the Palestinian community.

Dinner conversations emphasized the dire needs of the Palestinians economy and the effect of the enclosure of border crossings. As diplomats, they were forthcoming with the causes of the economic collapse of the Palestinian society and encouraged us to meet with political figures and businesspeople. With a regime change in Palestinian leadership, the delegation believed the time was ripe to make changes to the status quo. They suggested that one of the first initiatives should be to ease the crossing of people from town to town. Diplomacy was in the air as every word uttered was measured for fear of misinterpretation, but regardless of their measured words, we still got a glimpse of the reality of Gaza and the West Bank.

During dinner, State Department staff gave us a briefing of Palestinian political and business leaders we were to meet. I was filled with pride as the staff described the Palestinian leaders as brilliant and visionary people dedicated to advancing their people despite the occupation and hardship.

The next morning, security vehicles drove us to our first meeting with the Latin Patriarch of Jerusalem, Michael Sabah, about a half-mile away. He was short in stature but viewed as a giant in his community. He was the first Palestinian to be appointed by the Catholic Church as an archbishop in the region. He was shy but kind. Senator Levin told him about our mission and asked for his opinion. Patriarch Sabbah spoke deliberately and truthfully about the sadness of his community and the violence perpetrated on the Palestinian population. He did not mince words or shy away from describing the horrible situation on the ground. Despite his pessimism, the Patriarch gave his support to our proposed program.

Following our candid discussions, Senator Levin asked him about the future; the Patriarch responded that his faith gave him hope for a brighter, non-violent future. This brief visit set the tone for the rest of our meetings.

We had a few minutes to spare before our next meeting at the Consulate General's office. So, we walked the streets of Jerusalem and headed to the Holy Sepulcher. Since it was early, the roads were not crowded. A sense of sadness came over me when I realized that although I was free to walk in Jerusalem at any given hour, my cousins who live less than 15 minutes away were forbidden from taking the same walk just because they are Palestinians.

Our next meeting was Palestinian Finance Minister Salam Fayyad. Amy Shedlbaur, an attaché at the Consulate General, briefed us on Fayyad's accomplishments and gave him a glowing recommendation. Waiting for us at the consulate was Council General David Pearce and his staff. We had a few minutes before the briefing and were introduced to a middle-aged, impeccably dressed Fayyad.

Although we were missing two members of our delegation, we started the meeting with the suave, articulate, and intelligent Fayyad, who spoke fluent English. After a brief introduction, Senator Levin addressed the purpose of our project and asked Fayyad his opinion regarding the mission. Since Fayyad was the minister of finance, he spoke about the financial state of the Palestinian Authority. To the best of my recollection, he presented us with the following statistics: the budget for the Palestinian authority is $2 billion. In comparison, Israel's budget is $90 billion. In addition, Fayyed stated that 75 percent of Palestinians live in poverty while 40 percent of the overall Palestinian population is unemployed. He told us that the $150 million allocated to help the Palestinians from the United States go to NGOs who work directly with USAID.

Fayyad recommended if we wanted to invest, we should invest in the olive, food processing, technology, and Jerusalem stone industries.

Fayyad echoed the concerns we already heard about the occupation, road closures and the collapse of the economy. Since he was a member of Fatah, the Palestinian ruling party; he sounded alarmed about the growing support for Hamas, a Muslim political party opposed to the peace process. It was his belief that Israel empowered Hamas and that the party was gaining ground because of the services provided in refugee camps. He talked about the lack of vision the Israeli government had regarding the peace process. He pointed to our delegation about the lack of coordination between Israel and the Palestinian authority vis a vis the Gaza disengagement.

When pressed, he truly believed that both the Palestinians and Israelis could live and thrive side by side in peace and prosperity, but Israel needed pressure from the United States. A successful businessman in his own right, Fayyad wanted to help the current Palestinian administration succeed and was sacrificing his business to guide Palestine into fiscal solvency.

Naïvely, our delegation had left the United States thinking we could go to Palestine and adopt a project by providing low-interest loans to projects, not fully knowing the terrain. But we were quickly advised by Fayyad to invest in projects rather than loan money. He believed the sectors he recommended would be successful so our investment would net profits and help expand existing businesses and provide employment to local Palestinians. We left the meeting with a sense of hope about an uncertain future. I believe that like the Phoenix, the Palestinian people will rise from the ashes of tragedy and despair and thrive.

Our days were consumed with meetings mostly with USAID and local American NGOs. The sessions were informative. Each spoke to us about the tremendous needs of the Palestinian community and about the effects of state closures and the prevention of an individual's movements on the economy and society. They talked about initiatives that the USAID and other NGOs worked in Gaza and the West Bank, which seemed plentiful but are minuscule in comparison to what Israel and other surrounding communities were doing.

To a person, everyone we met with touted the high level of education of the Palestinian people. Human resources were the best natural resources for Palestine. The education levels of the Palestinian people exceed those of the surrounding nations, including Israel. The next best resource they told us was agricultural, and when allowed to farm and export their products, the Palestinians could tremendously improve their economy. Unfortunately, as farmers, they were hampered by Israel checkpoints, lack of access to water and lack of seeds for crops. Although most businesses in Palestine are small and family-owned, there were a few public companies with investors that were thriving.

Each time we discussed our program, we were encouraged to either invest directly in existing companies or work with banks to guarantee loans by local banks. Besides the hardship of the closures set by Israel, a Palestinian entrepreneur had a difficult time securing a loan from local banks because of their stringent collateral requirements. For a loan to be processed, the bank required the borrower to submit 125 percent collateral, and the loan must be paid back within a year.

We gained many insights into the economy and the obstacles Palestinians faced daily because of the occupation. Despite these impediments, Palestinians achieved greater levels of education than all of their neighbors. This was an amazing achievement considering Israel's effort to close Palestinian universities and schools.

Before leaving the United States, we had requested, and were promised, that our delegation would travel through the checkpoints. The Palestinians in the delegation who witnessed the problem firsthand wanted the rest of the delegation to see for themselves. Everyone, including Senator Levin, agreed to the course of action we devised in the US. Upon arrival, our official delegation was denied the request by the State Department. They allowed us to travel to Ramallah through alternative routes designated for Israelis and approved foreign personnel only. We traveled on highways which rivaled the best in the United States and Europe. Aside from a few soldiers and a few Israeli cars, the roads were empty. For the most part, we saw the imposing wall from a distance; it did not look menacing. We saw no checkpoints.

However, on closer inspection, we noticed the villages were divided and would be further disseminated once the wall was completed. At that moment I understood why our policymakers were unaware of the obstacles Israel uses to curb the movement of the Palestinians and their economy. The Palestinian problem was hidden in plain sight.

I was outraged at the apartheid road and the false appearances presented to us by traveling this route. Some honest officials from the American Consulate told us most journalists and public officials who go to the region rarely see how Palestinians live because of these alternate routes that mask the problem. I concluded there was a deliberate effort to prevent our officials from getting a clear picture of what was going on. Via these roads, we entered Ramallah within ten minutes.

The pristine streets ended at the back edge of the City of Ramallah. It was as if I was in a foreign land. The contrast of the roads was glaring. The Israeli roads were manicured and surrounded by flower beds on the sides and in the median, while the Palestinian streets were full of potholes and garbage. We arrived at a restaurant owned and operated by a member of one of Ramallah's original families. Young boys and girls stood outside peddling gum. My heart broke to see children as young as four standing for hours, being abused by people who shoved them aside and screamed at them, just so that they could help their families.

The restaurant was clean and relaxing. Judging from the pictures on the wall, the place was visited by foreign leaders and celebrities, as well as the upper echelon of the Palestinian community. We met with an impressive group of agency heads and bank leaders who had their pulse on the Palestinian economy. Like the others, they talked of the obstacles Palestinians face that prevent them from growing their economy. They encouraged us to meet with the technology sectors in Palestine.

Despite the Israeli occupation, the Palestinian people had found ways to excel at technology in the Middle East. With fewer Israeli restrictions, they could have transformed the region. People were excited about the prospect of success. With enough resources, they could become the supplier of technical support to the whole Arab world. Again, the opportunity did not pass without a discussion of business failures and stagnation. Once again, the people we met told us about the inhumane closures that prevent commerce from thriving.

Before leaving for Jerusalem, Senator Levin asked if a meeting with representatives of the technology sectors could be arranged. Without prior notification, the people set up an impressive presentation about their work and their impact on the community. After this spur of the moment visit, we went back to Jerusalem, again shielded from the ugliness of the wall and the checkpoints. During our trip back, our escort talked to the staff in detail about the criminal aspect of the wall and checkpoints. I made sure to point out the hours of waiting I had endured at the checkpoints during my previous two days of traveling by myself.

Before leaving the United States, Senator Levin's office had set up a meeting between Prime Minister Ariel Sharon and our delegation. No one, Arab or Jew, from the group was particularly excited about this meeting, except me. I wanted to meet the butcher of Palestine and confront him in person. I was not intimidated by this criminal who ordered the killing of people without remorse. Unfortunately, before our meeting, Sharon sent a message that he would meet only with Senator Levin, his staff, and the US ambassador. The four civilians in the delegation waited outside the Knesset.

Once reunited, we visited the Wailing Wall in Old Jerusalem and continued with our meetings set up by the American Embassy. The people we met with were a mixture of Palestinians and American economic development gurus trying to build an economy under extreme circumstances. Everyone pointed to the problems of restriction of movements and closures of towns by the Israeli government. As I listened, I became angry and sad that although my country was aware of these human rights violations, it continued its unconditional support of an oppressive state against the interest of the American people.

Although the Palestinian people are resilient and had the capability of building a prosperous country, the world, led by the United States Congress, was deliberately aiding Israel in oppressing the Palestinians. Would our investment of assistance be worth anything? At the conclusion of the meeting, I realized that the Palestinian community had no shortage of needs, plans or intellect; they just needed someone to work on their behalf to free them from the chains of oppression.

The investment we hoped for was a symbolic deed that would plant a seed, and when it grew, it would nurture not only the economy but would affect peace and justice in the area. I refused to believe that people of goodwill, who were open to discussion, would intentionally close their eyes on the oppressed. I knew I would continue to educate and cultivate a relationship that would eventually help the Palestinians.

Before I left on this trip, many from my community warned me about the potential ill effects of the mission. I opted not to share the negative comments with the team. I was apprehensive. However, I wanted to give our group every chance to succeed. Everyone we met with, from both the Palestinian and American sides, wanted to help the Palestinians as much as our delegation did.

This point was brought home during a side conversation with one of my companions whose beliefs showed that no one was on a mission to trick the Palestinian people or conspire to prevent them from achieving their goals. Everyone wanted to help, despite their love for Israel or Palestine, and I was sure what they heard in the meetings affected them as much as it touched me.

I also decided I could not allow my fear to stand in the way of connecting with people. I am an avid believer in the philosophies of Jesus Christ, Gandhi, Martin Luther King Jr., and Nelson Mandela, who all worked tirelessly for peace and justice for the afflicted.

These leaders succeeded because they built alliances that stretched beyond their communities, sending their messages out to their enemies to perpetuate until eternity. Although I am far from their status, I humbly chose to try to heed their call of working with others. With all their adversities, the Palestinians we met with were working to bring the two communities together.

Sitting in silence as we drove to the restaurant that evening, I thought of the events and remembered that my energy was better spent believing in the goodness of people rather than in their failings. This may be naïve thinking, but I knew I could not be a passerby. If nothing else, in its own way, the trip gave a powerful senator and two influential Michigan Jewish men the opportunity to hear about Palestinians from a group of people who live on the ground.

The Palestinian people in the Diaspora (those who became refugees in foreign countries) had attempted to help the Palestinians and worked hard to try to help the people who live in Palestine and refugee camps all over the world. But our work did not make a dent in the lives of those who were, and still are, suffering. As I sat silently, I began to examine my impact. Had my accomplishments stopped any invasions or curbed any settlements? Did I build schools for my people? Did I provide comfort to our people when bombs were dropped? Was I able to foster American legislation that would help the Palestinian people? Like many of my Palestinian friends, to my knowledge we worked hard holding demonstrations, writing poetry and newspaper articles to spread the message of brutality and oppression, but we did not stop the wall, the expansion settlements or the reduction of the checkpoints.

Our work was done with good intentions, but all it did was change a few minds and briefly alleviate our pain. We felt good about ourselves because we worked toward a cause, even though not one hospital, school or home was saved because of our activities. As we go on with our comfortable lives in the US and Europe, we rarely took a moment to be in the shoes of the gum children, who peddled gum late into the night to help their parents put food on the table.

As I looked out the window while the car rolled on the pristine roads, I thought that we should take a lesson from the American Jewish community, which was very successful in aiding Israel. We could not stop the Jewish community from pouring money into Israel, but maybe we could match their zeal by helping our brothers and sisters in Palestine.

Right then and there, I decided we could outmatch Israel's supporters if we could convince ourselves that we could make a difference. For those who think we have neither the power or the means to help, please look around. We have the intellect, the money, and resources to outmatch anyone in the world. What we need is the willingness to work. We can do our part by standing as one and helping our Palestinian brothers and sisters get rid of the occupation and live in a prosperous land. We've worked defensively to help, but now it was time to go on offense to assist our families in gaining their freedom.

My daydream was interrupted when someone asked if the Palestinian community was working on selling bonds for construction and building? The person pointed out that the Jewish community built Israel by selling bonds (investing in the public work) to finance its construction. The Zionist communities around the world supported the building of Israel including all the settlements. The bonds were, and are, issued by the State of Israel, and its local governments, and are sold around the world with a profitable interest rate. Most states in America invest in Israeli bonds.

His words bothered me when I thought how he'd helped create a country that destroyed mine. But I wondered whether we could replicate it. The purpose of selling bonds seemed financially astute and must be explored, so I asked him to explain how it worked. He said the Jewish community bought bonds as a wedding, birthday, or holiday gift for friends and family, so the money they invested doubled and a whole country was built.

Imagine giving a bond of Palestine in lieu of flowers, candy, or money to help the fight against occupation. I tucked the idea of bonds in my heart to explore later, but I genuinely believe this brilliant idea will give us the incentive to build while fighting for our freedom.

Meeting With the Enemy

We departed the hotel and I prepared myself for meetings with people who had made strategic decisions to expel my family from their homes, people who continue to abuse the Palestinians. I told myself to remain calm, stay strong and say what's on my mind without fear or malice. This was my opportunity to confront these people about their actions and the ramifications of those actions for my family.

On the ride to the first meeting, the topics of state closures, checkpoints, and occupation were raised. I told my car-mates about my three-hour checkpoint experience and how the Palestinians must endure humiliation every single minute of their lives. I also explained that my cousins, who lived 15 minutes from Jerusalem, were denied the opportunity to pray in the Holy Sepulcher and had not been in the church since 1993. I explained that my cousin, a dentist, had lost most of his patients because they could not cross the checkpoints to see him.

We arrived at Shimon Peres' office on time. However, Peres was being interviewed by a local TV station regarding a Palestinian-Israeli soccer player on the National Israeli team. The buzz was that the Palestinian player scored the winning goal to defeat the French National team. Since Arabs are not considered equal members of Israeli society, Israel was stunned. The Israeli TV news wanted reaction from an Israeli official and Peres was excited to show there was no difference between Israelis. Not true.

Revered in the West as a liberal, civil rights icon, and a peace dove, Peres had been an active participant in the suppression of Palestinians since the inception of the State of Israel. An ardent Zionist and ambitious Israeli leader, he started the regional nuclear arms race when he initiated secret atomic weapons programs in the 1950s and '60s. He was responsible for establishing some of the first Jewish settlements in occupied Palestine in the '70s. He served in the notorious Sharon government and enabled the pro-settler government of Prime Minister Netanyahu.

Peres was cordial and friendly toward us. We spent the first few minutes talking about soccer and the interview. He tried to convince us that Israel was an inclusive society. He thought the fuss about the winning goal ridiculous. Senator Levin explained the purpose of the meeting. We talked about the Israeli disengagement from Gaza and the peace process.

I found Peres to be insincere, offering frivolous advice. One of his solutions for our group was to develop a joint sports venture between Palestinians in Gaza and Israeli children. I kept silent. I wanted to hear a just solution to the conflict. Instead, Peres talked about nonsense. As he continued to speak, I became amused by his comments, which demonstrated he was apparently a very weak politician or just a clueless leader. In a meeting later that day, former Israeli Justice Minister Yossi Beilin explained to us that "Peres is about Peres." He sold his soul to stay in politics.

A couple of years before our visit, Israel had dismantled an Israeli settlement near Gaza and rearranged the occupation to save defense money by closing out Gaza and the 1.5 million people from the rest of Palestine. They took the soldiers out, evicted a few illegal settlers, dismantled their greenhouses, and surrounded the area with a wall and made the area surrounding Gaza into a buffer zone. With this move, Israel continued to occupy and punish the people of Gaza with less manpower and money. They made Gaza an open-air prison.

The closure of the settlements received accolades from the West, which viewed the move as a first step to creating the two-state solution agreed upon in the Oslo Accords. However, this strategic plan was done to keep the troops out of what they called "dangerous refugee camps in Gaza," while maintaining full control of the border. It also saved a tremendous amount of money for the Israeli Defense Forces. At that meeting, Peres told us about the difficulty of the decision because it upset the settlers. He tried to convince us that he had staked his whole political career on the promise that the Gaza disengagement would be the first step in the roadmap to peace. Peres viewed the Palestinians as victims who needed to be liberated but wanted the US to engage in the process.

I came out of the meeting thinking Peres was a weak politician who cared only about his career.

It was apparent that the Palestinians may be Peres' enemy, but Sharon is a thorn in Peres's side. Peres had the power to topple Sharon's government, but for his own political career or maybe his support to the strategic expansion of Israel, Peres allowed Sharon to form a coalition government. Therefore, in as much as his rhetoric was about peace and reconciliation, his actions proved otherwise. He allowed Sharon and his severely racist government to oppress millions of people.

After the Peres meeting, our escort drove us to a meeting with Deputy Prime Minister Ehud Olmert. To my total astonishment, I discovered that Senator Levin and the other members of the delegation did not know Olmert. I mentioned to the group that I wasn't sure if I had debated Olmert or his brother twenty years earlier at the University of Michigan in Dearborn. To prepare for our meeting, I read up on Olmert; he was a rising member of the Likud Party, a former mayor of Jerusalem, and one of the most conservative and racist members of Israeli society. I did not anticipate our meeting would be pleasant. He did not disappoint.

Our handlers from the State Department told us Olmert was a political hardliner but had a pleasant personality. They were right. As soon as we entered Olmert's office, Senator Levin asked him if he had been in Detroit, at the University of Michigan Dearborn, twenty years earlier. With smugness, he answered that he had been all over the United States and spoken at many universities. Senator Levin then asked if he had a brother in Michigan and Olmert said no, establishing him as the one I debated. He was curious about the questions regarding his visit to Michigan. We told him about the debate at the University of Michigan- Dearborn. He was amused. He looked at me and asked me who won, I replied: "I believe I did since I spoke about justice and human rights." I worried I had broken diplomatic protocol, but I did not want to stay silent.

Olmert soon revealed his true conservative and fascist philosophy. He told us he was the architect of the disengagement from Gaza. He referred to the Palestinians as "them" with disdain. I remained silent for a couple of minutes while he talked. He also referred to the Palestinians as "terrorists." I asked about the killing of Palestinians by his government. He calmly explained that Israel had no other option but to kill "them." "There were no other solutions," he said. My anger rose as he spoke about the justifiable killing of the Palestinian people. "We had to kill them before they killed us," I lost my cool. My friend Samir Mashni, the other Palestinian on our delegation, asked him about his vision after the disengagement.

Olmert bluntly but explicitly told us what was being done was clearing Gaza and a couple other cities to suit Israel. He bragged about the wall and its separation of cities, which created a prison for the people of Palestine. It took all my non-violent training to keep from exploding in his face. I could not believe how proud he was of his agenda of hate. I wished for a minute that all our American friends could hear him spewing hatred toward the Palestinians or a courageous journalist could interview him uncut. His hate bothered me so much that I stopped listening to him. In as much as his comments were vile, I was glad Senator Levin heard them in person.

Sensing that Olmert was charming but obnoxious, our Israeli handlers tried to soften the blow by telling us that his wife completely opposes his politics. In fact, we were told that Mrs. Olmert is an active member of Women in Black, an international human rights agency that vehemently opposes the Israeli occupation. Hoping they would ease the situation, they also said the Olmert children took to the politics of their mother and not their father. I left that day thinking that despite his wife's courageous stand, we have no hope for peace. I was wrong. Later in his career, Olmert changed his tune and began to talk about compromises. Just before he resigned as prime minister, he gave an interview to the Yedioth Ahronoth, Israel's leading newspaper, about soul searching and said the following:

> We must reach an agreement with the Palestinians, meaning a withdrawal from nearly all, if not all, of the [occupied] territories. Some percentage of these territories would remain in our hands, but we must give the Palestinians the same percentage [of territory elsewhere]— without this, there will be no peace.

He went on to say that this compromise would include some part of Jerusalem. Today, after the invasion of Gaza, these comments are obsolete. They were just words.

After this sobering meeting, we left Tel Aviv to meet with Yossi Beilin, whom only Senator Levin and I had heard of.

In his 2001 book, "My Brother's Keeper," Beilin explains the critical elements that led to the crisis in the peace process between Israel and the Palestinians. He did not settle for blaming Arafat for taking advantage of the outbreak of the Intifada or not ending it immediately. He pointedly directed the blame at Binyamin Netanyahu. He accused Netanyahu of doing everything he could to prevent the implementation of the Oslo Accords to which he had committed himself. He also counted the mistakes of Prime Minister Ehud Barak and the debacle of the subsequent Camp David summit. In addition to analyzing the crisis in his book, Beilin implored the Jewish community to return to sanity and negotiate peace with the Palestinians in good faith. He wanted a genuine and equal solution to the Palestinian-Israeli conflict. His aim of achieving a just, lasting, and comprehensive peace in the Middle East was based on the implementation of UN Security Council Resolutions 242 and 338 in all their aspects. He was a faithful dove who believed in equality for all people.

We had an honest discussion with Beilin; he did not mince any words. He viewed Peres as a cowering and weak leader who espoused Sharon's agenda. He regarded the proposed roadmap as a prolonged process that was going nowhere. He told us Israel's policies were the cause of all the violence in Israel and the occupied territories. He was not impressed with Abu Mazen, he called

Mahmoud Abbas, "a weak and reluctant leader." Beilin admired Marwan Barghouti, a man Israel sentenced to life in prison on trumped up charges. He thought Barghouti an excellent leader who could lead the Palestinians with prosperity and vision.

He blamed and implicated the United States for supporting crimes committed through Sharon's agenda of suppressing the Palestinian people. He was worried about the religious fervent and fanatic Israelis and settlers dangerous to Palestinians and Israelis alike. He had a lot of respect for the Palestinian people and felt them a true partner for peace. He was worried about the gimmicks used by Israel, especially the deployment from Gaza, which he called the "restructuring of the occupation." He insisted the disengagement from Gaza was a ploy Sharon used to save face in the world. He said that "at the end of the day what Israel is doing to the Palestinian people is harmful to the Israelis as well as the Jewish soul."

The more he talked, the more I wanted to hear him speak. He left Israel's Labor Party and established a new party. His time in Parliament would end the following September when Sharon was expected to finish the final pullout from Gaza, but he thought he and his new party could topple Sharon's government. He honestly felt the only process that would bring everlasting peace was the Geneva Peace initiative, but both sides had extremists taking leadership. He warned us that unless something was done to help the Palestinians now, Hamas would take over. He talked about the upcoming local elections and how Hamas was moving in with its well-financed social service programs. He implored Senator Levin to help the Palestinians.

Beilin was animated and did not want the meeting to end. He shed light on the extreme Israeli agenda and the tragedy of the Palestinians. I had no doubt Beilin was a patriotic Israeli, however unlike most Israelis, he did not believe the suppression of Palestinians was healthy for Israel. He thought the Middle East would continue to be inflamed unless a genuine and just resolution to the Palestinian situation was achieved.

Ignoring the Palestinian by Design

After taking pictures with Yossi Beilin, we headed back to our hotel for our next meeting with Mazen Sinokrot and Samir Huleileh, two Palestinian leaders who worked for American NGOs at the US Consul General's residence. At the Consulate General, the Consulate General and his staff gave us an informational package with instructions about the do's and don'ts while visiting Israel and Palestine. The following are excerpts from the package. It aims at deterring people and American government officials from traveling to the Palestinian territories.

All consulate employees and official visitors were told that:

- Travel within the West Bank is strictly prohibited. Official travel into areas of the West Bank is considered on a case-by-case basis if deemed mission essential. Transiting any part of the West Bank for expediency is likewise prohibited. It is incumbent on the employee to know where the borders of these territories are to avoid crossing them.

- Travel on Route 44 (Moi'in Road) is permitted only under the following circumstances: travel for official purposes, an armored vehicle is used, and the travel occurs during daylight hours.
- Traveling to the Old City's commercial districts of East Jerusalem and the Mount of Olives continues to be authorized during daylight hours. However, the Old City is off-limits between 11 a.m. and 2 p.m. on Fridays and during the hours of darkness all week.
- Employees and family members are urged to remain vigilant while traveling throughout Jerusalem, especially within the commercial downtown areas of West Jerusalem and the City Center. As always, personnel are urged to exercise a high degree of caution and common sense when patronizing restaurants, cafes, malls, and theaters, especially during peak hours. Large crowds and public gatherings should be avoided to the extent possible, and personnel should be alert to street vendors who often aggressively harass tourists.

These directives would not be dangerous except for the fact the people receiving them are responsible for making American policy. I find it hard to fathom how a diplomat could learn the reality of the occupation if they don't witness it for themselves. Every time I go to Palestine, I find myself wondering how anyone can experience what I observe and continue to support the Israeli occupation. But then again, I realize our policies toward Israel are not based on reality but the politics of fear, bias, misinformation, religious zealotry, stereotypes of Arabs, and distortions of history.

Before Israel banned me from going to Palestine, I visited several times with people from the Ramallah Federation and Project Hope to work on our annual program. Except for a few brave Americans and Europeans, few people experience the daily humiliation and degradation ten percent of the lucky Palestinians experience every day.

This trip opened my eyes to the unfortunate circumstances and ways the United States views the Palestinian/Israeli conflict. Even people of good will who see wrong done by Israel refrain from fixing the obvious problem, which is colonialism and the Israeli occupation.

Israel had maneuvered and manipulated our foreign policies in the Middle East to the point we cease to see a difference between our policies and theirs. At the end of our trip, Senator Levin continued his official travel to Iraq, while I bid my family goodbye and headed home to my husband and family. My trip back coincided with the two Jewish people from my delegation. Not wanting to miss my flight, I arrived at the airport five hours early knowing I would be detained. Of course, I was flagged by airport security. They had me stand to the side while everyone else who was not Palestinian moved effortlessly. When my two Jewish colleagues saw me, they asked what was going on. I told them it was normal I was profiled.

They were upset and approached the security people to explain. They showed them the letter we had from the State Department. Security asked for their passports. They had them wait for less than an hour then let them go to the plane. As for me, it took five hours before they let me go. Five minutes before my flight took off, they finally let me board the plane and leave. I was pissed and delighted at the same time. I wanted my colleagues to witness firsthand the experience every Palestinian or Arab goes through at the airport. When they saw me, they gave a sigh of relief and expressed disappointment about what they had witnessed. I shrugged it off as "nothing new."

Although the trip was educational, upon returning to Detroit we began putting cooperative agreements together. We assessed the trip and agreed to work together and recruit others to join us. However, within months, the situation in Palestine deteriorated, and Israel attacked Gaza. I felt that unless my Jewish colleagues publicly condemned Israel's actions, it would be hard to recruit others and succeed in this project. Within two years, the project died with no accomplishments.

26 / Going Home to Serve My Homeland

I have never regretted the visit with Senator Levin. I don't know its impact on the people who went with us. All I know is that it left me with an indelible ache in my heart. It confirmed for me that people of good will continue to support Israel regardless of its abuses. The Palestinian occupation is hidden in plain sight. Sometimes, I wish I could forget the past and the present and look forward to a brighter future of genuine peace and justice for the Palestinians and Israelis, who are victims of colonial power and circumstances. I can't.

The abuse is constant. The neglect and the reclassification and demonization of the Palestinian people are ongoing. Not a day goes by without a child, family, man, or woman being harmed by Israeli policies and the silent voices of world leaders who allow the abuse to continue. Therefore, I find it my duty to keep the injustices against the Palestinian people in the open. The daily killing and numerous violations don't bother me as much as the checkpoints and the daily treatment of the ten percent of the "lucky people," who had to endure daily humiliations by teenage soldiers who hate the people they encounter daily.

Since Senator Levin's visit, I have visited Palestine many times. I've traveled with young Palestinian Americans to Ramallah to volunteer and give back to our homeland every other year or when I have had the opportunity. I also went with my husband and nephew and saw the differences in the treatment just because my husband did not have an Arab surname.

During my travels, I make sure that, besides my family, I also visit friends like Father Iyad, a young priest dedicated to his parish and community. During one of my visits to Berzeit, where he served for a few years, he took me on a ride around town and introduced me to people. He saw injustice daily and tried to correct them, but since he is an Arab, certain things were beyond his power. Nevertheless, he wanted me to witness the daily crimes that occur at the edge of his city.

After the fifteen-minute tour, he parked at the top of a hill overlooking a checkpoint between the city of Ramallah and Berzeit. To cross the checkpoint, people had to walk half a mile to the gate, and once approved had to walk another half a mile to catch a ride to their destination. The road was dug up, which made the way hard to walk on for people trying to deal with everyday issues.

The Israelis built the checkpoint at the bottom of a steep hill. I watched as people struggled uphill to reach a ride. As we sat in silence, I watched older men and women with canes struggling to make it to the nearest taxi. I saw women with young babies dragging themselves and their kids up the hill in the scorching sun. No one dared to help them. I saw the pain on Father Iyad's face, as he was unable to support the helpless because the Israelis control their lives.

No matter how awful the situation was, it never compared to the time I arrived at the Qalandia checkpoint between Ramallah and Jerusalem in 2013. It was a mild afternoon, and I decided to go to Bethlehem. I took a cab to the checkpoint. Since it was the middle of the day, the line was light. I decided to try it out. As I exited the taxi several young children ran to me peddling gum and other junk I didn't need. They surrounded me and pleaded with me to buy something. I took out a wad of single dollars I kept in my jeans pocket for this purpose and bought gum from at least four boys. As my husband always tells me, "They know a sucker when they see one."

My heart ached for these young children; I was in awe of their ingenuity. They knew how to tug at my heart. I walked to the checkpoint with a fist full of gum, disregarding the stench of garbage, the dirty sidewalks, the dust, and the roaming soldiers with their machine guns. I entered the area to wait for my turn. I heard the yelling before I saw what was happening around me. I heard a rude female voice yell in broken Arabic. "Rouh, rouh, rouh, (go, go, go)." I looked and saw a woman standing in disbelief, with tears in her eyes. She sounded confused but did not know what to do. On a nearby wall, a young teenage boy looking like he was about to fall, stood pale and in pain. It was apparent he needed emergency medical care. He and his mother had to cross the Israeli checkpoint of Qalandia to get to the hospital. In their haste to get there, the distraught woman had forgotten the ID card for her ten-year-old boy, a catastrophic mistake that often results in restriction or stoppage of movement. Unlike the ID cards we carry here in the United States, the identification card issued to the Palestinians by Israel is used to enforce apartheid on Palestinians. The type of ID one has determines how much of historic Palestine one can access. Israeli Jewish citizens are free to move and live in virtually the whole country, while at the bottom end Palestinians in the occupied West Bank and Gaza are restricted to tiny enclaves. If one leaves his or her card home by mistake, they literally cannot pass through a checkpoint or go to another town.

And that is what I stumbled upon when I saw the Palestinian woman pleading with a female soldier to let her son cross the checkpoint to accompany his brother to the hospital. The soldier, a young woman about eighteen, did not care. She yelled again and told the woman to move out of the way. The people in line stood helpless. Some offered words of comfort but could not help her. They feared the soldiers and did not want to jeopardize their chances of crossing the checkpoint. The woman stood in tears, not knowing what to do. She had to take her son to the hospital. The boy could not stand anymore and might die if he did not receive medical care.

Like everyone else, I watched. I could not believe the cruelty. The ten-year-old apologized to his mom for forgetting his ID. His older brother slid to the dirty floor as his legs buckled. The woman started to cry. I peered at the window; the heartless soldier continued to process other people's papers with rudeness. Just when the situation became bleak, a middle-aged man with a briefcase in his hand approached the woman and offered to help. I listened. He told the women he would take her younger son to her home if she gave him directions. In his eloquent Arabic, he said: "Madame, my name is," I did not hear his name. "I own a business in Ramallah. Here is my business card." He reached for his wallet and showed the woman his ID. "Here are all my numbers." He asked her name. With tears in his eyes, he said to the woman, "What is your son's name?" The woman gave him the name. He went on to say, "I have kids of my own, I cannot imagine what I would do if this was my son." He continued, "I want you to put your faith in God and trust me, your little boy will be safe with me, if you give me your address and names of people I can deliver your kid to, I will do it for you. You need to take your other son to the hospital. Madame, please trust me, I consider your son my son."

Other people in line urged the woman to trust the stranger. A woman trying to cross the border offered to go with the man. Overcome with anxiety and gratitude, the woman reluctantly allowed the boy to go with the stranger.

Watching the exchange, people in line let the woman go ahead of them, people helped her and her boy as the soldier stamped their permit to go to the other side. The mother thanked the strangers who helped her. I stood in disbelief.

The two strangers took the younger boy as they once again assured the mother her son would be okay. With my American passport in hand, they let me pass without a problem. I was ashamed of myself for not jumping in to help. I was disgusted with the cruel soldier whose hate toward the people made her heartless and evil. Even if I wanted to help, I did not know how.

I had often read and heard stories about the cruelty of the checkpoints but reading and witnessing are different. To this day, every time I think of this woman, I cry. I remember the kindness of the strangers who abandoned their tasks to help. I still see the pale face of the sick teenager and wonder if he was medically saved. I think of the ten-year-old who made a grave mistake by not taking his ID with him. And I think of the mother and what she would have done if the stranger had not stepped in to help her. As for the soldier, she was conditioned to hate Palestinians through her military training and therefore, I doubt if she had any remorse. The noose on Palestinian lives tightens daily, while US support for Israel intensifies.

I am haunted by this and many other images I witnessed while visiting my homeland. Nevertheless, I always want to go there to witness the truth for myself. But that stopped when Israel banned me from going to my birthplace on July 8, 2014.

27 / My Husband Encounters the Israeli Occupation

Throughout my life, I considered myself lucky to have many gentle males who supported me with their love and compassion. My grandfather, father, and uncles always had my back. So I was particular about the men I dated. I wanted someone a thoughtful, sincere, honest, and an all-around kind man. I found all those qualities in my husband, Bob Morris, whom I met at work. I am a lucky person who found pleasure and friendship in public service. No wonder, I found the man who will stand by me for the rest of my life at the Wayne County Executive Office. He and I differ on when the spark of our love ignited. Nevertheless, in 1997 we pledged our love to each other in a small ceremony at his house near Lansing, Michigan.

Our childhoods were so different. Yet if one looks closely, one can see the similarity of how we were molded into who we are. He grew up at the knees of his father, Ken, whose family was Jewish. But their religion was put on the back burner in order to survive the economic difficulties of the Great Depression. Ken moved to Detroit and became a labor leader. Bob's mother, Doris, came from Nebraska and always supported her husband's activities.

I grew up wanting to bring justice to the Palestinian people. When I married Bob, I knew he would have my back and I would always watch out for him. Throughout our marriage, he has supported and encouraged me to stand up for what I believe even when I wanted to give up. He had been to Palestine and Israel long before he knew me, and was always sympathetic to the Palestinian cause. My insights helped bolster his position.

He has enjoyed a distinguished career as a public servant who worked for the state of Michigan, Wayne County government and Southeast Michigan Council of Governments. He gave valuable insight into how to reach out to influential leaders regarding Palestinian issues. Besides being my best editor, he stood by me as I traveled throughout the United States for meetings with the communities and public officials to lobby on behalf of the Palestinian cause.

As a young man, Bob, who grew up supporting Israel, traveled around Europe and Israel in 1975 after a two years stint as a teacher and before he started his career in government. He came back from Israel conflicted about what he saw. He started to question the discriminatory practices of the State of Israel, but since this was not his focus, he set this issue aside until I came along.

Throughout our dating and marriage, I talked to Bob about my childhood, family, and teachers in Ramallah. We both knew it was a matter of time before we would visit. The opportunity presented itself in 2008 when we took our nephew, Tony Dawson, a member of the Tennessee National Guard, to celebrate Easter and explore Jordan and Palestine.

We traveled to Jordan, where we visited my Aunt Salma and her husband and Nawal, who retired in Jordan. We spent a few days exploring historical sites and left for Palestine. It was Tony's first visit to the region. It was Bob's first visit to Jordan. We hired a driver who stayed with us on all our tours. We were free to go anywhere we pleased.

Jordan was a land of striking contrasts. The country mixes bedouin traditions with modern lifestyles. We saw ancient ruins of past civilizations, intermixed with contemporary buildings. We saw the magnificent landscapes as we visited the Dead Sea, the lowest point on earth; Jerash, an ancient Roman city; Petra and Aqaba. We even stumbled on a parade for King Abdullah of Jordan. We traveled with no limitations. No one stopped us, there were no checkpoints. The people were gracious and hospitable. We felt welcomed.

After a few days, we left from Sheikh Hussein crossing to northern Israel. The security was a little lax, however, my nephew was exposed to extra search and scrutiny. With the name Tony Dawson, he did not go through the usual five to seven hours of interrogation like Americans with Arab surname usually go through. Even with the lenient security, young soldiers and security officers in plain uniforms were all over the place.

We decided to tour and visit holy places and some family in Israel. There were no checkpoints or army patrols. Their highways were modern and well maintained. We saw the contrast between Arab towns and Jewish towns, but we did not see the overwhelming presence of the military. We visited Nazareth and Yaffa, In Nazareth, I insisted on visiting my former teacher who was then the Catholic Bishop of Nazareth. The driver was reluctant to take us since we did not have an appointment. I wanted my husband to meet the man who was an influential part of my life when I was a pre-teen. As we arrived at Bishop Marcuzzo's residence and office, the driver warned us not to be disappointed if the bishop refused to see us. The driver told my husband that the bishop is a very busy and important man. We received the same warning from the bishop's secretary, who told us he had a very busy schedule, but agreed to check with him anyway.

The secretary returned to the lobby moments later, then ushered us in with a welcoming attitude. the bishop would be with us in five minutes. Suddenly, our driver's and the secretary's attitudes changed regarding we three Americans. They were impressed by this welcome. Bishop Marcuzzo did not disappoint; within minutes, he was coming toward us with a great smile and extended hands to greet us.

I introduced him to Bob and the driver (who still could not believe his eyes). We went down memory lane. After exchanging stories about the good old days, the bishop talked about the discrimination his parishioners faced in Israel. He talked about the difficulty the priests and nuns encounter daily. After an hour, we left to continue our tour.

In Yaffa, my mother's birthplace, we stopped to see her aging aunt, Sister Marie Stella, a nun, who dedicated herself to helping cancer patients in Jerusalem. She was surprised to see us. She was in enthralled with us, especially Bob. I told her he was a lobbyist. When other nuns came into the room, she told them "Bob tells Congress and the president what to do." My aunt was clearly impressed with my husband! Bob and I glanced at each other with smiles.

After a great visit to Yaffa, we headed to Jerusalem, where Father Shawki arranged for us to stay at an inn inside the ancient walls of Jerusalem, near the New Gate.

This unique hotel is used by guests of the Latin Patriarch of Jerusalem. The Gothic hotel reminded us of an era gone by. The icons on the walls are from centuries old. The hotel was charming and convenient. We checked into two adjacent rooms and went out to explore before dark.

The streets were full of tourists who came from all over the world to celebrate Easter and Passover. Bob haggled with shopkeepers. He believes that negotiations with shopkeepers are part of the fabric of Jerusalem. I, on the other hand, know the pressure imposed on these vendors. Despite these people having their business for generations, Israel is trying to squeeze them out by imposing new policies and taxes.

Upon learning I was Palestinian, the clerks went out of their way to serve us. As we walked from one alley to the next, we watched how some tourists were ushered away from the shops by their Israeli tour guides. This ancient and historical city, considered by many to be one of the holiest places in the world, is filled with a treasure trove of historical architecture, religious culture, and tradition.

Many world powers, including the Greeks, the Romans, the Ottomans, and the British, have tried to take over but failed to change the hearts of its indigent inhabitants, who provide the heartbeat and the smell of the city. With the exception of the soldiers who walk around with their hands on the triggers, Jerusalem marches as it has since ancient times. As we walked the streets, we watched and heard the sounds of joy, sadness, love, and hate intermingled. Jewish settlers hurriedly walked by Muslim and Christian Palestinians as if they did not exist. Muslim and Christian Palestinians looked at the Orthodox Jews with disdain. There are many reasons for this scorn. These settlers are stealing their identities and their land.

This ancient and holy city can tell thousands of stories of people who lived and still live there. Most who are Palestinians can trace their lineage to pre-biblical times, yet are denied citizenship by the Israeli government. Among those living in the old sector of Jerusalem inside the walls are friends and family members. They steadfastly stay in Jerusalem despite all the hardships. The city is surrounded by stones that were built on top of ancient stones. Jerusalem and its inhabitants saw many conquerers prosper and then be doomed. The restrictions put on the people by the Israeli government are as harsh as those of the Roman Empire. The Christian and Muslim residents are threatened daily with expulsion and prison simply because they are Palestinians.

The city is visited by millions of pilgrims, but few if any truly know the people of Jerusalem. We walked from the New Gate through the narrow streets; we sat at a café in the Christian sector and watched the people of Jerusalem go on with their lives. We always wondered when pilgrims come to Jerusalem what do they see? As we walked around the vibrant, yet sad, city, we saw Christian, Muslim and Jewish residents walking on the same cobble streets, going on with their daily lives. While Muslims and Christians live in harmony together, their Jewish occupiers rarely see their humanity. Jerusalem is called the city of peace but rarely experiences tranquillity. Its conquerers hold all the power, with its inhabitants struggling to survive. Its ancient stones reflect its spirit, strong and enduring despite the constant struggle. Jerusalem and Jerusalemites will themselves to be resilient.

Within the ancient walls, we walked with our nephew as we told him tales from our memories. Bob talked about his stay in Jerusalem at a hostel in 1975. As we walked, we saw a kaleidoscope of people. The tourists sat at popular cafes, as directed by their guides. Catholic monks, in various uniforms, strolled or hurriedly walked to their destinations. Closer to the Holy Sepulcher, we watched Russian Orthodox nuns huddled in corners talking to neighbors. And of course, everywhere we went there were Israeli policemen and soldiers with their automatic weapons.

We did not let the sight of soldiers disturb us. With Bob and Tony present, it was unlikely I would encounter a problem. We attended some of the Easter festivities. We walked the way of the cross behind the Franciscan procession, just as I did as a child. The Saturday before Easter, we attended the festival of lights with the Christians of Jerusalem. I took Bob and my nephew and walked them into my memory lane I showed them St. Louis Hospital where I spent my last months working with my aunt before I left for the United States as a teenager. We went to the Holy Sepulcher and watched the tradition of a Muslim clerk locking its door.

Unlike many of the tourists who come on pilgrimage to the Holy Land and leave without seeing its true beauty and its people, we saw the irony, fury, scorn, and despair of the city. We also saw the tender moments of neighbors talking to neighbors about the Easter festivities. We paid attention to the old women who sat all day at the corner of Bab-ALamoud trying to sell their vegetables. Vendors like them are not there for the amusements of the pilgrims, they are just trying to live in a cruel world that sees them as a nuisance.

With the help of Father Shawki, we took part in the official Easter ceremony. We were enthralled by the festivities and various processions during Holy Week and celebrated with our nephew Tony as he attempted to drink his first beer.

We left Jerusalem behind and went to Ramallah, then to Bethlehem. Bob and Tony saw the massive apartheid wall for the first time. At Bethlehem, they noticed the oppressive wall surrounding the cities we traveled to. We went through checkpoints and experienced the callousness of the young soldiers who mistreated the Palestinian people. Going through the checkpoint is not like reading about them. It dehumanizes the occupier and the occupied. The sight of soldiers with their fingers on the trigger was menacing. The people were moved like cattle. Some went through the checkpoints with scrutiny, others were rejected without an explanation. With our American citizenship, we went through without a problem. A family in line behind us was banned without explanation. They had all the proper permits, but the soldiers did not care.

As we left the Bethlehem checkpoint in a bus, we saw tears and dejection on one particular family. The man and woman in their thirties walked to the bus holding their children's hands. Witnesses to their rejection tried to soothe their pain. They climbed into our bus, the people around them tried to ask what happened. Through tears, the young man, a Christian pharmacist from Gaza, told us it took him five years to get a permit to travel with his family to Bethlehem during the holiday. It was the first time his family had left Gaza since his children were born. He described the joy of receiving the permit. He did not understand, how foreign soldiers can disregard an official Israeli permit. He kept saying through tears "they gave us permits, this is their stamps." Many on the bus, told him not to despair. They told him to wait an hour and try again. One person said, " It's arbitrary, the next soldier, may let you enter without a problem." I translated for Bob and Tony the conversation on the bus. In his naïve way, Tony whispered, "It is not fair." Bob was angry and sad just as I was. Bob often mentions this family when talking about the Palestinian-Israeli issue. Bob did not need to see what is happening to the Palestinians to believe. He is well read and understood the conflict and understands America's role in it. As a believer of justice for all, Bob was one of the first people to advocate a one-state solution for the Palestinians and the Israelis with one person one vote and equal justice for all.

Bob and I took other trips to Palestine together. The last was in 2014, when we went to the American Federation of Ramallah, Palestine's first convention in Ramallah, just a couple of weeks before I was banned from traveling to Palestine. Like me, Bob believes in the power of witnessing what is going on in Palestine. Upon my ban from Israel, Bob worked tirelessly with our Congressional members to persuade Israel to lift the ban, to no avail.

28 / Banned from my Homeland

In my recurring nightmares about soldiers running after me, my young sisters, and brother, I try to scream, but nothing comes out of my mouth. I turn to look for a second and my family disappears. I wake up with sweat, and I thank God it is only a dream.

The nightmare became a reality at the Allenby Bridge between Jordan and Israel. We had spent the previous three days visiting Petra, Wadi Rum, and Amman. I returned to Palestine with Project Hope on July 8, 2014, and found myself surrounded by soldiers and plainclothes border patrol clutching their guns, inspecting and directing us.

Wherever we went, the gun-toting officers eyed our group. The Allenby Bridge and Sheik Hussein border are well known as painful and uncomfortable border crossings. Complaints about the ill-treatment and harassment of people by the border patrol are legendary. I went through several bouts of humiliation at this border, but was never afraid until July 8, 2014.

I suppose my nightmare began the moment I received the call from the president of the American Federation of Ramallah Palestine, asking me to sub for one of the Project Hope leaders, who could not travel with the group for personal reasons. As one of the founders and coordinators of this program for many years, I agreed to return to Palestine with a new batch of Project Hope candidates. I did not want to delay or cancel this excellent program. But I would have rather not traveled so soon after my June visit to Palestine.

***

Earlier in June, my husband and I were in Palestine to attend the first historic Ramallah Convention in Ramallah two years after the American Federation of Ramallah Palestine voted to hold its annual yearly convention in Ramallah, Palestine. Since the vote took place while I was president of the Federation, I was ecstatic. Bob and I were going to Palestine for the convention, then traveling to Greece for our annual vacation. We opted to go through Tel-Aviv. Upon landing, I became a little agitated knowing I would be subjected to harassment by the Israeli border patrol and immigration. I was ready for it, but nothing happened; it was a breeze.

As a seasoned traveler to the area, I anticipated the drill. I knew I was not welcome in my homeland. We walked off the plane and stopped at the border police. My husband went first. The young immigration officer smiled at him and asked the typical questions. She stamped his passport and welcomed him to Israel. It was my turn. I was ready for the interrogation. She looked at my passport; she checked me out. She began to ask questions. When she turned her face, I mumbled to Bob something like "here we go again." The young lady asked me "What did you say?" I told her, "You did not ask my husband any questions, but you are asking me questions." She gave me a "whatever" look, stamped my passport and wished us good luck. I was floored. I wanted to kiss her. I wanted to yell at the top of my lungs: "I am Palestinian," but knew better. I kept my mouth shut.

The organizers met us at the airport. We had to wait for other conventioneers who were detained for an hour or so and left for Ramallah without any difficulty. Bob and I had a great time in Ramallah. The Palestinian people went out of their way to be kind to the visitors. They treated us like royalty. The prodigal sons and daughters were home again. The governor, the dynamic Laila Ghanim, mayor of Ramallah, and other dignitaries greeted and welcomed us with open arms. President Abbas spoke at the main event. We had four days of pure joy. We partied, sang, and walked the streets of Ramallah. Nothing stopped us, including the massive ugly wall which sections Palestine and makes life hell for people.

We met people from throughout the United States. We got to experience Ramallah through the eyes of Palestinian Americans who were returning to their homeland, either for the first time since they left in the 1950s and '60s, or for the first time ever. We visited our cousins and went sightseeing.

I was a frequent traveler to Palestine. Bob had also traveled to Palestine three times with me and once on his own in 1975. Since I was on the board of directors of the American Federation of Ramallah, Palestine, I had to attend meetings and work on the convention business. While I was busy, Bob roamed the city on his own or with people. He befriended people from the US and Ramallah. He went to the local bakery and ate Timriya, a tasty Palestinian pastry made only during specific holidays. Alone or with others, he was treated well. He did not fear, on the contrary, he felt as safe as in any other place.

The people who organized the convention did not disappoint. Among the festivities, we participated in an old-fashioned reenactment of traditional celebrations with parades from the city hall to the Boy Scout headquarters. Despite the tensions growing between Israel and Hamas in Gaza, the outdoor ceremony lasted until midnight. Memories of this event still give me goosebumps.

I reconnected with some classmates from elementary school. I also reconnected with alumni from Project Hope, who came back because they felt a connection to the land.

Bob and I sneaked out to Jerusalem, Bethlehem and other towns and met with our friends, including Father Iyad Twal, a dear friend who visited us in Michigan. As a bonus, we attended the ordination of a young priest in my old church, the Holy Family Church in Ramallah.

During the stay, I participated in official meetings with American Consul General Michael Ratner, who took time to meet with our delegation. He encouraged us to work with him and his staff on projects in Palestine. We talked about collaborative work between the federation and the State Department. We set some goals, including the continuation of Project Hope. He assigned a staffer to work with us. Via an email, I introduced Dr. Jessica Haddad and attorney Natalie Qandah to the staff at the consulate general.

Haddad and Qandah, who had led the project before, were thrilled at the invitation to meet with the State Department while in Jerusalem. They had already established a line of communication with the White House Engagement Office and the State Department. Since they had both led the program previously, they provided details of their travel to members of the Palestinian/Israeli desk at the department.

After five days in Ramallah, Bob and I left at night to Tel Aviv, on our way to Greece. We rented a local van with a young Christian Palestinian driver who had an Israeli ID. The young man wore a large crucifix, intended for show. He was full of confidence. He bragged about never having trouble going to the airport. We believed him because he came highly recommended by our hotel. He was sure that we would "not have trouble." He took the less congested back roads with fewer checkpoints. He did not count on the temporary checkpoints Israel set up whenever they saw fit. He reassured us more than once that all was well. "I have all the proper documents, don't worry," he said with confidence.

He told us about his family and the difficulty of being a Christian. Several times he mentioned he was Christian. With the large cross on his chest, I wanted to say, "No shit, Sherlock," but stopped myself. We talked about the cost of living. Like all cab drivers in the Middle East, once he gained the trust of the passengers, he didn't stop talking. And, of course, we spoke about Israeli occupation and the illegal annexation of Jerusalem.

He clearly saw the discrimination between Jewish and Arab Israeli citizens. Although born in Jerusalem and tracing his ancestry for several generations, he was only considered a resident and not a citizen. Israel has the right to revoke his residency without cause any time it sees fit. Our trip was a lesson on the ugly facts on the ground. He had a college degree but could find only menial jobs. He used his car as a taxi during the evening to make ends meet. He pays his taxes but does not have the same access to services as an Israeli Jew.

The distance between Ramallah to Ben Gurion Airport is only 32 miles. On a typical day, the trip should take not more than an hour. But since most roads are segregated for Israeli use only, traveling to the airport is an art. Ninety percent of Palestinians cannot use these Israeli segregated and direct routes. Although our driver was not Jewish, he had permission to go on the road with his Israeli ID. The hotel management recommended we leave for the airport about five hours early. We did as directed. The driver arrived in the lobby on time. We knew that Israel could erect barricades to complicate the lives of Palestinians whenever and wherever they see fit, so we decided not to chance it.

Along the way, we saw a makeshift checkpoint manned by several soldiers. We shifted in our seats, but the driver remained calm. He assured us that all was well. "It's normal don't worry. Take out your passport," he said. We complied. A young soldier carrying a machine gun approached the car. Two other soldiers were right behind him. They had their fingers on the triggers. They spoke in Hebrew to the driver. He gave them his ID and got out of the van. The soldier turned his attention to us. We gave him our passports. He asked us in perfect

Australian English "Where are you going?" We told him we were on our way to the airport. He followed the others toward the driver, who was surrounded by soldiers, with one of them pointing the barrel of his gun directly under the driver's chin. Bob became nervous, feeling like he was behind the Iron Curtain in the 1950s. I was familiar with their tactics, so I was concerned but not terrified. In fact, I had come to expect this abusive behavior. After a few minutes, the driver returned, got in the van and began to drive as if nothing happened. He looked in the rearview mirror said, "Don't worry, it's normal." I muttered, "Goddamn, there is nothing routine about this."

We continued to the airport without incident. Our van and passports were briefly inspected a mile from the airport, standard procedure in Israel. We entered the airport and walked to the airline counter as we do at all other airports around the world. We were happy because we were first in line. The smiling attendant motioned us to approach. She began the process and stopped when she discovered we did not pay our exit tax. She told us how to go about paying the taxes. She also assured us we would not lose our place in line. Bob left to pay, and I stayed in the vicinity as she directed us to do.

I was amazed at the ease of this process. I wanted to pinch myself to see if I was awake. The controversy over the mistreatment of Palestinians is noted throughout the world. I was the subject of abuse at this very airport. I was in shock at the courtesy afforded to us that day. I deduced the new conduct was because I was with Bob. We had unusual and exceptional service. Everyone was polite.

Bob and I commented on the ease of entering this secure airport without a problem. We noticed a line with hundreds of people in one of the corners. We thought the line belonged to another airline. Seeing Bob, the airport attendant ushered us to the front of the line. She examined our luggage and asked us about a tag from the security line. We looked at each other, then at her; the look on our faces told her we did not know what she was talking about. Simultaneously, we all realized we did not go through proper security checking. She pointed at the long line and asked us if we went through it. We said no.

She apologetically told us she could not proceed with check-in until we went through security. Our flight was leaving in an hour and the line was so long. Sensing that we were frustrated, she asked someone from security to come over. She explained the situation. The stars must've been lined up right that night. The security officer took us to the front of the VIP line, and within minutes, we were cleared to go. We passed every hurdle except the last station, where an attendant took me for further interrogation. We made it to the plane with time to spare and without scrutiny. It is so unusual for me to go through this. Bob and I joked about the experience. We left for Greece and had a great vacation.

Upon my return to the United States, I received an urgent call asking if I could substitute for one of the leaders of Project Hope. Since I worked as a consultant, and my schedule was flexible, I agreed to return to Jordan and then to Palestine. I was still jet-lagged when I again boarded the plane to Jordan. I met the group and went to Wadi Ram. We had an excellent orientation. I got to meet impressive young people who were eager to begin the program. At Wadi

Ram, we ate delicious rice and lamb cooked in the underground hot sand. We drank Arak and danced the night away. At 4 a.m. we ran barefoot in the desert to the east to see the magnificent sunrise.

We did not leave to go to the bridge until the afternoon. The group was fluctuating between nervousness and euphoria. They had heard the horror stories of Palestinians crossing the Israeli border and were afraid. Dr. Haddad and I assured them all would be well if they didn't respond to the abuse.

I felt sorry for the participants who were not used to ill treatment by authorities. Most grew up in American middle-upper class suburbia with little or no interaction with law enforcement or border patrol. Since I already had my visa, I did not think I required another permit. Technically, I should have been allowed to come and go without a visa since I was born in Palestine. But that was not the case. I was allowed to stay in my birthplace for only three months at a time. I could petition the Palestinian authority to give me a residency, but it must be approved by Israel.

As we drove toward the bridge, Jessica drilled everyone about how to avoid getting delayed. "Be polite, cooperate, don't respond to their abuse," were some of her instructions. We said not to be afraid and stay calm. We tried to lighten the mood by cracking jokes. The Arabic bus driver and the Jordanian police officer dropped us at a building where we boarded another bus to the "no-man land" to go to the Israeli side of the bridge. They wished us luck and introduced us to someone in uniform who took our passports, and to check if we had current Jordanian visas. He asked me to follow him. It was scorching hot. The air was suffocating. I could smell the cigarette smoke from miles away. Since I am allergic to cigarettes, I felt a migraine coming. The building was dusty, men in uniform were milling around. Porters shuffled luggage from one side to another. The man who took our passports escorted me to an office in the back of the building. A man with a pressed uniform stood and shook my hand and asked me to wait. He had a cigarette dangling from his mouth. The ashtray on his desk was full. His office was dusty and reeked of smoke. He asked how long we had been in Jordan. I responded three days. He asked the purpose of the trip. I said, "We are American Palestinians traveling to volunteer in Palestine." He stamped the passports, extended his hand to me, and wished us luck.

We rode to the next stop. Before we approached the Israeli sign, the bus stopped for inspection. We noticed some coaches were lined on the side of the street waiting for a guard to usher them forward. Our driver told us our bus would go to the front of the line. The people waiting were Palestinians and therefore had to wait longer. Someone in uniform directed the driver to move forward. Several soldiers with mirrors on long selfie sticks and other equipment searched underneath the bus. Two officers came on board and asked for our passports. After a few minutes, they communicated with the bridge. They gave us the green light and off we went.

Jessica and I again tried to ease the tension with a few jokes. Within minutes we arrived at the central office at the border. Plainclothes patrols greeted us and directed us to go to the right line. A few Arab porters helped us take the luggage to the chutes in front of the main building. Two young undercover security officers walked around checking us out. Other young men with machine guns paced back and forth among the people arriving at the building. We stopped at a line and waited our turn at a window outside the building. Jessica was first in line, and I was last. We cleared the first hurdle with no problem. An undercover police officer asked one of the participants to go with him. I asked him politely if I could join her. He was kind and said yes. We sat for a few minutes. He checked her passport and let her go.

The line to the immigration queue was short. It was late in the afternoon. The attendant, whom we dubbed "the one-eyebrow Barracuda," was rude. Except for Jennifer Patterson and Helen Hyde, the two members of our group without Arab surnames, she gave us all a paper indicating we would undergo further inspection. Jennifer and Helen almost got through without a hitch, until the Barracuda discovered they were with the group. She made them sit with the rest of us. They took our passports and told us to wait in a section mostly dedicated to Palestinian travelers. Jessica and I knew the routine. To ease the tension, Jessica quipped "We are in the Arab VIP section, we are privileged." She mimicked someone who spoke broken English.

After a few minutes, they began the interrogation. They first called Jennifer Patterson. After half an hour, Jennifer came out crying. One by one, they took the participants. Jessica tried to ask what was going on. A young civilian woman came to speak to us. She asked for the leader. Jessica got up to meet her. She demanded we give her our itinerary. Based on experience, we knew better than to have any papers that might create problems at the border. Jessica told her that she was happy to provide her with our schedule if she would give us access to Wi-Fi. Of course, she did not agree. She left for a few minutes and came back asking for our plans during the trip. We explained to her, and she knew because they had all our luggage, that we didn't have any paper with us. Without access to Wi-Fi, we could not provide them the information they needed. The report was on our laptops or tablets. She looked at us with disdain and said, "Either you give me your schedule, or you will be denied entry."

The authority already had access to our luggage, and they had already searched our belongings. They used these tactics to intimidate us. We had only one or two working phones. Our international service was not working. We could not talk directly to the American Embassy. Initially, we tried not to disturb our families, mainly because it was night in the US. We maintained our composure and tried to find a solution. I was mad but knew better than to show any emotion.

When the interrogator came back to talk to Jessica and me, we asked her kindly to connect us to the American consul general in Jerusalem. She refused. The clock was ticking. We watched as people went through without a problem as we languished on the metal seats. By then most of the group was separated and put either in different rooms or in different sections of the hallway.

Concerned, I went to one of the offices and asked to see the supervisor. He told me it appeared we were lying and unless we produced a schedule, we would be denied entry. I explained to him that we were happy to comply with their request for our agenda if we have access to our emails. "That is not my problem," he said without lifting his face to look at me. I asked again if we could call the American Embassy. He told me he did not have a problem with my calling anyone, but not on his phone. We had a significant predicament. The one or two phones still working after three hours of waiting could not make local calls to Israel. After his interrogation, Alfred Siniora found a way to charge his phone, it was about 9 p.m. Jordan time so we could not call the State Department in Washington. I called my husband in Canton, Michigan, and told him what was going on.

In the meantime, an angel from heaven, in the form of an Israeli border worker, secretly gave us her phone and helped us call the 24-hour hotline at the American consul general in Jerusalem. We left a message and received a callback within minutes. We explained our problem. We verbally gave the man on the phone our agenda, which he offered to type and send to the authority. We gave him a number to call us back on, and he did. I asked him to speak to the supervisor and he agreed. I took the phone to the director's office and kindly asked the supervisor to talk to the consulate representative. They spoke for a few minutes. The manager gave me the phone back and told me to go wait.

Before we left on the trip, Jessica and Natalie had given the information to the State Department. Upon learning I was going to be back in Palestine, I sent messages to Richard Buangan, chief, Public Diplomacy Section, and Steve Bitner at the American Consulate in Jerusalem, the two staffers I had met while in Palestine a few weeks earlier. I told them our plans and requested a meeting with the consul general. They were happy we reached out to them. They gave us the number of the Special Consular-Services and asked us to call if we encountered a problem.

As we were going through our ordeal, I related my conversation with Richard and Steve and asked him to notify them of our dilemma. He agreed. The staffer from the Consulate General tried to help, but the Israelis did not budge.

One by one, the team came out of the cross-examination with horror stories, including threats of possible imprisonment if they did not cooperate. These officials accused them of lying to the authorities. They asked them questions about their grandparents and parents. They questioned Jennifer why her mom had left Palestine for the US She replied, "She was young, and her parents wanted to leave for a better life." They told her not to be stupid like her mother who left Israel and did not think Israel is a good country. Andrew said they threatened him with jail. They separated members of our group and forced them not to talk to each other. They asked them if they spoke Arabic and they responded no, they were accused of lying. They wanted to know where their grandparents lived when they were in Palestine. Most did not know the particulars but knew what city they lived in before immigrating to the US.

Undercover security people walked around us. We fluctuated between pacing and sitting trying to pass time in the designated area. We kept calm. There was no reason to panic. We knew the drill — at least I knew the drill — several hours of harassment and then released with no explanation. Their actions were predictable, or so I thought. Crossing the border into Israel is always a journey of abuse and bigotry. But I never thought they would deny us entry. After several hours of questioning and intimidation, the supervisor came out and told us we were denied entry and would not be allowed in Palestine for five years. I felt like someone stuck a knife in my back. I wanted to cry, but I kept my emotions in check. Jessica and I could not afford to fall apart. The supervisor berated us for lying about the trip. "You did this to yourself, you lied to us." I looked around the room and saw the hurt on the group's faces. I also noticed that we were surrounded by more people with guns. They told us to collect our luggage and go out to wait on the curb for a bus that would take us back to Jordan.

Jessica and I hugged everyone and whispered to them to stay calm and not say anything, "the walls have ears." Outside, waiting for the bus with undercover cops and guns pointed at us, one of our participants could not take it and began to sob. He came to volunteer with us and was looking forward to seeing his grandfather who lived in Jerusalem. Jessica, Amanda, and Sonya tried to comfort him. In the meantime, I was talking with the authorities about transportation. They told me that a bus would take us to the Jordanian border and then we were on our own. Jessica called her dad in Amman and asked him to help with transportation and hotel. He arranged for taxis to take us to the hotel he reserved for us after crossing and clearing Jordanian immigration. On the bus to the Jordanian side, everyone was deflated. Jessica and I could not afford to deal with our emotions. We sprang into action to make alternative plans and notify the proper authorities.

I got on the phone and talked to the American Embassy twenty-four-hour emergency service in Jordan and alerted them to our situation. We spoke with the staff person for a few minutes and told him we had to clear the Jordanian border. He promised to stay in touch. Jordanian security was waiting for us. They were sympathetic. They said Israel was denying more people than usual lately. Throughout this, I kept my composure for the sake of the others. After a brief conversation with the Jordanian border patrol, they stamped our passports and off we went to the hotel. It was after midnight.

The taxis were waiting for us. Jessica's dad and uncle and the hotel staff knew we were coming as well. They offered us water and asked us if we wanted food. We declined. We were extremely depressed and tired. Before we went to bed that night, we called our families and the Federation president and told them about our situation. We emailed the American Embassy in Amman and wrote to them about our status.

Jessica and I penned a note to the State Department

Dear Secretary of State Kerry,

It is after 4 a.m., we are now settled at the Le Meridian Hotel in Amman. Per our communication this evening. Below is a summary of what happened at the Israeli borders. We attempted to make phone calls to the American Consulate to no avail, the immigration officers refused to allow us to talk to you. Our phones were dead since we had to wait for six hours. Attached is a list of people who were denied entry for five years and were accused of lying. The following is a summary of the conversation.

Per conversation with Terry Ahwal here is a brief synopsis of to-day's events:

We arrived today at the Israeli-Jordanian border — 15 people in total and some of us cleared security within 15 minutes. However, the entire group was questioned, intimidated and harassed for five hours to be later denied entrance. We traveled with a group of youths from around the country from ages 17-28.

- threatened to be arrested because youth were "lying."

-phones were not in service and denied use of the phone to call consulate general.

- the group members were separated and not allowed to talk to one another."

- refused to give water to two members of our group who were fasting for Ramadan when fasting was complete

- asking for documentation however not allowing us the resources to get the information (email, phone)

- asked about our grandparents, when they left Palestine, etc.)

Quotes from youths:

"So the very beginning of the interrogation — the first question was where are you from? I answered Arkansas - they then checked my passport. Then they asked where my grandparents are from where they lived. I answered "they are American and live in America, and they left Palestine in the 1920s - 1950s, I don't know the exact dates, but I kept repeating.

They asked for my itinerary over and over, and I told them I had it on my phone and I could show it to them if they allowed me to use a computer or have access to the Internet.

They laughed at me and said you are lying, we know you are going to visit a refugee camp. They then threatened to arrest me because I was "lying."

They asked me if I spoke Arabic and he asked me why I was lying. They asked me what I'm doing going to Ramallah and how long I was staying.

He asked if I spoke Arabic and I told him no and he laughed like he was mad, like he was mocking me.

She asked the same questions over and over, and then we went inside and immediately were told to separate. Then a guy from outside came inside and asked about what our itinerary is and if I'm lying some people are going to be sent back and not to be able to go into Israel so you better not lie to me.

They asked me what my name was - I stated Alfred, and they asked what my father's name is. They asked me who were my relatives in Ramallah. They asked me who my grandfather was, my uncle and his wife's name.

They said that the group leaders told me to lie. That we were going to refugee camps and not to the holy sites as we said.

So a female soldier asked me where my mom was from and where she lives, and I told them she moved to San Diego when she was seven for life-threatening heart surgery. They asked why, and I told them because my grandma didn't want the Israelis doing surgery and so she moved to the United States. They said your mom is stupid for not trusting us to do surgery. Don't follow in your mother's footsteps.

May we please set up a conference call, please. Today's experience was awful, to say the least. We were threatened and did not feel safe and had no way to contact the outside world. I am an American citizen traveling with 14 other US citizens and to be denied access to the holy land is such a shame. I was humiliated, harassed and discriminated against. This is an unacceptable way for any human to be treated.

Thank you,
Jessica Haddad

During my visit earlier at the convention, I established a relationship between the American counsel general and his staff. They told us what to do in case we encountered a problem at the border. We called the number they gave us. They were accommodating. They were familiar with the harassment of Arab Americans at the frontier and were eager to help. We briefed them on what was happening. We told them that Israel banned us from entering. They jumped in with both hands and feet to help us. The border patrol did not give a damn about our American citizenship.

It turned out we were not the only ones banned at the border. The State Department had dossiers of Palestinian Americans denied entry to Palestine. The security people who were guarding us ushered us outside to collect our luggage. It was dark, we did not have a hotel lined up, nor transportation to a hotel. Everyone was traumatized but kept their emotions in check until they got on the bus. We tried to give them hope, even when we knew there was no hope. I was not sure that our government would come to our aid. I knew they did not have any leverage with Israel. The ban hurt me to the core. The lie as to why we were denied entry was beyond belief. I was confident they had cameras throughout the compound; they could present the evidence to show the State Department officials if we were belligerent. They did not care. The Israeli's strategic plans continue to prevent Palestinians from returning to their homeland, and they continue to execute their agenda. That day the border patrol may have stopped us from entering our home in hopes that we forget about Palestine. They were and will continue to be wrong. We were all determined to inform the world about the atrocities committed by Israel wherever we go. They awakened our allegiance to our ancestral homeland. Our hurt did not compare to the daily trauma of the Palestinian people who live under their occupation.

After our ejection from the border, we went to bed without deciding what to do next. Of course, it was hard to sleep. While we slept, my husband, Bob, contacted Senator Carl Levin and Senator Debbie Stabenow and told them our problem. Since both senators knew me, they assigned a staff person to help us.

After less than an hour of sleep, I woke up to a phone call from Ian Hopper, the chief consul at the American Embassy in Jordan. We gave him the details of what transpired and informed him of the ban. He promised to follow up and keep us posted.

I went to the lobby to meet the group. Still puzzled and upset, we discussed the latest information with the US State Department and the embassy. We collected data and sent it to the American Embassy in Jordan as instructed.

Over a late brunch, and in between fielding phone calls from various officials, we decided to stay in Jordan to volunteer and tour the country. After clearing our decision with the Federation president, I set out to find us an alternative project. I contacted the Palestinian ambassador in Washington to ask for help. He connected us with Palestinian leaders from various refugee camps in Jordan. The turn of events worked out for us better than expected. We met with a liaison from the Palestinian Embassy in Jordan who helped us set up a program in various refugee camps. We also decided to take two days to relax at the Red Sea in Aqaba.

Before we left for Aqaba, we heard from Richard Buangan, the chief, Public Diplomacy Section, at the US Consulate General in Jerusalem He wrote to let us know what the consulate was doing on our behalf. Before we left for Aqaba, we also contacted our members of Congress asking for help. No one except Levin and Stabenow responded.

Going to Aqaba was like going from despair to enthusiasm. The Red Sea was the cure for our melancholy. We booked a hotel and off we went. The place was paradise. We swam, sunbathed, drank, ate fresh fish, and some went scuba diving. Throughout the whole ordeal, the group bonded together in this ancient city, made famous by Lawrence of Arabia.

Jessica's father came to the rescue by providing us with a local cell phone. Staff from the American Embassy in Jordan and the Consulate General in Jerusalem kept in touch with us and advised us on what to do. With a connection to Wi-Fi, we discovered that Israel had attacked Gaza. Our families were extraordinarily concerned but very supportive. Despite the unrest in Gaza, they encouraged us to stay. Working with a small budget, we found a cheaper hotel for the rest of the journey.

After a brief rest, our new organizers provided us with eye-opening programs and introduced us to another segment of Palestinian life. They took us to the Palestinian refugee camps in Jordan. The camps opened after the expulsions of the Palestinians from their home in 1948 and 1967. The first Palestinian refugee camp was established in Jordan in 1948, after the Nakba, when the state of Israel was created. Back then, more than 700,000 Palestinians had to flee their homes and run somewhere safe. Some went to refugee camps in the West Bank, inside Palestine, but lots of families went to neighboring countries, like Egypt, Jordan, and Syria.

The first camp created by the United Nations in Jordan was Zarqa, in Amman. We noticed it was small. As we walked the streets, we saw that most people lived in shacks with their families. The streets were filled with raw sewage and trash. There was no garbage collection, one organizer told us. It seemed like neither the United Nations Relief and Works Agency for Palestine Refugees in the Near East nor the municipality was interested in taking good care of the camp.

The list of problems, besides the garbage, was overwhelming. Shanty homes without green space, high unemployment, lack of opportunity outside the camps, and poverty. We soon discovered that all the camps had similar features, but one thing stood firm from the first generation to the third-generation refugees: they all dream of going to their homes in Palestine and believed their housing in the refugee camps was temporary. Despite the lack of resources, most everyone thought education the most critical weapon they possess.

Our host took us to women centers and introduced our group to energetic women who help women and children in the camps become successful. They had programs for the elderly and babies. The more we toured these camps, the more I disgusted I became with the inability of the UN and the powerful countries to find a just solution for the Palestinians languishing in these miserable places.

All the camps had similar ugly features, but when we arrived at Baqa'a refugee camp, I was not prepared for its bleakness. This camp, with more than 100,000 residents, looked like a shanty town. It was the first and largest refugee camp in Jordan. Like the other camps, shanty homes were built in small places on top of each other. The people were amicable, especially when they found out we were Palestinians. They all invited us to their homes. As we walked the dirty and smelly streets, shopkeepers offered us coffee. Little children with dirty faces followed us and wanted their pictures taken with us.

We arrived at Baqa'a after the noon prayer. We asked our host if we could visit some of the homes. He made a couple of phone calls, and off we went. From the outside, the places we visited looked like garbage dumps, but inside they were bare but meticulously clean. The first house had three rooms for a family of seven: a living room, a bedroom, and a family room. It was lined with white plastic chairs, with mattresses stacked in one corner. Next to the main room was a small private bedroom for the parents. They had a little kitchen on the side with a small fridge, a cupboard, and a small burner. They had no indoor plumbing and shared an outhouse with their neighbors.

Since it was Ramadan, the families we visited apologized for not offering us coffee and treats as tradition dictated. They also insisted we come back and share iftar meal with them (iftar is breakfast served in the evening when people break their fast during the month of Ramadan). We felt terrible walking in a place where people sleep. Although the houses and the situation looked desperate, they took pride in telling us that the four older children were in college. They saw their misery as temporary.

We saw strong and educated men and women of all ages. Their hearts beat with the hope of going back to their homes one day. They educate their children so when they go back to Palestine, the country will be prosperous. They were bitter about their current situation, but grateful for the educational opportunities they had in Jordan.

Unlike the refugees we met in the camps, the Israelis continue to have everything: support, money, and all the modern conveniences. They continue to be armed to the hilt. They continue to have un-feathered unfettered power but are afraid of their shadow. Not the refugees; they continue to have dreams of going back where they came from. Children as young as five knew where their families came from. They knew their history. They eloquently recited poems about their homeland. At one meeting, we asked the children what they wanted to be when they grew up. One by one, they talked about their dreams of being doctors, lawyers, police officers, firefighters and other occupations that require college educations. As a Palestinian who never lived in a refugee camp, I was in awe of these people. Although their lives are bleak, collectively they keep the Palestinian dream of a homeland alive.

After two weeks in Jordan, we came back to the United States. I vowed to follow up on our case with the State Department and Congressional leaders. I set up several meetings with the State Department and our Congressional delegation. At our request, the State Department followed up on our ban with the Israeli Embassy in Washington, D.C. Our hopes were dashed when after three years of constant communication, the Israeli Embassy told us the prohibition would take its course. As I suspected, the State Department was powerless. We tried every avenue possible, including appealing to members of Congress, the State Department, the Israeli Embassy in Washington, to no avail. Today, as my Jewish cousins and friends who have no connections to the region whatsoever can go live in my homeland, but I can't. I am waiting for the five years to be over so I can go home.

After my ban in 2014, I was determined to continue my service to the community. Besides volunteering in Michigan, where I live, I traveled to Jordan and spent a month with the Syrian refugees now suffering the same fate as my family did in 1948. I cannot help but feel for them. Their stories reminded me of the stories my grandfather and mother told us about their experiences. As time passes, I continue to monitor the situation in Palestine. I always hope that people of goodwill will come to the rescue. When Barak Obama was elected president, I was thrilled. I thought finally someone would know about the suffering. I was excited by his inaugural address.

I stayed home to watch the speech on TV so I could capture the moment without interruption. With his election, I felt a deep sense of commitment to justice. Until he appointed Rahm Emanuel as his chief of staff the day after the election. Emanuel served in the Israeli Army, and his father continues to be an ardent Zionist who wants to expel the Palestinians from their homeland. But true to his values and practical political ambition, President Obama tried to pressure Israel to compromise, yet provided them with outrageous military aid to satisfy the Israeli lobby and its supporters in Congress.

At a photo op encounter with President Obama, I politely thanked him for trying to support the Palestinian people and the peace process. He replied with honesty, "I need to do more." Oh, how I wanted to scream yes, but that was not the proper venue.

Earlier that day, we met with one of his top advisors at the White House and spoke in detail about the deteriorating conditions under the Israeli occupation. At that meeting, Ben Rhodes, the deputy national security advisor for strategic communications, tried giving us the usual rhetoric about Israel's right to defend itself. But I felt he was not convinced by his own argument. I tried to push back, but he kept to his bullet points. But unlike after other meetings with both the Bush and the Clinton administrations, I felt there was an opening for change.

Although I was very critical of Obama's lack of courage on the Palestinian issue, I felt it was a matter of time before the tide of support for Israel would turn. Sure enough, at the end of his tenure, his administration did not stop a UN resolution condemning Israeli settlements. Instead of vetoing the resolution, the United States abstained. It was the first non-veto vote on the Israeli settlement issue since March 17, 1970. At that time, Secretary of State John Kerry, who tried very hard to push both sides to negotiate a peace agreement, blamed Israel for the collapse of talks. In a New York Times article, Kerry accused right-wing Israelis of deliberately thwarting efforts to broker a peace deal with the Palestinians.

This was a harsh statement coming from a former senator and a diplomat who always stood by Israel. But Obama, like other US politicians, relies on funding for elections and let's face it, not many people involved in politics are keen on the Palestinian people. Years of dehumanization of the Palestinian people has created an environment that allows politicians to carry on the façade that allowed the occupation to thrive.

As an eternal optimist, I viewed Obama's and Kerry's small change in policy as a sign of hope. Then the election of President Trump happened, and every positive change in foreign policy began being dismantled. Today, I can't bear watching the news about Palestine or the Middle East. My heart breaks daily as the killing of the Palestinian people who protest their awful conditions continues and I listen to the silence of the American media and members of Congress on both sides as the slaughter goes on.

Before the Iraqi overt invasion, the Libyan, Syrian and Yemenite proxy war, the Palestinian people garnished support from European, Arab, Asian, and African leaders. Today all attention is focused on ISIS, and the refugees from these countries, and little or no attention is given to the plight of Palestinians. This is precisely what the neoconservatives and Prime Minister Benyamin Netanyahu intended in their 1996 white paper, *A Clean Break*.

Colonial powers come and go, but the will of the people to be free from the shackles of oppression is stronger than all the powers and military might.

The Palestinian people are not alone. Israel's policies are pushing not only the Palestinians out of their homes; they also are driving their best and brightest to leave Israel for the US and Europe. Over one million Jewish Israelis now live outside of Israel. They wanted a better life and can't find it in Israel. As for me, I still dream of a day when I open the news and see a story of Christian, Jewish, and Muslim children living in Palestine free of military, wars, and oppression. My dream and people of good will keep me going.

29 / 2018-Present Day

It has been seventy years since my mother was evicted from her home at age twelve. She now has dementia and can remember little from recent history. But her memory of her childhood floods her life. We take solace that in her old age, she reconciled with her past and maintained only the beautiful vivid reminiscences of a time gone by. Every now and then she sighs and wonders if she will ever go back one more time to her beloved Yaffa.

Before her dementia, my mom spoke about the horror she encountered when she was driven out of her home. She talked about the children who cried because they were separated from their parents as they escaped the violence exacted on them by the Irgun, the Jewish terrorist group that later became the Israeli Defense Forces. She talked about the bodies she and her family saw while trying to shelter themselves from the bullets. She reminisced about the sea of 750,000 people who wandered to an unknown destination for safety.

Today she repeats the stories of her family in Yaffa. She describes details of her neighborhood and the daily routine she had with her aunts, uncles, cousins, and neighbors. She talks about the fresh food taken from the Mediterranean Sea by her father and uncles. She yaks about when her brother was born on Christmas and how a British colonial brought them the largest turkey to celebrate his birth. My mother never lived without foreign occupation. She was born in Yaffa under British rule. Her memory of this occupation was pleasant. It was not that the British or the Ottoman regimes were better than the Israeli occupation; her recollection of it is from a child's point of view.

Those who lived through the first eviction of the Palestinians under the Israeli occupation still remember. Some who live in Israel, Gaza, and the West Bank are still living the nightmares. The Israelis still maintain their power over the people they evicted with guns. The original 750,000 grew to 14 million throughout the world, of whom 5.3 million are in Palestine, 1.7 million in 1948 territory, 6.3 million in Arab countries, and around 750,000 in other foreign countries.

For seventy years, Israel has tried to erase us, to obliterate our existence. And, yet we grew and thrived under extreme circumstances. Not a day goes by without Israel killing, injuring, or imprisoning a Palestinian. They labeled us terrorists to justify their crimes. They even enlisted the support of other countries that allowed Israel to blatantly abuse the Palestinians. In the name of security, Israel has been forging its colonial power with a strong army supplied with an endless flow of cash from well-meaning benefactors and their supporters who believe Israel is a safe home for the Jewish people.

They are also supported by corrupt foreign politicians who, although they privately rebuke Israel, are afraid to speak out for fear of retribution from their political donors. But most of all they are supported by the evangelical Christian right, which believes modern Israel is the fulfillment of Biblical prophecy. They made alliances with the extreme Jewish community and the fascist Israeli right-wing government to maintain the occupation and the killing of the Palestinian people.

Israel does not fear our weapons; we have limited, antiquated weapons for defense. Israel fears our numbers. They want us to wither away, similar to what happened to the aborigines of Australia and the Native Americans in the United States. They want us to live on our reservations with limited rights.

As I was writing this, Prime Minister Netanyahu was sitting with President Trump's son-in-law Jared Kushner and his wife, Trump's daughter, Ivanka, and extreme members of the Israeli government cutting ribbons for the relocation of the American Embassy to Jerusalem, on Palestinian land stolen from the Fetyan family. While they were celebrating, Israel launched a continued attack on peaceful, unarmed protestors in Gaza who seek freedom, the ability to go to their homes in accordance with the Geneva convention. More than 150 people were killed, and thousands injured. I am sad and disgusted, but still somehow hopeful.

If the Palestinians have common traits, one would be our lust and love for life. We cherish our families and the land we lost. No matter how much Israel tries to wipe us from the face of the earth, we stand steadfastly with our heads high and refuse to give up. Every time I feel discouraged about our misfortune, I look to my fellow Palestinians who remind me that no one can take away who we are. We are people with a strong history, a prominent presence, and a fantastic future. We are counted among the most educated population in the world. We are builders, not destroyers.

Even in Gaza, where everyone lives in an open prison, stories of survival and perseverance are inspiring. Take, for example, the two young women who subverted a crippling Israeli blockade that makes importing construction materials a demeaning, expensive, and time-consuming process and developed their green bricks from the rubble. Their goal is to help Gaza residents rebuild their homes from the ruins of the bombs Israel throws at them.

Our pain is temporary. Israel, with Netanyahu at its helm, is desperate. Its government is spending millions if not billions of dollars to silence any criticism of Israel. Although thousands of miles away, I feel I am still under the Israeli occupation, yet I still think I have more power than they do. I have truth and justice on my side. The BDS (Boycott, Divestment, and Sanctions) of Israel is catching steam despite the Israeli campaign to stop it and criminalize it.

With all its arms and defense, Israel fears every peaceful Palestinian who stands for his or her freedom. I am heartened by the courage of Israeli soldiers who would rather go to jail instead of serving in the occupied territories. I am in awe of celebrities such as Pink Floyd, Steven Hawking, Richard Gere, and many others who are speaking out against the crimes committed by Israel.

Between tears for those who continue to die because they are Palestinians, I celebrate American students who are pushing their universities to divest from

Israel. I am in awe of the young Jewish Americans from "If Not Now," Jewish Voice for Peace, and J-street who protest Israel's actions daily and are willing to get arrested for it. When the dust is settled, and the truth becomes a reality, I know the Palestinian people will owe a debt of gratitude to Israeli Jewish reporters like Gedeon Levi, Amira Hass, and Marion Benevensity. These reporters, and many like them, continue to write about the facts of the Israeli government to the detriment of their lives. I am grateful for Israeli historians like Ilan Pappe, who is exposing Israel's lies and history by bringing to the surface mountains of evidence disputing Israel's twisted history.

As a Palestinian American, active in politics, I have little hope for change on this issue unless we have campaign finance reform where politicians on both sides are not relying on lobbyists to fund their campaigns. But even with millions of dollars pouring into election campaigns, in support of Israel, more courageous members of Congress are speaking out. Senator Bernie Sanders, a Jewish American, did not abandon his heritage nor his core values to support Israel. Like me, he measures human rights and justice with one yardstick. Frankly, if one is opposed to apartheid in South Africa, one must oppose the occupation of Palestine.

I wrote my memoirs to tell the story of my family and to keep our Palestinian heritage alive. Many Palestinians are doing something to keep our culture alive. Not a day goes by without a Palestinian talking about the villages that were erased from the face of the earth to make room for the Israelis. Not a day goes by without the Palestinians throughout the world celebrating the memory of the country that made them; or dancing to a Palestinian song that was part of their ancestry. Not a day goes by without Palestinians eating the food passed on from generation to generation. Palestine is in our hearts and veins. Israel, with their fears, can try to stop us, but we are survivors.

So, if Israel wants peace, let's live together in one state with total equality, regardless of religion. For that to happen, Israel must shed its fear, abandon its military might and live in peace. Once they give us our freedom, they can achieve their security. My dream is to go to sleep and wake up to a world bestowing justice to the Palestinian people.

Epilogue

The war to eradicate the Palestinians and their aspirations to live free in their homeland never ceases. Not a day goes by without Israel and its allies working on criminalizing the Palestinian people. In Israel, the targeting and killing of Palestinians never stops. Every day, families are separated, homes are demolished at record numbers, settlements are erected on land owned by Palestinians and confiscated. But that is not enough. While Israel refuses to allow Palestinian refugees to go back to their homes, they launched a campaign to reclassify them as non-refugees to exclude them from receiving aid from the United Nations.

In the United States and Europe, Israel's supporters are weaponizing hate for Palestinians by declaring criticism of Israel should be included in the definition of anti-Semitism. I take comfort that many young people and many organizations from Jewish communities are leading the fight against the new, lethal definition. Yet, American and European leaders are pushing to legislate this new definition, even though the genesis of anti-Semitism stems from white and religious supremacists who allowed the Holocaust and pogroms to occur. Their support of the Jewish people is hollow and disingenuous.

As for the mostly European leaders of Israel, they advocate supremacy based on religion. They enacted laws declaring Israel a Jewish State, despite the fact all its prime ministers have been secular Jews. They also believe their power is everlasting. They believe their power stems from oppressing others. They are hurting not only the Palestinians, but have, like all brutal leaders, lost their own souls.

Honest observers of Israeli politics can attest to the function of the Israeli government. The latest government espouses fascist beliefs. They had five elections in five years. The last four Israeli prime ministers were charged with corruption. I frankly think they should be charged and convicted of crimes against humanity. There is ample evidence that Israel is committing crimes and assassinations without any repercussions, including journalists like Shireen Abu Aklah, a Palestinian American journalist.

But I feel the tide is turning. In the last few years many well respected human rights agencies, including Human Rights Watch, Amnesty International and B'Tselem, have labeled Israel an apartheid state. Human rights advocates and descendants of holocaust survivors, like Ken Roth, called Israel an apartheid state. This gives me solace that there is justice in the world. I know that the wheels of justice are slow, but the day will come when Palestinians will live free in their homeland; I just hope it comes sooners than later.

As an American, I believe in the power of possibilities. But until justice and freedom are achieved, I will keep fighting for my rights to be free and to stop the Israeli occupation. I am not afraid nor fear the accusations and hurdles put in my way. Fighting for my rights as a human being requires a 24/7 commitment. I hoped the invasion of Ukraine might shed some light on the occupation of Palestine in the media and political circles. But of course, it did not, for in these circles Palestinians are viewed as people of a lesser god and Israel is a promised land for Jewish people only. These beliefs are not only dangerous for Palestinians but Israelis as well. I believe no religion is supreme over any other. In my heart, I know we will rise. But until then I will continue to advocate on behalf of the Palestinian people until my last breath. We will rise and we will be free.

Not a day goes by without my receiving a note from a human right organization asking me to support their initiatives to help the Palestinians. The notes usually start with "We need your voice to act immediately." Although I am tired, I still carry the torch to help my people achieve their freedom and aspirations.

In 2019, I attempted to visit my family in Palestine, only to be told that my ban was not over. It is just another tool Israel has in its arsenal to prevent Palestinians from visiting their homeland, even with an American passport. Currently, they enacted a law that puts more hoops to prevent anyone, especially Palestinians, from visiting family in the occupied territories. I find it ironic that my husband's family, with no connection to the land whatsoever, can live in my homeland because they are Jewish, but I cannot even visit.

After finishing this manuscript, I went on with my life. I retired from my work, but still help non-profit agencies in Michigan. I continue to travel all over the world as a volunteer with Habitat for Humanity and other organizations. In 2021 I climbed Mount Kilimanjaro with my friends Pearlette Ramos and Tammy Johnston to shed light on the possibility of overcoming obstacles for people of color. With pride, I wore my Keffiyeh, the symbol of Palestinians' connections to their earth, and to honor the Palestinian peasants who taught me the love for the land stolen from us.

My mother is still alive and I visit her often. Her memory of the present is gone, but her memory of Yaffa and her wedding is still intact. We watch clips from YouTube about Yaffa. She talks about her neighborhood and her neighbors. She also watches clips of Palestinian weddings and sings along with them. The distant past is her solace and torment. She talks of Ramallah and Yaffa as if she still lives there.

Like most Palestinians, I am still steadfast in my determination to let the world know that Israel is responsible for the ethnic cleansing of my family and the Palestinian people. A friend from the Jewish community once told me that every Jew dreams of reclaiming their ancestors' homelands and that I am denying their dream. I responded that if their dream is the cause of my demise, I will fight it until my last breath.

As I finish updating this memoir, I take my energy from people who dare to speak about Israel's human rights violations and its apartheid regime. I take my energy from the 38 percent of American Jewish people who refuse to let Israel represent them. My hope rests on the young Jewish people who stand shoulder to shoulder with the Palestinian people in their fight to live free and independent in their homeland. Although the oppression and killing of innocent Palestinians intensified in 2023, I hope I will see justice for the Palestinian people in my lifetime. I can only hope!

About the Author

Terry Ahwal is a native of Palestine who lived under Israeli occupation until 1972, when as a teenager, she was sent to live with her uncles in Detroit.

She was born in Ramallah, Palestine, where her mother and maternal grandparents relocated after being forced to leave their home in Yaffa in 1948.

She holds a Bachelor of Arts degree from the University of Michigan, as well as certifications in leadership training from Notre Dame University, Michigan Political Leadership Program, and Michigan Leadership Program. Now retired, she served as the executive director of the American-Arab Anti-Discrimination Committee. She worked more than fifteen years in Wayne County (Michigan) government, where she rose to be an assistant county executive. She also worked as a Director of Development at Madonna University and Vice President of Development at the Detroit Medical Center.

She has broad experience in comprehensive fund development and worked on more than twenty national and local political campaigns, including the Bill Clinton for President campaign. She was a convention delegate for Clinton.

Terry has extensive volunteer experiences in the United States and abroad. She is a former president of Habitat of Humanity in Detroit, vice president of the YMCA in Livonia, president of the American Federation of Ramallah, Palestine, and numerous board positions. She volunteers with four nonprofit agencies in the Detroit area.

She also climbed Mount Kilimanjaro in September 2021.